Willing to Love

ADVANCE PRAISE

Most books by therapists are about their clients. This book is unique in two ways. First, it is a collection of essays written by therapists about their marriages. Second, using the perspective of Psychosynthesis, it includes the spiritual dimension of intimate relationships. Both make an interesting and in depth read about many variations of love. Informative, stretching, and inspiring. We recommend it to all couples as a mirror of their own relationships and as a guide to their deepening.

— Harville Hendrix, PhD, and Helen LaKelly Hunt, PhD,
Co-founders of Imago Relationship Therapy and Co-authors
of *Getting the Love You Want: A Guide for Couples*.

When we meet happy long-term couples, we are often unaware of the difficulties they have traversed over the course of their many years together and the individual and interpersonal growth required to reach the happiness they know today. Here we have the raw and real stories of 11 couples who have walked their own unique paths beyond power struggling into trusting a deeper source of wisdom, true intimacy and relational joy.

— Chelsea Wakefield, PhD, LCSW;
Director of the UAMS Couples Center,
Author of *The Labyrinth of Love –
The Path to a Soulful Relationship*

Of the many paths to spiritual growth and personal healing, few can be as perilous, potent, or profound as the path of conscious relationship. This book of inspiring stories is an extraordinary gift filled with lessons, guidance and hope. An amazing essential for couples with a shared intention to evolve together, the insights here are overflowing, and many can be applied to other relationships and situations. Wonderful!

— Jonathan Ellerby, PhD, author of
Inspiration Deficit Disorder

Tender...vulnerable...courageous. Here are intimate revelations that show us the depth of what it means to be a couple. I was inspired by the diverse journeys the individuals in these relationships have traveled in their commitment to love. Perhaps most poignant is how each became a "beloved witness" for the other. The couples do not hold back the challenges they faced, and they share how the central principles of Psychosynthesis supported them in meeting the obstacles they encountered.

— Ann Gila, author of *Stay Present and Love Him,*
and co-author of *A Psychotherapy of Love*

In those moments when you find yourself staring out the kitchen window, wondering how you are possibly going to survive another night with your partner and their anger or your sadness, their criticisms, your fear, calm yourself, make a cup of tea and pull this book out...again. Guidebook, diary, textbook and prayer - this work offers the reader profound and hard-won templates for understanding in relationship, exploring that powerful and necessary balance between being accountable for one's own way in the world and responsible for the health of the chosen partnership. Each author addresses this commitment with courage in the face of imperfection and a stunning, consistent dedication to growth. Nothing is taken for granted here. The assaults of childhood, the intensities of falling in love, the painful differences between us, the descent into deeper understandings that require effort and care, the relief of finding our way together; all are addressed under the expanse of an overarching question: "How might the principles of Psychosynthesis bring us to a better place?" This transcendent model provides a map for each writer through these territories, and because of such honest, thorough, inner examination, we are each gifted a hope... that we, too, might find wisdom and uplift in the very rooms of love we inhabit today.

— Maria Sirois, PsyD, author of *A Short Course in Happiness After Loss (and Other, Dark Difficult Times)*

A great introduction to Psychosynthesis and Assagioli (an under celebrated contemporary of Jung and Freud) experienced through vignettes of long-term marriages and relationships. Fascinating reading if you want a less academic approach to depth and transpersonal psychology.

— Tom Butler-Bowdon
Author of *50 Psychology Classics*

Being invited into the lives of diverse couples, as they reflect on their journeys together, is a rare privilege. As their stories unfold, bound together by the shared experience of Psychosynthesis as a holding environment, they offer the reader their deep learnings on love, commitment, conflict, loss, and Self. We learn so much as we read, not through "taught" lessons, but through lived experiences. To follow these couples, with their deep self-reflection and honesty, is to see how people find their way to love and use that love to continue growing. The reader is invited into the private worlds of each couple, in service of exploring what goes into being willing to love, No journey is easy and all are profound. There is much to learn here, for all of us.

— Dorothy Firman, EdD, Director of Synthesis Center and Senior Trainer of the Psychosynthesis Life Coach Training Program, Author of *Daughters and Mothers: Making it Work; Living Well with Chronic Illness*, and Editor of *Call of Self: Psychosynthesis Life Coaching*

Isn't the most serious question: Who knows how to make love stay? This vital life skill finally has been authentically addressed by eleven couples all of whom are grounded in Psychosynthesis which is one of the most complete maps of the human psyche ever conceived. Seriously, imagine what you can learn!

—Neal Klein EdD Associate Professor
Holistic Psychology, Lesley University
Publications and Videos (Multi-Media)
Trance-endingtimes.com

The Psychosynthesis model, from its origins, has been designed to be applied in diverse fields that complement each other: psychotherapy and psychosomatic medicine, child and adult education, self-education, and interpersonal and social relationships. This wonderful book addresses the fundamental aspect of interpersonal and social relationships. Human relationships, and couples' relationships in particular, constitute one of the most demanding challenges and greatest opportunities for human beings, and perhaps the most valuable stimulus to their psycho-spiritual maturation and development.

Willing to Love is a unique and touching book because, in it, the authors, all experienced psychosynthesists, share and reflect, not so much on theoretical issues, but on their compelling firsthand experiences as part of a couple. The richness of the topics addressed is truly amazing. In this period of history, we have been called as never before to take responsibility for attending to and taking good care of our relationships. I am overjoyed and grateful this book has been published and I am sure that many will benefit and be greatly inspired by it!

— Petra Guggisberg Nocelli, psychotherapist (ASP, SIPT), trainer and author of *The Way of Psychosynthesis* and *Know, Love Transform Yourself*

This book is a big heartful of love. It is a collection of intimate travelogues of love's learning journey, each couple on a different path, all using the wisdom of Psychosynthesis as a map and their soul's knowing as a compass, and all with the same destination—a committed, authentic, expansive, renewable, truly mutual, and soul-suffused love. Each chapter beautifully illustrates Kierkegaard's remark, "For marriage is and remains the most important voyage of discovery a human being undertakes." What shines through each couple's story is their emotional and spiritual courage and their gradual growing faith that love is trustworthy, that it can be learned together, that the quality of loving attention can be consciously practiced, and ultimately that love has no limit and no opposite—because it includes everything. For us, and for anyone travelling the marathon path of marriage this is a truly inspiring book!

— Rich and Antra Borofsky, co-directors of the Center for the Study of Relationship, Cambridge, MA

Willing to Love

Stories of the Couple's Journey as a Path of Transformation

Edited by Anne Yeomans, Diane Rossman, Janet Messer, and Judith Broadus

Postscript by Piero Ferrucci

A Psychosynthesis Approach

Visit www.willingtolovebook.com

Cover and book design by Asya Blue Design.

Cover art by Lovetta Reyes-Cairo
www.lovettareyescairoart.com

ISBN 978-0-9913196-5-7 Paperback
ISBN 978-0-9913196-6-4 Ebook

CONTENTS

INTRODUCTION

Diane Rossman and Anne Yeomans

The authors of this unique book are delighted that you have found your way to it. We wish we had found something like it years ago when we were starting out on our own relationship journeys. We would have benefitted from reading the personal stories of people who were devoted to making their marriages rich and sustaining over time. Our book is more than a self-help manual, and different from a theoretical textbook about relationships. *Willing to Love* is unusual among books about marriage and committed partnerships because it is written by a group of seasoned psychotherapists and teachers about their own lived experience as part of a couple.

This book is a collection of love stories—not the pie-in-the-sky, romance novel kind, but real-life, bread-on-the-table love stories. Each of the following eleven chapters offers an intimate glimpse into a couple's life together. They are brave stories, because making a long-term commitment to another person requires self-awareness, humility and a generous spirit. As each story shows, being willing to love over time will wake you up, and grow you up too.

Along with the joys that come with long-lived relationships, we have aspired to write honestly about our fears and longings, our vulnerabilities and disappointments, as well as the strengths we draw on in difficult times. We know that the path of relationship is challenging. Some of us are in second marriages and were unable to resolve the difficult issues encountered the first time around. We've all felt discouraged and lost at times. Our book is a testament to the idea that it's never too late to do the work it takes to recommit—whether one is trying to improve an existing relationship or starting a new one. Even those of us whose first marriages are still going strong understand that sustaining a vibrant connection with a partner takes a willingness to love and to continually learn and grow.

Several of us describe our first meeting with our partner as both life-changing and unexpected. Two authors address the challenge a serious illness poses to a marriage and poignantly describe the decline and ultimate death of their husbands. We write about choosing to have children, choosing not to have them, infertility, and step-parenting. Two of us broach the issue of infidelity. The challenges of patriarchy and women's equality weave through several chapters. All the stories reflect our natural inclination toward psychological and spiritual development.

We range in age from 50-something to 80-plus. One couple has been together for four years and another for 56. Most of us are from the United States, but some are from Canada, the United Kingdom, Switzerland, the Netherlands, Italy and India. We are nine heterosexual couples and two same-sex couples. Some of us write from a cross-cultural perspective and two from the perspective of interracial marriage.

While our stories differ, we all have been deeply influenced and inspired by Psychosynthesis, an approach to psychological and spiritual development conceived by Roberto Assagioli, an Italian psychiatrist, who articulated his view of the human psyche in 1910. Assagioli lived through two world wars and was imprisoned for a time by Mussolini's fascists for his pacifist views; however, his faith in the human spirit never wavered. It inspires us to this day.

Psychosynthesis has enhanced our personal lives, our relationships with our partners, friends and colleagues, and–for those who are parents–our relationships with our children and grandchildren. It has informed our work as psychotherapists, counselors, psychologists, teachers, and writers. Many of us have designed and offered training programs in Psychosynthesis for professionals in various fields. As experienced practitioners and educators, we have found that Psychosynthesis has stood the test of time. In fact, we would say that psychosynthesis was ahead of its time because of its emphasis on the spiritual dimension of human development.

At the heart of Psychosynthesis is an invitation to discover and identify with the deepest part of ourselves, our essence or core. Assagioli calls this the Self, or the Soul. He believed this is who we essentially are. He also recognized the deep suffering that comes when, as a result of childhood wounds and traumas and trans-generational patterns and beliefs, so many of us lose touch with our true nature. This suffering is amplified by living in a materialistic and outward-focused culture. Assagioli's framework offers us tools and practices to reconnect with the Self and to heal our broken parts, so that we can create a life of meaning and purpose that expresses who we are.

Our book grows out of the understanding that having a companion on the journey of awakening is a great blessing. What happens when two people make a commitment to this process together? What happens when they learn to support the deepest and best in each other? And what happens when they strengthen the capacity to accept what is wounded and undeveloped in themselves and each other? These are questions that the stories of all of our couples explore. By living into these questions together we have realized that our being willing to love over time is a blessing beyond measure.

All of the authors have worked together to create this book. We found that each of us gravitated to our right place in the whole process where we were able to contribute our particular strengths, abilities and experience. Without consciously intending it, we realize now that we were practicing the very Psychosynthesis principles that we had written about in our chapters: inclusion, deep listening, mutual respect, and trusting the unknown. Making this book together has been a unique and rewarding experience for us all.

We offer you the fruits of this labor with the hope that it will provide encouragement, guidance, and inspiration for your own life and for your relationships.

PREFACE

Molly Brown

I find so much wisdom, joy and hope in these compelling stories of long-time couples. On a personal level, they reaffirm how vital the support of my partner, Jim, and our 60-year relationship is to my own life, as well as to my current work in the field of ecopsychology. The stories also remind me of the profound and ongoing gift of Psychosynthesis, a guiding framework for much of my life.

Yet one might well ask what the relevance is of a book about couples, in the face of the enormous global challenges before us: the climate crisis, international and domestic violence, systemic racism, pandemics, destruction of ecosystems, and the breakdown of civil discourse in so many places around the world. The answer, I believe, is that how we treat one another in our intimate relationships directly relates to how we treat others in our larger community and in our world, as well as how we relate to plants, animals, all living creatures, and the Earth itself. The same patterns of relationship operate on all these levels.

In addressing the enormous crises we face today, many leading thinkers call for an awakening to love. And this is what this book is about: how eleven couples found their way to commitment and enduring love through the challenges and difficulties life holds. All these couples were inspired by Psychosynthesis.

One of the central teachings in Psychosynthesis is the principle of "disidentification." This refers to the process of learning how to step back from a particular feeling, thought or habitual reaction, in order to see from a more neutral, spacious, and compassionate place. Disidentification can help us see where we are overly identified with our own point of view, and allows us to hear more clearly the point of view of another. In other words, it deepens our capacity to listen to what we truly need and, at the same time, to hear the needs of another person. These are essential skills, which greatly contribute to the health of ongoing relationships, as well as to any respectful and productive dialogue.

Developing the capacity to disidentify allows us to create more space, to slow things down, to take a breath before we respond. It gives us the opportunity to be more skillful in response to the actual situation rather than reacting quickly in accordance with old habitual ways or past traumas. Many of the following chapters name disidentification as key to working through both intrapersonal and interpersonal conflict.

As an ecopsychologist, I often think about how the capacity to disidentify could transform not only our personal relationships but also our social and political lives and our relationship with the natural world. We might then be better able to recognize our interconnectedness with all of life and take our place as responsible members of the Earth community.

As this book illustrates, successful life partnerships also depend on an individual's ability to disidentify and to consider a larger context, that of the couple and/or family. The authors show us how they learned to listen to both themselves and to their partners, to bring both their strengths and their vulnerabilities to the relationship, and to hold it in a greater context of love. These engaging stories offer instruction and inspiration to anyone seeking to deepen their relationships, beginning at home and extending outward in ever-expanding circles.

FOREWORD

Psychosynthesis and its Relevance to the Couple's Journey

Thomas Yeomans

The first phrase I learned when I studied Ancient Greek was ἀθάνατος ἡ ψυχή, which means "the soul is deathless," and, when Anne and I married we had this phrase inscribed inside our wedding rings. To us, it expressed the core of the commitment and adventure of marriage–learning to live deeply, soul with soul, as a couple.

A few years later, we discovered Psychosynthesis and this perspective on psycho-spiritual development became the framework within which we came to do our professional work and live our personal and family lives. In it, we found this same core orientation–to learn to live as souls on earth--and we applied its principles and practices to our individual lives as well as to our marriage. In this endeavor, we learned to take the soul seriously as a central organizing principle that does not depend on any religious orientation or tradition but exists as a vital, energetic center of life seeking fuller and more mature expression through us.

What then is Psychosynthesis? Historically, it is an orientation to human development, first formulated in 1910 by the Italian psychiatrist, Robert Assagioli, and now widely practiced in Europe, North America, Australia and New Zealand. It exists within the larger conceptual framework of Western depth psychology and existential, humanistic, and transpersonal psychology. Assagioli was a contemporary and colleague of Sigmund Freud and Carl Jung, and was, later, sympathetic to the humanistic developments within the field of Western psychology, particularly the work of Abraham Maslow, Carl Rogers, and Eric Fromm.

More subjectively, Psychosynthesis grew from Assagioli's awareness of, and deep trust in, the natural process of human development, a movement toward greater harmony, integrity, and maturity that exists within the psyche. His term for this natural process was "psychosynthesis" (lower-case p.) Around this focus, he and those who have continued his work over the last 100 years, developed a comprehensive set of principles and practices which make up the field of Psychosynthesis, (capital P.)

In the introduction to his first book, *Psychosynthesis: A Manual of Principles and Techniques,* Assagioli states, "The basic purpose of Psychosynthesis is to release, or let us say, help to release, the energies of the Self. Prior to this, the purpose is to help integrate, to synthesize, the individual around the personal self, and then later to effect the synthesis between the personal ego and the Self". To Assagioli, Self and Soul were synonymous. The presence of the spiritual Self, or Soul, in human nature, and its increasing influence and expression in our daily lives, is the key to this way of working with oneself and others. In this book about the couple's journey, it is also the key to the emerging depth and quality of the couple's relationship over time and to the enrichment of their shared journey. Within the perspective of Psychosynthesis, the heart of the couple is seen as an increasing experience of deep Soul connection and growing mutual respect between two maturing human beings. To my knowledge, this is the first book within Psychosynthesis to address the application of its principles and practice to couples.

The journey of a committed relationship is never easy. Two personalities need to find their way to an experience of integration and synthesis around a spiritual center, so that there is both a deep connection between the two people *and* a full individuation/maturation of each individual. There is much work to be done, suffering to be learned from, and joy to be had, all along the way. In this book, Psychosynthesis serves as the context for these eleven couples to tell their stories. It is also the means they use over the years to explore, understand, nourish, and strengthen their relationships.

Why is this book relevant to us now? We need only consider the rampant loneliness and the widespread suffering within relationships. At the same time, we are also aware of the deep longing for mutual respect and love, and of the valiant efforts couples make to rekindle the love and joy between them. There are myriad resources available: self-help books, workshops, psychotherapists, and life coaches. Yet, what is unique here is Assagioli's recognition of the soul and the spiritual dimension in relationships. This is one of his great gifts to the field of psychology. When the spiritual dimension is acknowledged, we can call on it to guide and support ourselves as individuals and as a couple toward a fuller realization and expression of the deep love we are seeking.

In this book, "Willing to Love," eleven couples describe how Psychosynthesis has enriched their individual lives and their marriages. Their intimate stories reveal glimpses of the soul at work in us and between us. They remind me of the inscription in Anne's and my wedding rings. The soul is deathless; it is also the central and steadying force in the gradual ripening of committed relationships.

Jon and Lyn

In this first chapter, Jon presents a clear and accessible introduction to Psychosynthesis. Through poignant and sometimes humorous anecdotes from his marriage, he shows us how working with the seven core principles has helped him and his wife, Lyn, become more self-aware and more conscious, loving life partners.

CHAPTER ONE

Assagioli's Seven Core Concepts and the Life of the Couple

Jon Schottland

I don't know why, nobody told you how to unfold your love.
—*George Harrison, While My Guitar Gently Weeps*

Beginnings

"You seem pretty content," I said to Lyn the first evening we spent together. "I am," she replied casually. "Good, stay that way," I said, sensing right away a relationship between us was possible. I'd like to believe two people can share a life together without losing sight of the things that attracted them to each other in the first place.

As we got to know one another, I could see that Lyn was grounded and took things in stride; nothing seemed to phase her much at all. This was something I admired, coming myself from a warm and loving Jewish family that nonetheless had some generational anxiety running through our veins. We were capable in any moment of "catastrophizing," which is really just the imagination running wild with the idea that bad things might happen. Or, as one of my sisters put it, we sometimes start from the grave and back up from there.

I'm generally a pretty grounded person too, and yet I've seen how being in a relationship can turn ordinary people into desperate, needy, confused, (fill in the blank here) human beings. If Lyn and I were going to be together, I wondered, how might we do that in a way that deepened our connection to ourselves and each other over time? That seemed like a useful guiding question to start us out on our journey as a couple.

One year later Lyn and I became engaged, on a remote windy beach on Block Island, with huge waves and a pounding surf as our witness. Two years later, in the summer of 2017, on a beautiful hilltop in southern Vermont, we were married in a twilight ceremony surrounded by family and dear friends. During the reception, towards the end of the night, my cousin Jim and I approached the band with a request to let us take the stage. Jim strapped on an electric guitar and I sang a Springsteen ballad, "If I Should Fall Behind," to my new bride:

> Now there's a beautiful river in the valley ahead
> There 'neath the oak's bough, soon we will be wed
> Should we lose each other, in the shadow of the evening trees
> I'll wait for you, and should I fall behind, wait for me.

Those who have devoted themselves to a loving relationship know that this is one of the great journeys of a lifetime. Rilke called it "the final test and proof, the work for which all other work is merely preparation."[1] A relationship is an opportunity to learn how to love someone really well, and I don't necessarily presume that I've got it all sorted out. A little humility seems in order when one is setting out on a great adventure that will no doubt include elements of mystery and uncertainty, and hopefully a little magic too.

This essay is about the enduring bonds of long-term relationships. It is about the ways we find and sometimes lose each other, yet through it all hold a deep, loving commitment to our shared journey. A relationship adds companionship, intimacy, meaning, and more to life. It opens us up to some of life's great joys and possibilities, and it will also show us where we're stuck or can't get out of our own way. My basic premise here is that if I pay close attention, the lived experience of being in a relationship will teach me a thing or two about love and, by extension, about myself.

Some of the chapters in this book describe marriages that span 30-40 years; Lyn and I have been married for only five. Yet I have been in relationships all my life, including a former marriage of fifteen years. I remember the first time I was kissed (at five years old, by a little girl named Ellen at Oakhurst Country Day Camp), and I have vivid memories of early teenage romances growing up at the Jersey shore. My adult life has included valuable lessons and experiences in the art of loving, some difficult decisions and painful setbacks along the way, and always love's promise to deliver something potent and life-affirming.

Now I take my place next to Lyn, having made a conscious choice to live out the rest of my life with this most wonderful, smart and sparkling woman as my partner. I don't have any illusions that it will all be smooth sailing, yet I do know that this choice carries with it my deep intention to stay the course. Perhaps this has something to do with getting married later in life, when both of us were in our fifties. There is nowhere else to go, no "greener pastures," just a desire to make a meaningful life together.

It has taken me a while to arrive at this point in my life where I feel more ready to show up with the whole truth of who I am—the bright and shiny aspects as well as my vulnerabilities and short-comings. Somehow this growing sense of wholeness gives me the confidence to commit myself fully and joyfully to the prospect of a long-term relationship. I credit that in large part to what I have gained from Psychosynthesis over the past two decades, as well as having the great, good fortune to come from a supportive family that still nourishes and sustains me to this day.

The Seven Core Concepts

Psychosynthesis, as developed by the Italian psychiatrist Roberto Assagioli, includes seven core concepts, or what he referred to as "experiences." These are: synthesis, disidentification, personal self, will, the ideal model, the superconscious, and the transpersonal Self. These experiences shed light on how we as individuals can become more vibrant and alive, living closer to the full promise and potential of who we may be. The same can be said about how Psychosynthesis can inform our collective lives too: our relation-ships, families, communities, and even the planet as a whole.

Psychosynthesis speaks to the need for conscious evolution and greater coherence from the personal to the global level, and this can be a tremendous support as we struggle with forces, both internal and external, that threaten to divide and diminish us. It is my hope that what follows will illuminate some of what these concepts can contribute to the understanding and experience of being in a meaningful long-term relationship.

Synthesis

Human beings are complex creatures. We experience ourselves as separate individuals, yet we long for connection and belonging. Our lives are relatively time-limited, minor events in the grand scale of a vast universe, and yet we hold fast to the hope that it matters that we are here. We are driven to find a sense of meaning and purpose. Internally, we experience a shifting and evolving set of motivations, feelings, thoughts, drives, needs, and desires. Given the existential challenges and complex nature of being human, it is no wonder that most of us find ourselves at times feeling fragmented, conflicted and confused.

Psychosynthesis is a process and framework that addresses the human condition and offers a path to wholeness. At the core of this process is the principle of *synthesis*. The word psychosynthesis literally refers to the integration of the various aspects of the psyche into a more whole and complete self. It is fundamentally an inclusive and love-oriented psychology in the sense that no part of the self is rejected or excluded; rather, the movement in psychosynthesis is always towards embracing both the light and the darkness, infusing life with love, including the most difficult and wounded aspects of who we are.

Every one of us is born of synthesis, the egg and the sperm coming together in a moment of dynamic creation to form the living embryo. Human life itself is dependent on this process. Similarly, a relationship is the coming together of two distinct people to form a new entity as a couple. In this sense, the process of synthesis is both a life-generating and love-activating principle.

Assagioli once referred to love as a "distant, dim recollection of original unity"[2]—as though love were deeply encoded in our genes, something we remember that serves as an attractive force, compelling us to join with one another, to exist not just as a separate individual but also within the context of relationships. From this perspective, entering into a relationship with another person might be viewed as a cosmic imperative to reconnect with that experience of original unity.

Synthesis refers to a dynamic, creative process in which disparate elements come together to form a greater whole. In the psychosynthesis of the couple, the two elements or "selves" coexist and mutually inform each other as the relationship develops, creating something entirely new and unique. From a systems perspective, my life with Lyn sets a context in which each of us comes to know ourselves as part of a larger whole. That means everything we do affects our shared environment.

This understanding helps us awaken to our responsibility for the health and vitality of that system. Since every choice we make can either elevate or diminish our experience of being together, it is fully within our realm of influence each step of the way to choose in the direction of love. In this sense, relationships are an up-close-and-personal experience of learning how to live a life for the greater good. From the microcosm to the macrocosm, we are reminded of the interconnected web in which we all co-exist.

Yet however close we become, we do not merge into one. Paradoxically, in the process of synthesis, each element becomes part of the larger whole while retaining its own essence and particularity. That principle is at the heart of any marriage: it involves a sort of new math in which $1 + 1 = 3$. There is both differentiation and unity, and over the long haul this process has the potential to produce a highly unified relational field that is richly differentiated: me, you, and us.

The process of synthesis, Assagioli noted, naturally includes a certain creative tension.[3] After all, the joining together of two separate and distinct human beings brings with it a mix of possibilities, challenges and vulnerabilities. Something will be required of each of us: to change and grow as we take into account the presence of this *other* in our lives. Our little routines and private lives are influenced by another human being.

One way to begin activating the principle of synthesis in a relationship is to shift from an "either/or" way of viewing things to a "both/and" mindset. For example, I am *both* excited *and* worried when Lyn tells me this week she wants to adopt another dog (and a Carolina rescue dog at that, an American dingo, wary of human contact). The both/and mindset allows us to hold different and what might seem to be opposing perspectives; in this way, it acknowledges the complexity of our experience. The either/or frame of mind can lead to divisiveness and fragmentation ("my way or the highway"), while the both/and approach supports collaboration and wholeness.

Synthesis is the way that complex systems grow more coherent. The both/and principle opens a portal for Lyn and me that leads from living only in our own narrow perspective to embracing the view or truth of the other person. It can cut right through the need to argue and be defensive, lifting us out of the painful world of blaming the other person for our resentments and unhappiness. The experience of synthesis helps us get beyond "me versus you" and "right versus wrong." It's like a salve that helps dissolve a compelling need to have things go your own way, because it recognizes that whatever constitutes "your way" is only part of the story.

Of course, in all relationships there will be times when the tension builds between two people and we find ourselves at odds with each other. We become disheartened and troubled, and we must learn to bear the hard times and some degree of darkness when our old wounds and fears reappear. In our marriage, Lyn and I acknowledge our difficulties when they arise, yet we also try to maintain a sense of perspective or proportion. Not everything is a disaster, and you have to learn not to sweat the small stuff, right?

Somewhere early on in our relationship, we rather humorously developed a tri-level classification system for our tensions and disagreements. In sequential order, from the most mild to most disturbing, we would identify troubling events as a "kerfuffle," a "debacle," or a "shit storm." I still remember our very first difficulty, when I decided Lyn was eating too much of the popcorn too quickly at the movie theater out of our shared bag and not thinking about me (an event later referred to as the "popcorn kerfuffle;" we now each get our own bag).

I'm not sure exactly how or why this seems to be helpful, but maybe it lets us accept the event as a moment in time, something that is part of the larger whole or synthesis of our lives together, and then let it go. I've shared this classification system with a couple of my clients who later remarked they found it helpful. Remember, synthesis is an inclusive principle and nothing needs to be excluded or rejected. We can even make room for the very occasional shit storm, and then get back to the business of learning how to unfold our love.

Disidentification

Psychosynthesis is a framework for understanding and cooperating with the natural drive in each person to fully express who we are in the world. For most of us, this journey includes being drawn into relationships with other people. When these relationships are sustained over a long period or even a lifetime, through thick and thin, the relational life of the couple becomes a crucible that stimulates and contributes to the growth of each person. For me personally, this has a lot to do with the fact that through my marriage to Lyn I come to exist not only for myself but also in the context of a shared life with my partner.

There are going to be times when these two aspects of my identity, the "me" and the "we," can lead to feelings of ambivalence or even conflict. I mean, really, do we need to adopt that second dog from the animal shelter when we already have Tommy Tom Toms, one of the all-time great canine companions? There is one part of me that resists the inevitable disruption to our established routines. Yet Lyn tells me she has more love in her heart available for this sweet but frightened animal who simply needs a good home, and so another part of me recognizes this is one way for Lyn to lean into a sense of purpose and meaning in her life.

Fortunately, there is a superpower in Psychosynthesis referred to as disidentification that makes it easier to navigate these different impulses more skillfully. Disidentification is a process that invites us to step back and create some distance between our immediate experience or reactions, on the one hand, and our larger sense of self, on the other. Whenever I am unconsciously identified with something (a belief, thought, emotion, impulse, pattern, etc.), then I am ruled by it in ways that can be self-limiting. Disidentification brings a shift in perspective and helps produce a greater sense of psychological freedom and possibility. Through this process, we come to realize that we are not completely defined by any particular reaction, role or even relationship.

So, applying disidentification to the question of the Carolina dog, I still acknowledge my worries and concerns (this is not about repression or denial), and, also, at the same time I understand that *I am more than* these feelings. I am a self, distinct, though not entirely separate from all that I experience. I have the capacity, on a good day, to disidentify from my narrow field of vision and see a bigger picture. In this case, I am able to connect more fully with the joy in Lyn's face at the prospect of bringing little Tilly into our home.

My marriage gives me a daily experience of communal living that adds a vital source of connection and belonging to my life. Most mornings, I start the day by bringing Lyn a cup of freshly brewed coffee, which I set on the table beside the bed. This simple ritual is a way for me to consciously attend to my relationship, and it brings a certain happiness to both of us. Yet at the same time, I also have a sense of myself as a distinct individual, a "me" who is getting ready for the day ahead. I have my own routine of exercises and stretching, walking and meditating, checking email, and then working on my writing projects or meeting with clients.

When I am only going about my own business, without connecting to the richness Lyn's presence adds to my world, life as "just me" eventually feels incomplete. Yet, if I am only identified with my relationship and lose sight of my own distinct self, then life also feels incomplete. The key here is that the drive to create and manifest our own individual lives is not by definition opposed to the force that draws us into relationships. They can mutually reinforce and support each other. My intention is to honor both: the path of becoming more fully and completely myself over time, and the path of being connected to a larger whole where my life is richly interconnected through relationships with my wife, siblings, friends, colleagues, and the many different communities of which I am a part.

To the extent that I develop the capacity to disidentify from my own reactions and attachments, I am increasingly able to show up for myself and in my relationships with love, compassion and understanding. Disidentification gives me the freedom and spaciousness to live authentically both as a "me" and a "we." Each of these ways of knowing myself adds something that makes my life feel more complete:

If I am not for myself, who will be?
If I am only for myself, what am I?
If not now, when?[4]

Personal Self

The discovery of the personal self, what Assagioli calls the "I" in Psychosynthesis, brings awareness and conscious intention into a relationship. The self is not our personality, mood or feelings; rather, it is our primary and fundamental sense of being. Anchored in self, each person grows more present and connected both to themselves and to their partner. It makes possible what Buber describes as an "I-Thou" relationship.[5]

Since the self is not the "content" of our lives but rather a source of being, the personal self also serves as a synthesizing and unifying center for the rich complexity of human experience. Thus it supports movement towards greater wholeness and integration over time, both on an individual level and within the relationship.

The personal self brings about a perspective shift; it can help us get out of our own way and see the bigger picture. I remember a time, not long ago, when Lyn and I were driving across town to a restaurant with some friends, and I suddenly felt compelled to point out to her where to park the car. When this micromanager takes hold of my brain, I might completely forget that Lyn is perfectly capable of parking the car without any input from me. Furthermore, she has been successfully parking the car for years (decades!). Fortunately in that moment I recognized the impulse of the micromanager, and with the awareness and conscious intention characteristic of the personal self, I was able to take a wiser course of action (keeping my mouth shut). Thus, a pleasant atmosphere was preserved for our dinner out with friends.

Many of these patterned behaviors are triggered by our own discomfort with the vulnerability that is inherent in our lives and in our relationships. Yet, in the face of our difficulties, the personal self is what allows and supports a bigger truth to emerge that is more aligned with our own values. From this perspective, I come into a greater sense of acceptance and ease in the present moment. I can drop all the various agendas of my subpersonalities; no longer needing to control other people or my environment, I find a sense of flow simply by being present to whatever is unfolding in the moment.

When I connect with the personal self, it is like pushing the reset button. It brings me back to myself and I feel more centered, grounded, and open. I get to give up whatever I may have done to myself with scissors and a glue stick and be whole again. The conversation I am having (with myself or my partner) opens up, warms up, becomes enlivening and life-affirming. When I am accessing this self, there's a different quality and feel to the conversation than when I am identified with a subpersonality (the people-pleaser, victim, perfectionist, etc.) and its reductionist worldview. The subpersonalities all have something to offer, yet by definition they tend to have tunnel vision and don't see the bigger picture. They can get us into trouble when they are loosely tethered or operate independently of self.

We all have moments when we lose our internal compass and can't get our bearings. Now and then, some subpersonality finds its way into the driver's seat, perhaps without us even noticing, and we are suddenly showing up in our relationship while "under the influence." Like a psychological DUI, we are hijacked by the particular mindset and strategy of a part of ourselves that seems more like an eight-year-old child driving the bus. When a subpersonality operates unattended and independent of the personal self, this is a recipe for trouble.

What is required at this point is to notice what's going on, disidentify from the psychological formation of the subpersonality, and find some way to reconnect with the personal self, the inner core of our being that has awareness and will. This is easier said than done. Yet it is only the personal self that has the capacity to transform the emotional turmoil and bring us back once again into a more expansive and loving space for authentic connecting and relating. It is at the heart of a deep relationship.

The commitment to a mature relationship requires some essential inner work on the part of each one of us: an ongoing engagement with the personal self. This commitment brings us fully into the magic of being a couple, the dance of self and other that unfolds not just in the small boxes of our subpersonalities but somewhere out in that numinous field, as Rumi noted, "beyond right and wrong, I'll meet you there."[6]

Will

What does the will have to contribute to the psychosynthesis of the couple? Will is the source of freedom and intentionality in our lives, the power to choose within one's circumstances according to our values. This is going to be fundamental to a healthy relationship: the ability to make choices on a daily basis that reflect my deep intention to love my partner and to manifest that love in ways that honor, respect and support our relationship.

Love itself is an act of will. That might not sound very romantic, especially if the will is understood in terms of "being willful" or pushy. But in Psychosynthesis, the will is no bull in a china shop. The function of the will is to direct and regulate the creative expression of self in the world. It is a refined, dynamic force that, when fully developed, includes not only the strength of the will but also higher qualities like goodness, patience, and joy.

Assagioli noted that a well-balanced will is strong, skillful and good, and that these three aspects complement and balance each other. If my will is unbalanced, dominated by strong will for example, I may become overbearing, stubborn and unyielding (not usually a successful strategy in domestic affairs). If my will is only skillful, I could become manipulative or disingenuous. Even the good will, which is the source of loving kindness, can be a distortion in the absence of strong and skillful will, in the sense that others may take advantage of me. Becoming a "yes man" in my relationship, wanting always to please Lyn, will serve neither one of us. It is the synthesis of the strong, skillful and good will that supports the health and vitality of our marriage.

In the context of the psychosynthesis of the couple, the synthesis of love and will is crucial. Generally speaking, people tend to exhibit differential development of love and will. This means that people who demonstrate a relatively strong will (decisive and empowered) may be less outwardly warm and caring, and those who possess more warmth of spirit and a loving nature may have a less well developed will. Assagioli suggested the way to address this imbalance is to cultivate the non-dominant aspect so that these two powerful forces can mutually reinforce each other.

For example, any time that our hearts are stirred, the will can be consciously activated. If I am grateful for the friends and family in my life, I can do the little things that let them know I care. Yesterday I went to Walker Farm, picked up a dozen ears of sweet corn, and visited some friends on the way home to share a little conversation and corn. In these simple gestures, love becomes manifest and expressed through action. Kindness is love in action, and it goes a long way to making our relationships more fulfilling.

Working from the other side of the equation, whenever one experiences a strong impulse of will, the task is then to consciously invite the energy of love or joy to inform the act of will. If I'm feeling motivated to get the house cleaned up over the weekend but I'm griping about it, our Saturday morning will quickly turn sour. No one appreciates a helping hand from a grouchy, resentful spouse! But turn on a little music and start dancing in the kitchen, suddenly the cleanup brightens not only the counters but everyone's mood as well.

The will can be consciously cultivated in daily life. In my relationship with Lyn, I draw upon my will to show up in ways that support connection, caring, and understanding between us; these are things I value, and it is the will that enables me to act upon them. Love and will co-existing in the daily life of the couple builds confidence in a relationship over time. Lyn and I have our difficult moments, but, guided by the loving will, we are better able to navigate these challenges and find our way back to a renewed sense of ease and flow. As Louisa May Alcott wrote, "I am not afraid of storms, for I am learning how to sail my ship."[7]

When Lyn and I find ourselves at odds with each other, we need to engage the will to reestablish a sense of harmony. This often signifies what is referred to as a "choice point" in psychosynthesis: the moment when either one of us might be feeling impatient or frustrated. The choice point entails invoking the will to *acknowledge* the underlying disturbance and then *choose* to behave in ways that are more aligned with our intentions to be respectful and kind.

Another way the will comes into play in our marriage has to do with gaining perspective. Whether it's making vacation plans or deciding how to save for retirement, Lyn and I both are willing to try to understand the other person's feelings, needs and point of view. This sort of empathy and perspective taking requires an act of will—a considered effort to see beyond our own lens and take in the world as the other person sees and experiences it.

The loving will is a powerful force that not only serves our relationships but can transform our world too, as evidenced in the lives of people like Martin Luther King, Mahatma Gandhi, Greta Thunberg and others. This kind of power is available to every one of us; with the energy of the loving will, we each can move our own mountains. When the will is infused with love, then our love is naturally made manifest in the world through acts of will. For the couple in a long-term committed relationship, this becomes an alchemical process that transmutes challenges and difficulties into deeper connection and joy. With the will and heart connected, not only do relationships flourish, but our collective lives come under the influence of a universal loving will that affirms and supports life everywhere on the planet.

Ideal Model

Soon after getting engaged, Lyn and I went to a friend's art exhibit and came across a fabulous painting that we both loved, called "The Conversation." We were drawn not only to its vivid colors and fluid brushstrokes but also to what it suggested about how we might spend our lives together: a rich, intimate and ongoing conversation with a beloved companion. We bought the painting, took it home and hung it in a prominent place in our living room as a daily reminder of how we wanted to fashion a life together.

"The Conversation" evolved for us into what is known as an ideal model in Psychosynthesis. An ideal model represents a vision for living and being in the world that most closely resembles our highest ideals. Lyn and I felt that the theme of the painting captured our aspirations as a couple beautifully. Our ideal model of a relationship is to be authentic with each other—this means sharing the depths of what it means to be human: the joys and disappointments, the darkness and the light, the full range of emotion and experience. It's an invitation to bring our whole self into the relationship; no part of who we are has to be excluded. If we can keep the conversation between us honest and open, then we trust that our connection to each other will be sustained and deepened over time.

Ironically, one of the keys to the ideal model is that it be *realistic* and not idealistic. Lyn and I both had enough experience in relationships to know that being a couple would test us at times. We also knew that a marriage involves work and would require an active commitment to grow and change, along with a willingness to admit missteps and make amends, in order to become the best version of ourselves. When we drop the secret daydream model of happily-ever-after and remember there's no such thing as "always" or "perfection," that opens a path to forgiveness, understanding and compassion both for ourselves and each other. In all these ways our ideal model serves as the foundation for a loving and healing journey together.

Just as our individual needs and desires change over time, so too the ideal model of the marriage evolves to reflect those changes. For Lyn and me, in the early stages of our relationship we went everywhere together. We played tennis as a mixed doubles team at the Brattleboro Outing Club, walked across Scotland side-by-side for three weeks, and shared birthday dinners each year with our close friends Ricia and Bill. Then one summer Lyn took a teaching job in Denver; we realized that sometimes life would pull us in different directions and that was a good thing. We decided to enjoy four days hiking and exploring the Rocky Mountains together before taking off to follow our individual pursuits, which led to meaningful adventures for both of us.

It turned out to be necessary for us as a couple to discuss our need to balance our collective and separate lives. From an ideal model standpoint, the task is for two people to find their unique and particular way to live together that meets the needs of both individuals. Lyn and I are comfortable being around each other while both doing our own thing. Yet we are also mindful of putting our phones down, not responding to the next text or email, and taking an evening walk together with the dogs or enjoying a nice meal on the back deck with friends. We appreciate the shared activities, which are many, and also both have our own separate interests, friends and work lives. It's all a matter of finding the right balance so we don't drift too far apart, on the one hand, or drive each other crazy, on the other.

The ongoing psychosynthesis of the couple includes this process of two people working things out in such a way that results in an experience of harmony and fulfillment: their own particular ideal model that is just right for them. There is no one-size-fits-all; an ideal model grows out of the uniqueness of each relationship. Some may lean in the direction of highly differentiated and separate lives, while others will be drawn to co-exist more as a unit. What is important is that the patterns within a relationship be consciously surfaced and addressed over time since our needs can shift as we move through different life stages.

Sometimes the process of visualizing an ideal model requires that we shake off what Assagioli called "false models," those based on internalized limiting beliefs of what a good marriage *should* look like. There are many qualities, intentions and routines that can inform an ideal model in the psychosynthesis of the couple. If you know people whom you believe have a good relationship, how would you describe what you admire about them? What is your own vision for an ideal model of a relationship?

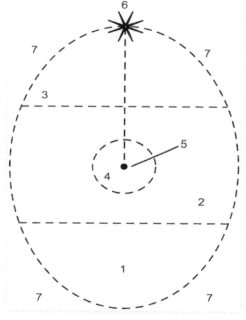

1. Lower Unconscious
2. Middle Unconscious
3. Higher Unconscious or Superconscious
4. Field of Awareness
5. Conscious Self or "I"
6. Transpersonal Self
7. Collective Unconscious

Model of the Human Psyche

Figure 1: Map of the Human Psyche – the "Egg Diagram"
Source: Roberto Assagioli: The Act of Will (1974)

Superconscious (the Transpersonal)

Psychosynthesis has a far-reaching vision of human development; it is a transpersonal psychology, which means that it includes the spiritual dimension and recognizes the human need to find a sense of purpose and meaning in life. This is part of what distinguishes Psychosynthesis from other frameworks in the field of psychology.

In his classic map of the human psyche known as the "egg diagram," (see Figure 1)[8] Assagioli depicted not only the lower unconscious (which Freud had identified) but also a superconscious or transpersonal realm. This dimension represents the unrealized potential in each person to mature over time, thus revealing the full blossoming of what we may be. This is a way of looking at both who we are now and also what is emerging (referred to in Psychosynthesis as "bi-focal vision").

The natural drive in all of life to reach this ripened state of development is evident when we look at the acorn and intuit the oak tree. We plant the grapevine and envision a bountiful harvest of sweet fruit. Similarly, when we walk down the aisle on our wedding day we can sense that we are setting something in motion that is full of potential. The realization of that potential can be consciously cultivated and informed by transpersonal qualities that point us towards our highest aims and values.

In the early morning hours on our wedding day, I sat quietly in meditation to reflect on the specific qualities and commitments I was stepping into as I began this next chapter of my life with Lyn. These included:

> Appreciation: To live each day with you fully and value our time together.
>
> Integrity: To be honest, faithful and true.
>
> Presence/intimacy: To show up, to listen, to be close and share what matters.
>
> Happiness/joy: To laugh, to dance and play, to cultivate *la dolce vita*.

Wholeness/acceptance: To bring all of who I am and to accept you fully for who you are.

Patience/understanding: To take time with each other, to allow for things to unfold and trust the process.

Love: To open my heart to you.

There is another way of framing the transpersonal dimension that takes us in an entirely different direction. Several years ago I attended the Casa Assagioli symposium in Florence, Italy, an annual event to promote further study and research in the Psychosynthesis archives of Roberto Assagioli. On the final day, I was sitting outside at a breakfast table talking with a French colleague named Serge. He spoke with great enthusiasm about the meaning of the transpersonal realm. "It's about the horizontal," he explained, extending his arm out across the table towards me to make the point, "not just the vertical."

Serge was emphasizing that transpersonal development is more than a vertical journey into higher states of consciousness, which is the conventional view. It is also about reaching out beyond ourselves to deeply connect with others, to gain a sense of belonging in the greater human family, and by extension, to see ourselves as one small yet integral part of the larger cosmos.

Entering the complex world of human relationships is like transpersonal boot camp where we learn how to grow beyond our own individual concerns and preoccupations. Yes, I can sit in a state of calm awareness on the meditation cushion, but can I navigate those moments when I'm annoyed, frustrated with or attracted to another person?

Certain spiritual longings may prompt us to go up the mountain to meet the wise being, and yet we might also discover that crossing the street to spend a few minutes chatting with our neighbor can bring its own sort of fulfillment. From this perspective, the transpersonal dimension is not "up there" but rather right here in the spaces between us where we co-exist with all other life on the planet (what the Buddhists call "interbeing").

Long-term relationships are one way we come to know ourselves as part of a larger whole. In terms of the psychosynthesis of the couple, when two people choose to share their lives, this generates a dynamic relational field in which everything is interconnected. Not a word gets spoken that does not reverberate in the field. Every glance, an expression of affection, a momentary impatience, the holding of hands—all these things take place in and inform the relational field of the couple. To deny or ignore the significance of this reality would be equivalent to throwing a stone into the middle of a pond and saying "no ripples, please."

The opportunity here is to develop a systems perspective, to get beyond our tendency to see things solely through the lens of an individual self. For, in reality, what I do to the relationship I also do to myself. All the warmth and love we pour into the pond, and all the grievances or resentments too, ripple out across the relational field. The reverse is also true: what I do to myself I also do to the relationship. If I let myself get overworked, stressed and generally don't take care of myself, then this can't help but impact my relationship.

In my marriage with Lyn, we both intuit the importance of this field. We do the little things that are not so little: we greet each other when arriving home, we express our love in words and, through being affectionate, we do our best to not blame the other person for how we're feeling or take things too personally, and we demonstrate genuine interest in the other person's life and work.

We also both recognize that it's up to each one of us individually to figure out how to keep ourselves healthy and happy. Recognizing the existence of this relational field compels us to be more intentional about how we behave and interact: we learn through experience that we do indeed reap what we sow.

The transpersonal dimension and the principle of interdependence apply to the natural world as well. While hiking in the high Sierras, the naturalist John Muir wrote that "when we try to pick out anything by itself, we find it hitched to everything else in the Universe."[9] So we are "hitched" not only to each other, but to the Earth and the non-human world as well.

Transpersonal Self

The process of psychosynthesis helps us explore who we are in the largest possible context. It invites us to get to know ourselves on many levels: our thought processes and patterns, emotions, physical sensations, desires, dreams and longings, etc. The early stages of psychosynthesis involve learning about our particular personality and how to direct and regulate its various elements. Then there is something more: as a spiritual psychology, Psychosynthesis also invites us to come to know ourselves as a soul on Earth. This is what Assagioli referred to as the transpersonal Self.

The Self is who we are beyond our feelings, our body, our age, where we live and work, or any other characteristics that seem to define us. I may be a very different person at 61 than I was at 21, and yet there is still a sense that it's the same "me" that's been here all along. We might say that the Self is who we are beyond any conditions or circumstances, and yet at the same time it is ever present, illuminating our life journey.

What does it mean to relate to yourself as more than just a personality but also as a soul seeking to express its essence over the course of a lifetime? Assagioli raised this potent question without answering it; he recognized that relating to one's own soul is a deeply personal experience and part of the great mystery of being. For me, this soul dimension implies there is a spiritual guiding force operating in my life, sometimes referred to in Psychosynthesis as "the call of Self."

The question then arises, how might I become attuned to this Self, learn to trust it, and in this way cooperate with the natural unfolding of my life as it is informed by my own soul? This perspective changes how I envision my sense of being on a path in life; rather than forever seeking to *find* myself, I realize I am already on that path of *becoming* myself. The soul is both guiding and embedded in our everyday life experience.[10]

We may not know at any given point how or even where this call of Self is guiding us, and the journey won't always be easy or comfortable. But over time this connection with Self brings a greater sense of vitality and confidence as we come to understand what is real and true for us. As one of my students in the Psychosynthesis training program noted, I may not know exactly where I am going, but I know I am on the right road.

In terms of the psychosynthesis of the couple, imagine a relationship in which two people see each other not just as a personality, with its charms, algorithms, dramas, etc., but also as a soul on Earth. I believe we are all on some level seeking an experience of belonging, and this is both the soul's great mission and also what it has to reveal to us. One way to achieve this sense of belonging is through being in a long-term, committed relationship in which two people are willing to witness each other in all dimensions of their human experience: their joys and fears, their accomplishments and disappointments, the burdens they carry as well as what lights them up and brings them a sense of fulfillment.

As we begin to experience a sense of belonging, the personality (with its various agendas and defense mechanisms) can gradually relax and recede more into the background, while an experience of soulfulness becomes foreground. This shift happens as we grow more comfortable in our own skin and get on with the business of genuinely being who we are. It might be said that the soul is patiently waiting for us to recognize our own light and express it in the world. The purpose and primary aim of psychosynthesis, essentially, is to help release the energies of the Self. When I see Lyn in the context of her soul, I am witnessing her journey to grow more whole over time, to belong not only in her relationship with me but in relationship to her own soul.

Another aspect of the transpersonal Self has to do with an experience of freedom that is beyond or independent of circumstances. Sometimes people leave a relationship or situation in an attempt to get free, yet they remain ensnared in the trappings of their personality. Perhaps they find themselves in another version of the same story that keeps repeating itself over and over again. The reference point of the Self, on the other hand, is transformational; it brings about a decisive shift that loosens the grip of how we are *relating* to our circumstances.

Several years ago, soon after Lyn and I started living together, I woke up one morning feeling distressed. I was overwhelmed, tired, and simply not up to the task of going about my day. When I shared my woes with Lyn, she paused and then said in her matter-of-fact tone: "You seem to think you should be feeling good all the time. You're just a little suboptimal." Boom! "That's it," I cried, "I'm just a little suboptimal!" I wanted to jump up and down and shout from the rooftops: "I'm suboptimal!"

Remarkably, whereas a few moments earlier I was down in the dumps, now I was energized and set free, practically joyful. To the personality, feeling suboptimal is one more problem that has to be fixed. From the perspective of Self, not such a big deal: suboptimal, superoptimal, it's all just another day. And the point, as many have said in different ways, is to live *everything* fully.

Psychosynthesis offers a path to freedom, and this path runs right through the transpersonal Self. Freedom comes when we let go of our personal story about the way things are, or should be, and move into the more spacious realm of the Self. Here we always have choice about how we orient towards our circumstances. This is one of the great gifts of Psychosynthesis to my life and to my relationship with Lyn: I may not be able to control my circumstances all the time, but I can choose how I relate to those conditions in the moment.

Orienting towards a more soulful relationship is a way of seeing my partner not just through the lens of personality but also as a soul in search of realization. In my marriage with Lyn, for example, can I begin to look beyond my immediate preferences and reactions ("why didn't Lyn take out the trash?"), and consider also "what is it that Lyn's soul wants to experience and express in her life?" It's not that I don't still want her to take out the trash, but I also see Lyn under the light of her soul: the way that poetry moves her, the way that color and nature help her feel more alive, the way she loves the dogs, and so on.

Through the process of psychosynthesis, our personality becomes more infused with the energies of the Self over time. This includes the energy of love, which emanates from the Self through the personality and out into the world. The personality, however, is an imperfect instrument; in the context of a long-term relationship, our love can become blocked when we feel shut down or disconnected. Psychosynthesis can help us learn to integrate and harmonize the various aspects of the personality, restoring our sense of Self and bringing our love back online. It is the presence of Self that allows each person in the relationship to grow into a more mature, balanced and well-grounded individual.

Yet another aspect of the Self has to do with transpersonal will. The Self serves as an organizing principle that guides the unfolding of each person's life journey, and the transpersonal will moves us in a particular direction to achieve a sense of purpose, meaning and fulfillment in life. This is not a predetermined course of events, but, rather, a recognition of the drive in all life to manifest itself, to become in form and function that which most closely represents the truth of who we are. Think of this as a sort of "spiritual" DNA that informs our being and becoming. There's no need to teach the acorn how to become an oak, and so it is with us. It is a matter of learning to cooperate with the Self and the natural process of development that is already underway.

The psychosynthesis of the couple invites us to explore what it means to love another person on every level: heart, mind *and* soul. A long-term relationship gives us the necessary time for all of these dimensions to unfold, so that over the years we might gain a sense of each other as "soul mates." The Self acts within and upon the relationship, so that each person can draw upon all their experiences, the difficult as well as the sublime, to further evolve and deepen the experience of soul connection.

Assagioli envisioned the process of psychosynthesis guiding human evolution towards what he called "the supreme synthesis" in which all of humanity is united through "links of love."[11] Now more than ever we are being called, both in our relationships and the world at large, to recognize and affirm our sacred bonds with one another. Intimate long-term relationships, informed by the process of psychosynthesis, can help us further develop our capacity to belong to each other, to form an ever more inclusive and loving togetherness.

In the End

Lifelong relationships can be deeply nourishing and a source of loving companionship. And as those who have attempted this journey know, they can also be quite challenging at times. Yet it is these very challenges, from a psychosynthesis perspective, that frame the relationship as a whetstone for each person's self-development.

What I would suggest to any couple starting out is this: take your time, be gentle and kind, and give each other the benefit of the doubt. It can be hard enough to figure out who we are, what we want, and the proper way to load the dishwasher *without* taking another person into account (who is also sorting out their own "stuff"). Introduce someone else into the equation and things can get complicated pretty quickly.

Paradoxically, for me, marrying Lyn has actually seemed to simplify things. One day soon after our wedding, I turned to her and said, "All we have to do now is love each other, grow old together and die" (that sentiment didn't please her as much as it did me!). It means that there is no exit strategy anymore, no looking for a prettier view on the other side of the hill. In this place and time, on this piece of ground with this particular person, I will put my whole self in. And through this process I will come to terms with myself and with the great mystery of a deep, loving relationship with another human being. As John Lennon and Paul McCartney have it in "The End":

And in the end, the love you take,
is equal to the love you make.

This means being willing to engage in our marriage guided by the conscious intention to love my partner as well as I possibly can. I will spend the rest of my life learning how to do that; it's all part of the daily exercise of unfolding our love. So yes, I do believe my deep commitment to a long-term relationship with Lyn simplifies things. And we will both work at it, so that over time, our marriage may give back as much as we put into it and probably a whole lot more.

Stephen and Janet

Janet's compelling story of her long relationship with her husband, Stephen, shows how two headstrong, spiritually-oriented individuals worked together to build a vibrant and sustaining marriage and family life. She writes candidly about the difficulties she and her husband have faced over the years, including Stephen's recurring bouts with cancer and their unexpected cross-country move.

CHAPTER TWO

A Marriage of Strong-Willed Partners

Janet Messer

Writing about my marriage has been difficult for me. I have struggled with how much to expose of our private lives and how to balance the description of hurts and disappointments over the years with the joy of connection and the personal and spiritual growth we have experienced. After writing several versions that I did not like much, I finally asked my husband, Stephen, to talk with me about our marriage. The hour-long conversation that unfolded became a living experience of why we are still happily together after 45 years. As he talked, I became aware of my respect and admiration for him. He described his journey and understandings and then he listened to mine, and we found ourselves building on what each other said. We discovered new things about ourselves and one another as we talked together, even when we disagreed about some things. This, I realized, holds the essence of our story. The conscious experience of openness, curiosity, mutual respect, and affection built on a foundation of commitment to spiritual level goals has given us a lifelong partnership in which we are still growing and learning together. These goals have emerged from our individual and mutual involvement in many paths of growth that we have been privileged to participate in. We have embraced teachings from Buddhism, Psychosynthesis, tai chi, and Arica Institute, among others. Our commitment to our growth as individuals and a couple has not been casual or haphazard, but rather conscious and often disciplined and central to our lives. We also have faced unasked-for challenges that demanded growth. In addition, we have both had moments of spontaneous grace that gave us sudden gifts of mystical insights.

We were in our mid-20s when we married, and we still had a lot of developmental tasks to achieve, while also committing to spiritual growth. Back then, I had little idea of what real personal and spiritual growth would look like. We both just wanted to get enlightened, even though we didn't know exactly what that meant. Stephen now sees his part of our couple journey as moving from a commitment to individualism to being a team, a unit that is made of us both, but is more than either of us. My sense of our journey has been about softening and breathing, about continually drawing the circle bigger to allow each of us to be all of who we are, and about committing to our own authenticity while still committing to one another. In Psychosynthesis terms, we have tried to move from identification with elements of our personality to identification with Self. That Self is always present, whether we are aware of it or not. Remembering that we are both our personal selves and our Higher Selves and acting on that knowledge forms the context of our ongoing journey. We are also aware that our relationship and existence is a tiny part of a universe that we do not really comprehend, much as we wish to do so.

As Americans, we believed that it was good to be a defined and strong individual; we both also were feminists and believed

I should have an opportunity for education and career equal to Stephen's. In our 20s and 30s, in the developmental process of finding our own identities, we often fought to "be ourselves" and to avoid giving up too much of our own needs for the other. It is probably an understatement to say we are both strong-willed. We both came from families with one dominant and one very quiet parent. My mother and Stephen's father both dominated, and we each followed unconscious patterns that made us expect to get our own way. Combined with our commitment to open and honest processing, that means we have talked and argued a fair amount as we tried to work through conflict. For a long time, we believed that expressing anger verbally was a good thing. Our opinions on that have, thankfully, changed. We have never been physical or cruel, but earlier in our relationship, we caused some emotional harm to one another with angry words. Now, we try to moderate our dissatisfaction and express it with consideration for our partner's feelings. I also think that since my father and Stephen's mother were quite introverted, we both did not have a strong connection with one parent as children. We seek that connection with our opposite sex partner now, with one another in our couple.

When we first lived together, I thought that Stephen would be the one who had to change and grow, while I could "be myself." Ha! We could have gotten stuck at this point, as many couples do, if we had not had higher principles to work with, learned from the spiritual/psychological work we engaged in. Psychosynthesis offered the concept of identification and disidentification, which gave us practical ways to work with the Buddhist principle of non-attachment. Arica offered the concept of ego fixations (akin to subpersonalities) and a structured process called karma cleaning, to process past trauma, as well as many meditation trainings. We embraced all of this. We agreed that we wanted to "get enlightened" and that it was all right to confront the other when we noticed them identifying with a subpersonality or ego fixation. Instead of (or usually after!) defending ourselves, we tried to examine our behavior and beliefs with the purpose of recognizing identifications that keep us from identifying with our Higher Self. For example, recently Stephen had a strong reaction to a political opinion I expressed. He began to feel angry and I asked him why, and I wondered about why I was so attached to my opinion as well. We both were able to take a short break and deepen our insight into what we were really feeling and get beyond the conflict. We are a product of our personal histories, but also of our aspirations and our commitment to embodying them. As I write this, I am filled with gratitude to Stephen for his sincere efforts over all these years, and also with gratitude to all of our teachers.

Raising children was an important part of our process of moving from self-absorption to cooperating with the needs of others. Soon after the birth of our first child, I realized I would never be alone again. My connection to the baby lived inside me even when I was not with him. I remember being in awe and surrendering to that reality. We were strongly committed to doing our best for our two sons. In that process, we learned a lot about deep listening and unconditional love. For me, parenting was a spiritual path that demanded I slow down and be present almost on a continuous basis. We valued the souls of our children. We wanted to encourage their inner development as well as support their learning on the outer levels of achievement. Stephen and I reached a stronger level of cooperation in meeting the demands of parenting together and have shared the ineffable love we feel for our children. We could often translate what we learned from parenting into our couple relationship as well.

Assagioli's description of the development of the Will is one lens to describe our journey as a couple. I quote here from *Psychosynthesis* by Assagioli:

> There are many people who have an over-developed personal will—generally directed towards self-assertion and the domination of other people.... Therefore, it is important to consider how to minimize and offset these dangers and drawbacks.... Second—and more important—is that of developing other functions in the individual which would check and balance the will-function ... that is, development of humanitarian love, compassion, loving understanding of others, and the ethical sense, the sense of responsibility concerning the effect one has upon other people. The highest expression of this is harmlessness. The third and highest way, which partially includes the second method, is the awakening and functioning of the *spiritual will*, connected with the realization of the spiritual Self.... But, of course ... establishing of [sic] a direct relation to the spiritual will, to the Self, is the goal of psychosynthesis. This means the developing of a constructive, strong, persevering, and wise will ... the energy of will and the energy of love, so that we eventually have in operation a "loving will". [1] (p. 141)

Our Story

I met my husband, Stephen, through his resume for the job of biology teacher at the alternative public high school where I worked as an English teacher. All faculty were invited to review the resumes and attend the interviews of job candidates. Standing in the office, I read his resume, including the part about interests and hobbies.

"He's a Scorpio," I told a fellow teacher. "And he's vegetarian, and he does tai chi and meditates. I'm going to marry this guy!" I was 24 and living in a new city at my first job after college in 1975. I had dated a lot, but had not met someone who was as grounded in both the spiritual and practical realms as I was. The next day, I dressed for his interview in my best hippy sexy clothes, a tight turtleneck sweater and long skirt. Unfortunately, I was not impressed. Driving home, my co-teacher said she thought he was fine. "He's just a biology teacher," she said. "You don't have to marry him." To me, he seemed shy and soft-spoken. He was not hired at my school.

A month later, I went to the meditation center where he taught, Arica Institute.[2] I had previously had some significant meditation experiences at Arica in another city. Going there seemed like a good way to meet friends I might like. Again, I loved the meditation work and honestly, I would have hooked up with any of the "spiritual" guys teaching there. And, again, I was not specifically impressed by my future husband. A month after that, I went to a party held at Arica to celebrate the end of a group meditation training. When I arrived, I saw Stephen and he immediately welcomed me and kissed me hard. I was finally impressed. (I learned much later that he had mistaken me for someone else.) Later that night, we danced together. Like in the dance in the gym in *West Side Story*, the rest of the room seemed to disappear. After we danced, we left and went out to walk, ending up climbing the steps of the Philadelphia Art Museum (like in the movie *Rocky*—not yet made). It was romantic and exhilarating and Stephen remembers falling in love with me on that walk. I remember feeling excited and happy. We walked and talked for hours and when we got back, the party was over and the building was locked. Stephen and I kissed for real at that point. After, I asked if he remembered my name. Luckily, he did. A week later, on our first date, we drove two hours to his childhood home, New York City, where we saw Pir Vilayat Khan, the Sufi master, and danced with his dancers. We began to spend most of our free time together.

This series of events energized me on all levels. I was actively searching for a way to nourish my spiritual life. I had explored many paths by then, including Zen Buddhism, kundalini yoga, Gestalt therapy, Edgar Cayce and psychic channeling, and Judaism. Arica offered conscious exercises on physical, emotional, mental, and spiritual levels in a non-religious context and was a wonderful vehicle for my growth. This was not the first time I had followed my inner guidance to find spiritual teachings, but it was the first time I had met a man in a spiritual group whom I liked so much and who liked me.

While my spiritual life was being energized by my new meditation experiences, I finally began to experience the emotional intimacy and safety I had craved, but never found, with the many men I had been in relationship with. I remember one evening, soon after we met, Stephen was painting his bedroom in a house he had moved into. I laid on the bed watching him paint while we talked. I found myself confiding in him a painful experience of my earlier life. I felt safe to cry and to talk about the hurt I still carried from that time in my life. He listened so intently and with such focused attention and gentleness, I felt genuinely loved. I began to trust him, which was so deep and important for me. At the same time, he was dealing with the loss of his first committed relationship. His live-in girlfriend of five years had broken up with him just a few months before I met him and quickly moved on with someone else. He trusted me to listen deeply and consistently and support him in processing his loss, and we spent a lot of time in those first six months helping him grieve. We built a deep sense of trust.

Very soon we were a committed couple. Six months after meeting Stephen, I did my first residential Arica training, a 40-day training in the mountains of New Mexico, while Stephen did an Arica Advanced Training for three weeks in NYC. He had a brief romantic relationship there. The trust and commitment we had built paid off. He told me about the relationship while it was happening. We worked through it together; we looked for why it happened and what it meant to him. I was able to accept it and forgive him (although it took a few more years for him to realize how he hurt me and sincerely apologize). A month later, we got engaged. We left our jobs in Philadelphia and drove across the country to Oregon for him to start naturopathic medical school. We married about 18 months after we met.

Some principles began to emerge in our relationship. We were both fiercely strong-willed and independent. We were also in love, and happy to have found someone so compatible intellectually and spiritually. We respected one another as separate people. We believed in the principle of equality on the personal level, which was based in the ultimate equality of us as souls. We tried to explore our needs and feelings and understand one another instead of judging. We saw ourselves as being in a continuing process of growth, where often what looked like mistakes also had meaning that needed to be understood. This process of exploration, openness, and forgiveness continues to this day. I had no idea how demanding this would be and continues to be, even now. Even with our deep belief in these principles, we still mess up and feel and act selfishly sometimes, probably every day. I still have to observe my anger and expectations, breathe, and let go of my desire to have what I want all the time.

Stephen and I are similar in our commitment to our spiritual goals, in our commitment to processing with one another, in our ideas about children and money, and in our devotion to service through our professional work. We share a curiosity and love of learning. We also both love to go deep in exploring ourselves and others. But we were also different in ways that came as a surprise to me as we lived together. Stephen was an athlete in college, a lacrosse goalie. I was a performer, acting and directing plays and always in dance classes. We both returned to those activities in middle age. Stephen is a scientist; he is exceptionally mentally active and curious. I have always been intuitive and empathic, often having trouble shielding myself from the energy and emotions of other people. Stephen eagerly embraces the new and I hold back, clinging to the comfort of the familiar. If not for him, I would not have owned a microwave oven or a cell phone for years after they were available. We have tried to learn from one another and allow our differences to enrich our relationship. For example, I find performances and artistic experiences for us to enjoy. Stephen has coached our children's sports teams and taught them chess, which they still enjoy together. Stephen's extensive knowledge about health and medicine has allowed us to function at high levels of wellness. My emotional sensitivity and skills have supported us through many emotional crises. We have also learned from one another and developed qualities we did not have so much in the beginning.

Communication

We are talkers, as I have said before, and strongly believe in maintaining open communication. In Psychosynthesis terms, in my opinion, this is the best way to increase awareness in the couple as a unit. I am good at self-observation. I can easily be present to my body experience, emotions, thoughts, and will. But I cannot function as part of a unit with Stephen without being aware of his experience. Mind-reading and projection are poor substitutes for direct knowledge. This means we must ask how the other is and listen to the answers. And we have to do that again and again, with curiosity and suspending judgment. We have had to deliberately learn and practice this because we both can be self-involved. Sometimes, I don't really care how Stephen is, but I ask anyway. Every time, I am enriched by his sharing and glad I asked. Sharing and listening builds couple-based awareness. And it increases our empathy for each other and our ability to be good partners.

Alone/Together

I have always felt alone. I realized at some point, probably about ten years into our marriage, that I wished that Stephen was exactly like me and could understand me completely. This need must come from a very young part of me. I remember telling him one day how much I wished he were just like me, so that I would not have to feel alone. He was slightly amused and answered that that was not possible, because he wanted to be exactly like himself, not like me. It was the perfect answer. Instead of feeling ashamed of my admission of aloneness, I felt enlightened by his simple assertion. Of course, he wanted to be just like himself, and I also wanted to be just like myself.

Still, I wrestled with closeness and separateness, learning that I needed both to feel whole and happy. As much as I craved being emotionally connected with Stephen, I also wanted to just be myself, have my own friends and pursue my interests that were not the same as his. Sometimes I felt guilty for wanting that; other times I felt lonely when he pursued his interests apart from me. At a Psychosynthesis conference in 1984, about eight years into our marriage, in a workshop with Jeanette Rainwater, I was working on these issues using imagery (use of imagery in Psychosynthesis will be discussed later in this chapter) and an image emerged that symbolized a truth about our marriage. It seemed like a silly image, but it was a perfect one and has stuck with me all these years. I saw a rectangular object and saw it get split apart, as if with an axe, and then almost magically, heal again, becoming whole. This repeated several times, until I realized that the split was an illusion. The image transformed into a zipper, unattached to a piece of clothing. The zipper glided up and down, as is its natural function. If you sew, you know that a zipper is mounted on heavy canvas that surrounds it on three sides. This zipper was a symbol of something that is simultaneously two and one. Zipped up, it is one thing. Unzipped, the two sides seem separate, but are still joined by the fabric at the bottom. That was our marriage—two separate people, but joined at the foundation. We were always two and one at the same time.

We have done our best to support one another's independent activities. When Stephen wanted to spend Saturdays playing chess downtown and entering tournaments, I used that time to do my own projects (or just wander around the mall if I wanted.) When I would get a part in a play (once every few years) and had to rehearse most nights for six weeks and then perform for another month, every weekend, Stephen adapted and took care of the children and shared in my excitement. When I applied to PhD. programs, he promised to move our family to whatever city I had to move to. When I got into our hometown university, he spent six years taking care of the children part of every weekend, so I could study.

Throughout our first ten years of marriage, we faced challenges. We had two children in the first four years. While they were young, Stephen attended naturopathic medical school all day and I worked for my Master's degree in Counseling at night. When they were three and seven, I began my PhD. work in Psychology. It took me seven years to graduate, because I did some of it part-time. Stephen and I cooperated constantly on childcare, transportation, cooking, bedtime routines, homework and children's activities. I always felt loved and supported by Stephen's commitment to my education and career, and I was committed to his. I treasure the memory of him and the children surprising me at my office on my birthday, where I was, as always, writing a paper on a Saturday. They spirited me off to the park for a picnic, gifting me with a new picnic basket as a birthday present. When I finally had to actually write my PhD. dissertation and had a hard time separating from everybody to do it, Stephen loaded the kids into the van and took off for two weeks to give me time alone. I am still not sure where they went, but I am grateful for his concrete support. I also supported him when he left several times each year for weeks at a time to study or teach homeopathy. We both actually loved being at home without the other, since it was a time to totally expand into the space ourselves and not have to be considerate of the other.

Illness

About 12 years into our marriage, a big challenge emerged when we were in our late 30s. I was still in my PhD. program. The boys were seven and eleven years old. Stephen was practicing as a doctor in Oregon and already gaining a national reputation as a teacher of homeopathy. Then, he was diagnosed with colon cancer at age 36. We had to face the possibility of his death and a fact about his health we had not known for sure before. He was a carrier of a genetic disorder called Lynch syndrome.[3] A person with Lynch syndrome often cannot repair genetically damaged cells that can easily go on to develop into a cancer. Most of us have repair mechanisms in our cells that recognize and eliminate these genetic mistakes when they happen. Lynch carriers do not have that, and the result can be a higher rate of many cancers. We knew that some of Stephen's relatives had this disorder, and some had died at a young age. But we did not know until that time if he had inherited it. Now we knew. The day after he was diagnosed, I withdrew from graduate school for a year. Stephen had surgery that removed much of his colon, underwent radiation, and eventually recovered. But our lives were altered, and we could never return to the childlike sense of safety we had before. We walked through a door into a new universe we had not known existed. One bright light was that we found Patricia Norris, PhD, a psychologist who worked with cancer patients using Psychosynthesis. Stephen spent a week at her clinic in Topeka during his recovery and later she became my mentor as well.

For me, my love and support were tested. I learned to be a cancer spouse. That meant reading and learning about cancer and treatments, comforting Stephen through his fears, and letting go of many of my own needs while we focused on his journey. We also had to continue to parent and not scare the children. We entered a new world that our friends had not experienced and we stumbled through it together. We came through with more love and trust for one another. I had always been terrified of dying and thought about it a lot. Stephen had not seemed to understand my deep fear of death. But now he did and it made me feel more understood.

Six months later, when he had recovered, I reverted to believing he was OK, but Stephen never did. He developed some PTSD in relation to his diagnosis and had lost his denial of death, a common occurrence in cancer patients. Having a cancer diagnosis is traumatic, even if the person recovers from it and the treatments. Living permanently in a body that gets cancer frequently, or randomly, is beyond what most of us can imagine. But this was/is

Stephen's situation. This began an era of concern about his health on his part. But mostly, we returned to our busy, interesting lives.

Big Changes

Our professional work has always been important to both of us, more like a vehicle for our souls to express ourselves than just a job. We always balanced it with family life. But after the children left for college, our careers took up more of our energy. Stephen, especially, had a sense of mission about teaching homeopathy and training young doctors. He was a leader in national-level educational trainings for many years. I continued to develop my psychotherapy practice and teach Psychosynthesis locally. However, 22 years ago, our lives changed radically. Stephen was recruited to teach at a naturopathic medical college in Phoenix, AZ, far from our home in Oregon. His cancer was 12 years in the past and we were focused on the present and the future.

I had not been aware before that time how important this aspect of his career had become to him. I resisted moving away from my friends and community involvements, which meant so much to me. As is our way, we talked about the move for an entire year before I finally agreed to it. Teaching doctors, which had been a smaller part of his career, had taken on an urgency for him and become his new purpose. Neither of us knew if he would have moved without me if I had refused; that was too scary to consider. I decided not to risk it. I was faced with a choice of giving up my marriage or losing everything else that meant something to me. With tremendous grief, I chose our marriage. The day we drove out of town in our laden van, we were openly emotional. I wept uncontrollably as we merged on to the freeway, leaving everything I loved. Stephen was singing and experiencing a sense of tremendous joy as he set out for his new life. He did remind me, after reading this, that he, too, burst into tears as we drove past the freeway exit where our best friends lived. As always, we were together and apart, loving each other and trusting, as we made a painful, momentous change in our lives.

Because I often felt alone, the community we had become part of in Oregon was precious to me. We lived in a small city, where, during more than 20 years, I had become part of overlapping communities—spiritual, theater, professional, girlfriend and couple friendships. Leaving all this was terrifying to me and I felt very sad. In order to leave, I promised myself that I would be proactive in our new home and try to recreate some of what I left. In my first five years in Phoenix, I was depressed for the first time in my life. My husband walked into a college, full of colleagues and purpose. I had to build everything by myself. We did have adventures and explored our new surroundings together, which was new and fun. Our old friends visited us and we visited Oregon almost every summer. But I was changed by the move. I became more introverted and adapted to spending more time alone. I made some friends, but the relationships were more superficial than I liked. I built a therapy practice and became a respected part of the psychology community here. I even did some acting and joined a chorus. But Oregon still calls to me and I want to spend more time there when we retire. I sometimes want to hold it over my husband that I moved here for him, but I only rarely surrender to that meanness.

Before we moved, I also decided that I could replace my local community involvement with becoming involved with the national Psychosynthesis community, which I had avoided out of shyness and physical distance. I was the only Psychosynthesis practitioner in our town in Oregon and also in Phoenix, as far as I could tell. In 2003, I took a risk and applied to attend a gathering of old and new Psychosynthesis practitioners. Even though they didn't know me at all, I was accepted to attend. That experience changed my life. I felt welcomed into the group and found many soul-mates there. I soon joined the steering committee of the national organization, eventually becoming its co-chair. I found new friends, some of whom I feel deeply connected to. The move to Phoenix, my aloneness and need for new community eventually led me down a path to writing for this book. I still miss Oregon, but I can see how new things have emerged that are also fulfilling and nourishing.

Cancer Again

Five years after our move to Phoenix, Stephen was diagnosed with colon cancer again, about 18 years after his first diagnosis.

Since then, Stephen has been diagnosed with life-threatening cancers, some quite rare, at least ten times. He has had many surgeries, sometimes several a year. He has undergone radiation three more times and chemotherapy once. He also was treated with immunotherapy. And, of course, he has treated his condition with naturopathic therapies, diet, and homeopathy. Now, four years after his most recent surgery, he seems to be well and he continues to monitor, have frequent scans, etc. As his body changes, we have both had to learn repeatedly that Stephen is more than his body; he remains, essentially, a soul, who is alive and whole despite changes to his body. One miracle in this story is that genetic testing showed that neither of our children inherited the Lynch defect.

Living with Stephen's health issues has demanded that I surrender my expectations about how our lives would unfold. The journey of having and treating cancer involves devoting a lot of energy to things I had not imagined I would do as a middle-aged person, like studying medical research, visiting doctors, and spending a huge amount of time in hospitals. I never expected to focus so much time and energy on serious health issues. Mostly, I have accepted this journey, but sometimes not. I remember one night when it all was too much for me and I cried, demanding, "Can we please talk about something besides cancer? I have a life too, and I don't have cancer."

Stephen has, naturally, developed some anxiety about his health, which he works on in many ways. But we also have decided to value and accept his anxiety as an important subpersonality whose job is to save his life. I see his vigilance as one of the reasons he is alive and healthy at age 71.

Meanwhile, throughout the last 35 years, I have managed to be in denial about Stephen's possible early death. I have told myself that this is due to my accurate intuition that he is not dying yet, and partly to my determination to avoid rehearsing sorrow for what is not happening now.

But I think that my denial of his possible premature death also comes from a more vulnerable place in me. I don't want my husband to be ill or to be frail. It scares me. I feel sad and helpless when he is suffering physically or emotionally. I can also feel angry and abandoned; I want him to be all better. I think maybe seeing Stephen in pain or in physical danger threatens an essential agreement between us. I want him to be my partner, healthy and vital and full of energy the way he used to be. I hate that this condition has affected us both so much. I try to breathe and let go and be present to the reality of what is happening now. That reality sometimes includes pain, but also joy and love and continuing gratitude for each other, all the more so because we know we can lose this life together any time. This is a journey of maturing that all couples have to go through, but we started that journey much younger than most.

Will

Thriving through my husband's medical journey has demanded tremendous development of Will from both of us. Life has presented frightening challenges to us, usually suddenly and always decidedly unwelcome. We did not know that our wills would become so important in surviving and growing through this. Assagioli writes that the Will has several aspects—strong, skillful, good, and transpersonal (or spiritual). We have gained strength in each aspect on this journey.

It is easy to see the need for the strong and skillful wills in overcoming serious illness. As an example, Stephen has walked around the nurses' station after surgeries hundreds of times, even when he is tired and in pain. I have learned to change wound dressings even though I hate body fluids and smells. We have endured through exhaustion and fear and kept on doing research, questioning doctors, changing our diets and finding the energy to see our patients between tending to our own healing. Our post-surgery walks to the corner have become a sweetly meaningful ritual.

Our good wills have also developed through this journey. This would include Stephen's caring about me even when he is ill and me caring for him when I am exhausted and maybe upset that he is sick again. It includes our determination to reestablish our sexual relationship after every surgery, to laugh, and to still be delighted when the neighborhood roadrunner runs through our yard. It would include Stephen encouraging me to leave to fly cross country to be with my dying father, only three weeks after he himself had had major surgery.

Our transpersonal or spiritual wills are responsible for both of us remaining positive about life in general. It also underlies our dedication to our patients and students and continual return to our care for them. Remarkably, throughout his illnesses, Stephen continued to work as full-time faculty, training new doctors. He has just recently retired. Our sense of higher purpose infuses us with inspiration and energy to do our work. And we feel more connected to one another than we ever have before.

Active Techniques

We are unfortunately compelled to hurt ourselves or one another or to misbehave because of the pressure of our childhood traumas and our childhood/human needs. But we are also drawn to perfect ourselves by the pull from our higher selves. We have always had a vision of the relationship we wanted. Actualizing that vision has taken work, sometimes deliberate undertaking of exercises to support our goals. Assagioli expresses this well:

> What has to be achieved is to expand the personal consciousness into that of the Self; to reach up...to unite the lower with the higher Self. But this, which is so easily expressed in words, is in reality a tremendous undertaking. It constitutes a magnificent endeavor, but certainly a long and arduous one, and not everybody is ready for it... In favorable cases the ascent takes place to some extent spontaneously through a process of natural inner growth, fostered by the manifold experiences of life; but often the process is slow. In all cases, however, it can be considerably accelerated by our deliberate conscious action and by the use of appropriate active techniques.[4]

Our lives have offered ample natural opportunities for growth, and we have also sought out "active techniques" that supported positive change in us. I share below some of the things we have used to support our personal and spiritual couple process, in hopes that readers might find some they want to try.

Listening

Learning to listen well is key to overcoming self-absorption. When we were young, to learn to listen better, we sometimes practiced an exercise in which we set a timer and one person was supposed to talk for ten minutes. The other person could only listen and not comment at all. Then we reversed roles. We also learned to do active listening, which we needed to do for our work as well. That is a method of listening for and reflecting the feelings and thoughts of the other without adding your own point of view. We still sometimes use that now. For example, if I am upset about something, Stephen might say, "You are angry and hurt, right?" and, if I agree, he might say, "You feel hurt because I ignored you when you asked for…" and so on, until I feel accurately heard enough to let down my guard and be open to trusting again.

Learning

We keep learning, often through reading new writing about consciousness, health, therapy, history, current events, and poetry. We share new ideas with one another and try new techniques together. We still learn from each other and others and love that there is always something new to learn.

Gratitude

We often took one another for granted. We began, a few years ago, to say thank you for small and large things. It is now the norm and no longer something we have to remember to do. Thank you for paying the taxes. Thank you for making this pot of tea. Thank you for listening today. Thank you for telling me how you felt. This practice lets the other know that they are seen and their efforts are appreciated. It also draws our own attention to how much we are constantly being given, by one another, by others, and by the generous universe of which we are a part.

Tai Chi[5]

We have practiced tai chi for many years, about 45 for Stephen and about 35, sometimes off and on, for me. Tai chi is a martial art that encompasses breathing, slow movement and deep focus. Its motto is "Strength through softness." Tai chi is a concrete way to experience being connected to the earth and being quiet at the center while your body is moving, responsive to the environment and your partner, if you are doing it with another person. When I am doing tai chi with relaxation and deep concentration I feel like I come close to embodying the stability of the Self while being totally in my body. I can use tai chi practice to immediately connect with Self.

Imagery

Psychosynthesis has brought the use of imagery for personal growth to new heights. We have used imagery throughout our relationship for many tasks. We have used it in Stephen's cancer journey both for physical and emotional healing. For example, he has discovered a subpersonality who is a feisty, little mouse brandishing a sword, brave in the face of a threatening attack. I recognize the image of myself in a cave where I go to recover from hurt feelings and can tell Stephen, "I'm in my cave and not ready to come out yet." Imagery is an effective way we open to unconscious parts of ourselves and we use it deliberately as a way to understand and share our inner lives with each other. Images unite the conscious and unconscious minds and hold wisdom that can supersede concrete thinking. Images have provided us with deep insight and also served as inspiration for action.

Meditation

Meditation is multifaceted and serves many purposes in our relationship. In the most basic sense, regular meditation practice has taught us to observe ourselves and gain understanding of how our inner worlds function. We use it sometimes when we are in a bad mood or in conflict. We stop and meditate for a short time and see what is happening inside. Sometimes that helps us let go of the conflict or be more sympathetic to one other. It definitely serves as a pause or re-set mentally and has taught us to have better control of our monkey minds. Meditation also is a deep spiritual practice that can open the connection to our higher selves. Regular meditation practice increases the possibility of experiencing the sacred and opens us to the infusion of energy from the Self, which is transformative. Meditation connects us with our basic goodness and loving will and makes our couple successful more than anything else we do.

Conclusion

I consider us very lucky to have chosen one another as partners, especially at a period in our lives when we were young and not really aware of what we would want as we faced life's changes. I had dated and fallen in love with men who would not have been good partners for me, and I had no idea of that when I was young. But even with a wonderful partner, I have learned that marriage can be full of painful disappointments and hurt and giving up control. We have opened ourselves to wanting love and to being vulnerable and tender with someone else over a long time. Stephen doesn't always know what I need and sometimes can't give it to me even if he knows and understands. I also have disappointed him many times. But I believe now that if you choose a partner who embraces Good Will and each of you is open to learning and being taught how to be a thoughtful, kind partner, then many times, you can each support and be present for what the other needs. But it will never be always.

Relationships demand active attention. I have learned that my partner is not exactly who I thought he was when I married him. And even if I had known him totally (which is impossible,) he has changed over time and with new experiences. And so have I. Given how life changes all the time, we have to show up and be present every day to know what is happening now; and as soon as we get the hang of it, things change again, so we have to keep being present and open to learning.

There are events that have brought exceptional challenges to us, especially, but not limited to, having children and raising them, moving, aging, and serious illness in one or the other of us. I consider myself very lucky to have married someone who, like myself, is still excited about and committed to his own personal growth, even in the darkest times. But I have also had to temper my expectations and accept the imperfect person I married, because I, too, am far from perfect. I still struggle, not only with my unrealistic expectations of my husband, but with my own shortcomings.

When I finished writing this chapter, I invited Stephen to read it. He had just a few minor suggestions for changes. But his first reaction was relief that he "came off sounding better" than he thinks he was. Thinking more deeply, he said that reading this story makes him aware of how many times he let me and himself down and how much he regrets those times. He said it makes him aware of how grateful he is to me for the many times I was there for him and that it inspires him to be more present and loving now.

We all want to be happy and often think that the right marriage partner will ensure that. Although I would deny that I believe that, in daily life, I often blamed Stephen for not doing or saying the right thing for me. That tendency to blame him for my occasional unhappiness has been a problem for a long time and I am just getting a handle on it. I remember doing therapy with Laura Perls, one of the founders of Gestalt therapy, at a workshop in the 1980s, when, evidently, I was struggling with a relationship issue. Near the end, she asked me, "What are you asking for from someone else that you could give to yourself?" At the time, in my 30s, I didn't really understand her question. I felt a little chastised, and I thought maybe she was implying that I was too needy, or that if I had higher self-esteem, I wouldn't care if my husband disappointed me. But I never forgot her question and I respected her enough to know that the answer would be important. I am just beginning to be able to answer it.

Where I am in my life now, I think I finally understand what Dr. Perls was suggesting. I have grown to a point where I am so much more connected with my self/ Higher Self that I routinely hold myself with compassion and unconditional love. This sense of love is deep and profound. It sustains me through good and bad times. I can go inside and connect with my Self when I have difficult feelings and almost always find perspective and real comfort. I can give myself what truly is not possible to get from someone else.

My little child part is still in me and still wants to be totally loved and accepted by someone else. But I have learned that the only way to be certain of being loved is for me to be willing to be, for myself, the partner I am searching for—present, compassionate, forgiving and unconditionally loving. In Psychosynthesis terms, I must embody my Higher Self for and toward myself. No one can do this for me. I must do this, in fact, to be able to offer that deep love to my partner. We both must take responsibility for our own evolution as spiritual beings. Only if we accept that reality can we continue to inspire one another and increase our love and connection on all levels. And, for that, thank you, my dear husband, for your companionship on this journey.

Walter and Cynthia

Here we meet Walter, a white man in his 80s, and Cynthia, an African-American woman in her mid-60s who have been going strong together for over 38 years. The evocative image of "the three candles," which grew out of a conversation Walter had with his mother, reflects their perspective on committed relationships. In this chapter, they describe how their ongoing work with Psychosynthesis has helped them to maintain their individuality within the context of their thriving partnership.

CHAPTER THREE

Three Candles: Strategies for a Marriage

Cynthia Lashley and Walter Polt

Beauty, art, and music deeply move both of us. We love singing as chorus members in classical concerts with orchestras. We both Jazzercise, often together. We feel safe enough with each other to cry (Cynthia more so than Walter). We love cuddling and hugging. We try to snuggle and kiss whenever we can. We love the taste of good, organic food and try to eliminate nonfoods, particularly those built on white sugar, salt, and white flour. We love kombucha, warm summer nights, and cold winter evenings in bed.

And we are very different.

Cynthia: I am African-American and in my mid-60s.

Walter: I am German-Austrian-American and in my 80s.

From the get-go this relationship was not what either of us had planned.

Cynthia: I am an anxious person. I worry about things I have no control over.

Walter: I tend to be laid back. "What, me worry?"

Walter: I sometimes swear when I spill birdseed.

Cynthia: When I spill something, I think, "Oh, s%*^!" but say, "Oh, sugar!"

Cynthia: I consider clothes, shoes, and handbags to be art forms.

Walter: I would happily walk around in the same pair of baggy sweatpants for weeks. "Hey, I'm not going anywhere!"

We know that we influence each other by what we think and do. For example:

Cynthia: I was a germaphobe. He ruined my love for stamp collecting. He watched me soak stamps off envelopes, and commented that I was working with "reconstituted spit." (Remember the days when everyone licked stamps?)

Walter: Germaphobia must be catching. After living with Cynthia for 30-plus years, I have almost become a germaphobe myself.

Walter: I am a good, supportive listener.

Cynthia: I like speaking out, yet I typically try not to play blame games.

All of what follows comes from both of us together.

Walter has studied Assagioli for years. Cynthia has learned about Assagioli and the Psychosynthesis process through multiple trainings, group workshops, and vicariously. Psychosynthesis guides our lives, and Walter explains how we are and are not using Psychosynthesis as we move forward in our relationship. This couples-book project has been exciting for us because we hadn't really thought intensely about our relationship and marriage from a Psychosynthesis perspective. Psychosynthesis was just there. We have used and created Psychosynthesis techniques that have worked for us for 35 years. This project offered us an opportunity to leap beyond finding synthesis only in conflicts within individuals. We're moving toward more focus on the synthesis in our relationship as a couple.

We took time to look at our levels of relationships. Yes, there are many different entities and relationships within each of us, between the two of us, and, as we interact with the world, outside of ourselves. Assagioli was convinced that when individual psychosynthesis occurs (within the individual), then "right and harmonious interpersonal and inter-group relations" also exist.[1] We decided to look at our life together as one variation of those "interpersonal relations."

When we talk about synthesis and *our* relationship, we recognize that we are distinct individuals composed of internal entities and working models. We are shaped by each of our unique challenges and gifts. We keep our individual experiences, personality, etc. Then, when we interact, in many ways we start to function as a unit that respects the integrity of the separate entities within each of us. This "new" way of being (the unit) still maintains our individuality. We think of our marriage as we think of our country. We view it as "a salad bowl" instead of the traditional thinking that marriage is a "melting pot." The choice of whether the "new" way of being and interacting is positive or negative is up to us. When we help each other be our more-authentic selves, we can come together in more creative and energetic ways. These opportunities and interfacings then become a third unexpected possibility, a synthesis. As we write, this essay becomes more creative, as each of us gets clearer and more supportive of our own and each other's contributions.

We noticed that although we don't *always* function well, when we do it means that our individual mechanisms are listening and responding to each other in positive ways—even if the event that started the process was negative. We try to be realistic. We take a "one foot in front of the other" approach by agreeing to view our relationship as ongoing: a work in process. Our relationship is never finally perfect. We simply try to be open to hearing and giving new ideas a chance. We try to let go of comfortable but outdated habits and techniques that don't work. We use Assagioli's "synthesis of opposites".[2] We practice listening to and enjoying the other person's point instead of contradicting it. We're listening to each other and describing what it is that is trying to emerge, what that particular "it" is, in each conflict and difference that we experience.

Additionally, this process requires us to recognize the importance of pausing. We go through the actual steps of mindfulness, such as noticing our inner arousal, rating the intensity from 1 to 10, then asking about what we thought the other person said, and listening … before commenting. At times, it helps just to check our breathing. We are watchful of our instinctual alarms and the judgments that slip in with them, and we evaluate them before believing them (Polt 2021). We find ourselves backing off from prematurely voicing our sudden, impulsive trigger reactions. And then we wait a bit with awareness and will, conscious choice, so we can respond rather than react. We are thankful for this suggestion often attributed to Victor Frankl: "Between stimulus and response there is a space. In that space is our power to choose our response. In our response lies our growth and our freedom."[3]

That alert pause takes us to another level. From this other level, when we maintain it, we can much more safely discuss how each of us feels about the differences. For one thing, we're no longer just individuals but more like a team. For another, we're both showing respect for and interest in, the two different perspectives—both of them. We recognize that multiple perspectives exist about everything. When we talk about our relationship (for example, when issues come up) and when we are working with others outside our relationship, there is a process involved. We recognize that neither of us is totally right or wrong. It is not a competition. We may in fact just have different ways of thinking about the same thing, event, problem, or joy. We each can state what we prefer and simply look at the two sides without judgment. Often, we then begin to look at things from a comfortable place, one with more humor. That is a way of moving together to the "higher self" of our relationship.

From that level we see the multiple perspectives, and how each perspective has something of value. When doing counseling work "within" an individual person, Psychosynthesis therapists, counselors, and coaches often encourage clients to talk about subpersonalities. By subpersonalities we understand parts of a person that act up or want to go different ways. Psychosynthesists often encourage clients to see the value of *each* part, to talk about their values, and explore how to put the values together.

We believe that this also works when we view each other's potentially opposite views about something as part of a possible "unexpected third option." We both love the fact that at least one "unexpected third option" may emerge from disagreements. We consider it a synthesis surprise (Walter's perspective) or synthesis magic (Cynthia's perspective) that is always waiting to happen.

A sidebar is that we both find ourselves using these beliefs outside our relationship and marriage. For example, when Cynthia introduces to her students the possibility of the unexpected third option, they can move away from thinking that they have to be right about every interaction with the children in their care and their families and their communities—as if there is only one right way to be. These students may start to realize that multiple perspectives and possibilities exist when they listen and work with children and families and their communities.[4] So, our practices as a couple may be a gift for others too. That possibility of a new, unexpected "third" option already starts to inform our interactions even before we get locked into our individual differences. This expectation then becomes a part of a relationship foundation based in a psychosynthesis approach.

There are a lot of "pros" to this process. So, what are the "cons"? We don't want someone saying, "You're a hypocrite; you're acting like you never are angry or inappropriate." Oh, we get mad, disagree, etc., but we don't get really nasty with each other, even if we're angry. (For sure, physical violence is never remotely an option in our relationship.) We take our space. We take that pause and go to our separate corners. Usually that helps us see each other's point of view more clearly. We're able to readjust and remember that there is more than one perspective. We also take that space and time to check in with each other. Walter saw a way to help us both shape our wording when we have been especially hurt. When we feel tension, we usually ask each other, "Are we okay?" Either or both of us may feel bruised. If one of us does, we recognize that we need more time. We need to figure out *why*. We continue to learn how to use the synthesis of opposites.

To the Center

We deeply love each other. That seems like the center of Assagioli's star diagram (see Figure 2). As you see, it shows six psychological functions such as intuition, imagination, and emotion. We feel our love as one with the Will of the Self at the center. One of our strategies is to check in with each other about our conscious intention in the following manner. At the beginning of the year and then again on our wedding anniversary, we sit down together, over dinner or breakfast at home or in a restaurant, and we talk and listen. We both must agree that we are happy or at least satisfied with our relationship. We did not have traditional wedding vows. Instead, we made a different promise to each other on our wedding day. We will stay together as long as both of us are at least satisfied, at best happy. When we want to see changes for the next year, we describe and discuss them. This has worked for over 33 years.

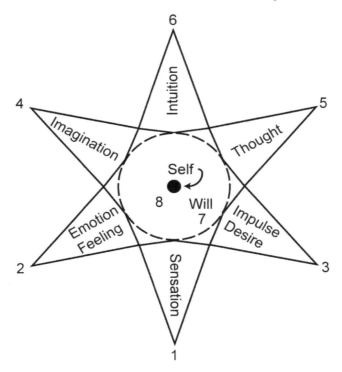

Figure 2: Assagioli's Star Diagram[5]

Source: Roberto Assagioli: The Act of Will (1974)

Walter describes this process as disidentifying from an individual position and moving to another level where you identify as a couple. It must begin with respect for each of us as individuals and for the characters within each of us. Then there's the overall interaction between the two at this relationship level. It is informed by deliberate choice. Walter labels this active, thoughtful, mindful deliberation about whether we want to stay a couple as part of Assagioli's "act of will"[5]. We look at our purpose. It is to be a loving couple. We deliberate how to be that, or whether we can be that. Eventually we make a choice. We both deeply appreciate how powerful that intention and choice is. That joint act of will is a higher level of unity. As we've said, our relationship is not perfect. And we're both committed to this process. The plan, the vision, is to stay together for the rest of our lives. To accomplish this we have viable options, such as couples' therapy, breaks from each other, etc. It is also true that if the relationship makes either of us miserable there is no point in staying together. But so far, knock on wood, so good.

Walter thinks maybe the reason our relationship is surviving and flourishing is that we've been learning to look at our differences from another level, together. From there, in true Psychosynthesis fashion, we identify what each of us wants, needs, and is trying to offer. Starting with differences in our loving relationship and feeling success gives us hope that we and our community may benefit from defining and combining differences we see in the larger world. Between us success may be easier because we often find there is less at stake, and winning-or-losing is not so vital. Besides, we already delight in joys, and jokes, and projects, and hopes, and goals. These help us balance out mistakes and heal wounds. We are finding it refreshing and nurturing to stick with the love, the humor, and the "I get what you're saying." If the heater got left on in the office all night, it's far less important to figure out who's to blame, and much more important, and easier, to figure out how not to waste the heat next time.

Additionally, the "imagination" point on Assagioli's star is big for us. We "get" and enjoy each other's points, jokes, puns, and corrections. After more than three decades, we're both pretty good at understanding what the other means. We use our imagination to have fun with each other's whimsical imagery—at least in private—no matter how wild.

Experiencing in our bodies the "sensation" star point, thanks to Assagioli's guidance, we notice that our physical feelings and imagery clarify and broaden our understanding of each other. As a couple, when we have agreements or disagreements, we continue to tap into a whole world of reality by taking time to explore. For example, we can allow a sensation or image to emerge to answer questions such as: Where am I now (with life, or this issue)? Where do I want to be? What in me is stopping me? What quality in me would get me there?

The sensations and imagery that emerge are enlightening. We are constantly sharing our humor and creativity, our struggles and pain. We follow whichever of us is the natural leader in a particular moment. For example, Cynthia plans, plants, and weeds the garden. Walter drip-irrigates it, rakes the weeds, and lugs branches that New Mexico winds fling down from our tall elm trees. We each sometimes drive. We make sure we feel safe.

Sure, in our loving relationship we have bad moods, real mistakes, serious misunderstandings to discuss, fears of being too tough or too weak or not being taken seriously. These will always be genuine concerns. We see each other and ourselves at our best; our worst is a small fraction of who we are. And in a loving relationship we have much more opportunity to uncover each other's beauty, and our own, at multiple levels. The funny secret is that conflicts and differences are also opportunities for differentiating from each other—and for synthesis, for combining opposites.

Synthesis emerges from a key learning for us: not to correct each other until we have acknowledged what is true or valid in what our partner did or said. Then we also acknowledge what is valid in what we ourselves did or said. To do this, synthesis requires that we ask for more information. Whenever I (Walter) remember to ask her why she didn't turn at that intersection—instead of telling her she should have turned—it's easy for her to answer freely, and we both feel great.

Three Candles

Walter's late widowed mother remarried at age 80. Before the wedding, she sat Walter down to ask his opinion. She and Alphonse, the groom, a high-school classmate of hers, also 80, were considering a surprise in the wedding ceremony. She and Alphonse would each hold a lighted candle. Together they would light a third candle to represent their new marriage entity. Then, she said, they would blow out their two candles. Walter said he loved it, but wondered if they might want to keep their own candles burning. This would respect their individuality. Three lighted candles would light up the ceremony. The center candle would represent their marriage—as a developing synthesis of two strong, independent individuals who would also continue to develop. They liked the three-candle idea and used it.

We believe this three-candle story of Walter's mom and her husband represents our process as a couple and individuals. We've had many experiences, both positive and challenging. We continue to use them, when we can, to produce a third expected or unexpected synthesis of who we are as a couple. We feel that every challenge and gift in our relationship is precious. Each builds our foundation as partners, lovers, spouses.

Diane and Jeff

In this soulful reflection on their 44-year relationship, Diane and Jeff each write about the joys of falling in love and starting a life together as well as the struggles they faced as a young couple, including personality conflicts, gender inequality and infertility. Five years into their marriage, their "chance" encounter with Psychosynthesis introduced them to what would become the formative framework and guiding light of their personal healing and spiritual development, the deepening of their marriage, and their professional work.

CHAPTER FOUR

Growing Together: Reflections on Our Marriage as a Psycho-Spiritual Path

Diane and Jeff Rossman

Introduction

We first discovered Psychosynthesis in the early 1980s and studied with Tom Yeomans, who had worked with Roberto Assagioli and had also trained in California. He had recently moved to the Boston area to set up a professional training program in Psychosynthesis. Several years later, in 1990, Tom founded the Concord Institute and shifted his work to what he called Spiritual Psychology.

Rooted in Psychosynthesis, Tom's teaching took a more experiential, process-oriented approach to therapeutic and group work. We then studied Spiritual Psychology with Tom for over twenty years and completed advanced training in both individual work and group leadership. We were part of the professional community that gathered around the Concord Institute during those years and participated in the Concord Institute/Harmony

Institute Russian Project. All of this work was infused by the spirit of Psychosynthesis.

Section I: Ground Work

Part 1: This Meeting, One Chance[1]

Diane: Rabbinic eyes, silver-blue, soft and intensely kind. His eyes, like the smaller ends of two finely calibrated telescopes, the larger ends opening inward. Knowing eyes I instantly knew and knew knew me. On a muggy, late afternoon in the summer of 1978, in the foyer of a dilapidated duplex in Georgetown, my eyes met the eyes of the man I would marry. I was 21 years old.

He is unexotic, I mused to myself, as familiar as my hand. My heart was not pounding; I was not breathtaken. Yet when he spoke, the door to an exotic, secret place swung open and in wafted the fragrance of another world and time—a scent like the taste of water drawn from an ancient well: stone dust, verbena, pine—his scent exactly. It was not intoxicating: I inhaled his scent and all of my scattered pieces rushed together and settled in my body. I grew calm. I was wholly there.

Jeff: I was totally unprepared for meeting Diane. When I appeared at her door, I was already in a relationship and planning to move to Long Island to start graduate school at the end of that summer. Beginning a new relationship was not on my agenda, but love and destiny had other plans. I was immediately drawn to Diane's beauty and intense presence. Once our conversation started, I felt an instant familiarity, as though we'd known each other for many lifetimes and this was just one more instance of finding each other again.

Diane: We spoke for three hours straight.

His words: Philadelphia ... Jewish background ... psychology ... Frankl ... Fromm ... Transcendental Meditation ... James Taylor ... in service to the world ... family and children ....

My words: Iowa City ... Jewish background ... poetry, especially Rilke ... Kundalini Yoga ... Jung ... life purpose ... Titian (my Irish Setter) ... biking ... family and children ....

Now, 44 years later, I realize that our prismatic first encounter was more conjuring than conversation. Each word would serve as a magic place-holder for the prismatic story our lives would tell. This meeting also quickened and externalized what had previously been, for each of us, a mostly private soul yearning and inquiry. From that point on, we became serious spiritual seekers together. In fact, a few days later, when Jeff invited me to go on a road trip to visit a new Sufi community in North Carolina, I enthusiastically agreed.

Jeff: I was not a devotee of Sufism, a mystical and more universal aspect of Islam, but I was curious. I had learned about Sufism from a friend I'd met at a Transcendental Meditation course in 1976. At that time, I had embraced TM practice and philosophy for about a year, and found it tremendously liberating. It freed me from my very rational and at times obsessive mind, and enabled me to experience my inner and outer life in a fresh and uplifting way. I loved the daily practice and having a curriculum for living life consciously. I spent one month in that residential TM course and almost entered a two-year program to become a TM teacher, but opted to go to graduate school instead. Although I didn't become a TM teacher, I continued TM meditation twice a day for the next several years.

My desire to visit the Sufi community grew out of my friendship and my willingness to assist in the building of my friend's house.

I'd read a few books about Sufism and found aspects of it intriguing, but I looked at the trip to Asheville more as an adventure than a pilgrimage. It was scheduled for a few weeks prior to the start of graduate school—the last stop on my odyssey of psycho-spiritual exploration before embarking on immersive professional training. When Diane agreed to join me, it made the trip more exciting and offered us the opportunity to deepen our connection before my departure to Long Island and our transition to a long-distance relationship.

Diane: Three weeks later, we drove thirteen hours to a 90-acre, wooded property in the Smoky Mountains outside of Asheville. There, Jeff's friend and several other American Sufis were totally absorbed in the early stages of building a spiritual community from the ground up. We were put to work immediately, Jeff helping the men with construction, and me chopping organic vegetables with the women in the outdated kitchen. On the second morning, one of them introduced herself and asked my name. "Oh, you're one of the lovebirds," she grinned. Apparently, the fact that Jeff and I were newly in love had not gone unnoticed.

In the afternoon at 4:00, everyone gathered in a large community room for prayer and various experiential Sufi practices facilitated by a young American Sufi teacher. On the third day, the teacher asked us to line up. Walking up and down the line like a drill sergeant, he called out three or four people at a time, assigned them to a particular "angelic plane," and demonstrated a gesture and a chant for each one. Then he called up the small groups, one by one, to perform for the rest of us. I was the only person not assigned to an "angelic plane."

After the first six groups had completed their routines, the teacher approached me and signaled for me to stand. I felt his eyes, fiery and penetrating, slowly take in the full measure of my body. "I don't know what you are or where you belong," he sneered. Everyone was staring at me, and I vividly remember the heat rising into my face. He practically spat, "just go with the seventh plane angels."

I stumbled toward the center of the room and forced myself to sweep my arms over my head while leaping and trying to make the foreign sounds I heard the others chanting. The teacher rushed over to me, cupped his hands around his mouth and yelled, "We can't hear you!" I broke down, and, sobbing uncontrollably, ran all the way back to the barn.

Still hyperventilating, I agonized over what I might have done wrong to make myself the target of a public shaming. I worried that since a powerful spiritual teacher had found me unworthy, so would Jeff. Heartbroken, I convinced myself that our seemingly fated relationship was over and started packing to leave.

A little while later, Jeff found me in the barn; he told me he loved me, for the first time. He reassured me that the inexperienced teacher was likely reacting to the fact that we were more focused on each other than on being a part of a fledgling spiritual community. On the way back to Georgetown, I remember admiring Jeff's keen insight and his calm, steady presence. I reveled in our deepening love. But, I couldn't help wondering why that teacher had singled me out and not my boyfriend.

Our foray into Sufism may seem unusual, but Jeff and I were not unique among young people in our attraction to alternative religious and spiritual paths. At that time, the synergy of the 1960s civil rights movement, the women's movement, the anti-war protests, the proliferation of psychedelic drug use, the influx of eastern spiritual traditions and the human potential movement in psychology, was breaking open the structures of mainstream American culture. Like so many in our generation, we were idealistic and uninspired by the vision of the future our culture prescribed and what we had experienced within our own religious tradition.

Here is a picture of what was happening in Georgetown in 1974: on my morning walk to the boutique where I worked part-time, I regularly passed by American Hare Krishnas wearing saffron robes, chanting, drumming and dancing down Wisconsin Avenue. Disciples of the Reverend Sun Myung Moon (the "Moonies") huddled on the street corners handing out brochures, and followers of Elizabeth Clare Prophet were eager to "share the light" with passersby as they tacked up their posters.

A few blocks away, The Golden Temple Emporium, established by disciples of the Sikh guru Yogi Bhajan, sold Shakti Shoes (Birkenstock knock-offs) and Wah Guru Chews (precursors of Kind Bars) and served delicious vegetarian lunches. I was drawn to the serene environment and the radiant men and women in white robes and turbans who worked there.

Several weeks after our time with the Sufis, Jeff moved to Long Island to begin his doctoral program in clinical psychology. Having arranged to graduate early from college, I moved in with him that January. In love and freed up from the under-stimulating, but considerable demands of being an undergraduate, I poured myself into our relationship.

Root

Some new part of me writes
in verbs not yet conjugated
they are so innocent.
I have slept inside the fist

of an iris in a glass
room and I have been warmed
awake by sunlight here
where my breasts turn
lavender, where your tongue trembles

green. If I could live with you
the poem I have always dreamed
of writing, all of the words would root
in the dark earth of our bodies:
there would be nothing left
to say.

We worked and studied hard, and continued our Sufi training by attending workshops and retreats in the New York area, but our hearts weren't in it. My interest had waned, and Jeff was consumed by his academic work.

Jeff: I was deeply immersed in my clinical psychology training program and I loved it. I appreciated the rigorous academic approach to understanding people's inner lives and relationships. While I enthusiastically embraced my role as a psychologist-in-training, I also felt something was missing. Much of the training focused on identifying psychopathology and using psychotherapy to treat what was wrong with people. Very little of what I learned had to do with identifying people's strengths and providing approaches to nurturing those strengths. There was no reference to the spiritual dimension and ways to help people access it. This was before positive psychology and mindfulness had made their way into the mainstream of psychology and psychotherapy.

My program was heavily oriented toward psychodynamic theory and practice. Humanistic psychology and contemplative practices, which I was drawn to, were not part of my program and were regarded with skepticism. Of the 25 students in my program, I was probably the only one who had a regular meditation practice. Although I felt a strong connection to my fellow students and the faculty, I felt like an outlier.

Nevertheless, I was strongly identified with becoming a psychologist and eventually being part of a professional community. Although Diane also pursued graduate training, and obtained her M.A. in Education, she did not identify as strongly with her professional role. This disparity created tension that challenged us to grow in ways we could not have imagined at the time.

Diane: By the end of those three years, we had crossed the threshold into marriage, Jeff had completed his doctoral coursework and I had completed my second year as a high school English teacher.

Part 2: This Ache In Your Heart Is Holy[2]

Relocating to Cambridge, MA was a dream come true. Jeff had landed a psychology internship at a Harvard-affiliated psychiatric hospital and we moved into a cozy apartment near Harvard Square. Knowing I would be unable to find a teaching job due to spending cuts to education, I viewed our move as an opportunity to find less stressful work, write more and explore further training. Eventually we hoped to realize our shared dream of becoming parents.

I found a job at a trendy café nearby, enrolled in the C.G. Jung Institute and started Jungian analysis. I wrote poetry and rode my yellow Fuji ten-speed around Cambridge. A year later, we bought a condo in a converted three-family house down the street from where we were renting. Even sweeter (at least, to me), we got

Daisy, a four-month-old Great Pyrenees puppy. We were settling into an idyllic period in our married life.

Occasionally, I had the fleeting awareness that I was living someone else's dream of an idyllic marriage. Jeff was preoccupied with starting his career as a psychologist. I struggled with his unavailability and envied his certainty and single-pointedness. Sometimes I found his calm, rational manner irritating. My intensity would spark and flare in my consistently unsuccessful attempts to feel met in kind.

Jeff: For me, the first few years in Cambridge were all work, all the time. My internship year consisted of 70-hour work weeks, caring for severely ill patients and writing psychological evaluations at home in the evenings and on weekends. The training was fabulous and I loved the experience, but it required a tunnel vision commitment. I realized it wasn't sustainable long-term, but it was only for a year and there would be light at the end of the tunnel. What I didn't fully realize was the negative impact that my professional dedication had on Diane and our relationship. That I was surrounded by colleagues working as hard as I was further clouded my ability to appreciate how lonely and neglected Diane felt.

Unfortunately, I didn't learn the lesson from my internship experience. At the end of that year, I was offered two jobs, one full-time and one half-time. They were both attractive to me, and after a week of obsessing about which to accept, I chose both! While I rationalized that these were both good opportunities and we needed the income, the choice was driven in large measure by the part of me that is drawn to overachieve.

I had internalized my parents' strong work ethic. My mother taught English in a public high school and got her master's degree at night while raising three children. My father got his M.B.A. and law degree at night while working full-time during the day. Their evenings and weekends were filled with grading papers, preparing lesson plans, studying, writing legal briefs, cleaning the house and taking care of us kids. My inner marriage template was of two partners focused intently on their work and their goals, supporting each other implicitly and unequivocally, with little time to share feelings or explore their inner lives together. There was always more work to be done.

My strong identification with working hard and achieving produced tangible rewards and personal satisfaction, but it also had a dark side. When I wasn't working hard, I perceived myself to be lazy and unworthy. It also locked me into an overly narrow definition of what it meant to be successful and fulfilled. Even worse, it drained precious energy and attention from my spiritual life and my relationship with Diane.

For better or worse, I was locked into my beliefs about hard work and achievement and my implicit model of marriage. In those early years together, I wasn't aware that I had a choice about whether to continue to accept those beliefs; it was just what you had to do if you wanted to be successful and have a good life. My approach was painful for Diane and, fortunately for us both, she expressed how much she missed having a more intimate relationship and how much more our life could be. Over the years, she has reminded me of that, and supported my efforts to be more present to myself and to her. The prospect of having children also helped me realize that I needed to change.

Diane: While Jeff was diligently pursuing his calling, I was struggling to find mine, vacillating between the call to serve people and the call to serve the poetry muse. I took graduate courses at Harvard's Divinity and Education Schools, Lesley College and finally ended up in a well-respected M.F.A. program in creative writing where I managed to catch my breath. I shook off those ominous intimations of inhabiting someone else's life and carried on in what seemed then like a perfectly appropriate (though, admittedly, impractical) direction.

The Wife's Song

The husband singing in a breathy falsetto
places the last dish into the groove
of a wooden rack. His song rises
to a whistle and an immense white dog comes
bounding across the oak floor, nuzzles
his hip and begins to bark and growl.
They are doing the dance they do
every night before their midnight prowl
through the sleeping neighborhood, before
his last stroll through the little house.

On any other night, you would be the wife
undressing in the bedroom, turning
back the sheets and waiting.
But tonight, you are the old song their lives
sing to each other as they sleep entangled
on the bed they built when he was twenty-five
and she was too young to recognize the song
he was singing:

we are pitched so high only the dog can hear us.

The highest point of this high time came in the winter of 1982 when I learned I was pregnant. We were ecstatic. I had the mysterious, yet distinct, experience of simultaneously opening into the divine and the divine opening in me—lifting me out of my little life in Cambridge and revealing my true location in the sacred web of life. I was shown—and wholeheartedly stepped into—my place in the luminous, unbroken line of women circling back to the original ancestors and arcing onward beyond my imagination. I heard angels singing.

During this sweet and catalytic interlude, something else opened up in me, bringing with it strange powers. For example, one afternoon while standing in the grocery store check-out line, I suddenly realized I was looking at the skeleton of the man in front of me. Specifically, I saw a small, kidney bean-shaped tumor at the base of his skull. Part of me was flipping out, wondering what was happening and what to do with this information; another part was completely relaxed, as if this were the most natural experience in the world.

I was unsettled and intrigued by this and other emerging transpersonal phenomena, but mostly I was too busy to delve into it. In addition to my job, my poetry classes, my fitness routine and my housewifery, I was hyper-focused on shopping around for the best alternative OBGYN and books on baby names and prenatal care.

"The bottom fell out" are the words that come now. The double-entendre is not lost on me. The heart-searing double-losses of that first miscarriage and the accompanying energetic opening remain visceral. Right after the D&C, I started falling. I fell through layer after layer of dirt and dung and then *that* bottom fell out, and I fell further: through rot, pitch and ash. And then *that* bottom fell out and I fell further into nothing—lifeless, bottomless, nothing. At one point, it occurred to me that I had not only miscarried an embryo, I had also miscarried my embryonic, adult self.

My poetry turned dark.

For The One Who Would Have Been A Leo

The lion-pod asleep among my bones
and decomposing leaves divides himself
alive unwillingly and like an elf
who hungers for a human shape, he owns
a piece of this unruly cave—his den—
until his transmutation is complete.

Brave son, whose paws would flower into feet
and hands, whose crowny head would awaken
into teeth, nose, eyes—I feel you creeping
out the way you came. What has frightened you?
Stay! Or like a ghost I will seep through
the dark world you leave and leave it sleeping.

My dreams turned nightmarish. Soon the poems and the nightmares dried up. And, for a long while, I lost everything, became pregnant again and lost everything again. I, or the not-I I had become, was lost. Once in a moment of overwhelming self-pity, I begged Jeff to find another wife so he could have children. In his characteristically droll, non-reactive way, he said, "You never know, it could be me, and besides, I don't want another wife; one's more than enough!" I see now that while I went missing, Jeff, and our relationship, held me like a womb.

Jeff: I did the best I could to help Diane move through her grief. I bore witness to her pain and reminded her that we would eventually become parents. When she was in a very dark place, I sometimes felt frightened for her; her capacity for intense feeling is much greater than mine. I accompanied her as well as I could into the depths she fell into—but I kept one foot on the shore as she descended far below the surface.

As a child I had developed the capacity to be sensitive to others' suffering. My mother carried a deep reservoir of emotional pain from her lifelong experience of taking care of her mother, who suffered from severe depression. I knew my mother loved me dearly and was deeply wounded. For my mother's sake and for mine, I tried to empathize and support her when she was overwhelmed.

When Diane went through her dark night of the soul, I was her companion to the extent that I could be. I was empathic and supportive, but I had my own emotional limitations when her pain was more than I could handle. I resorted to self-protective avoidance when I felt that Diane was directing her anguish at me. When I felt helpless to help her, I trusted in her capacity to heal. I tried to be patient and simply hold a space where she could begin to trust in that herself.

Diane: Other well-meaning people tried to be helpful: my mother's unwavering refrain was "relax; it'll happen." My Jungian analyst called it important "shadow work" and gave me a book by Laura Huxley called *The Child of Your Dreams*. A famous poet teaching in my graduate program tried to convince me that my Persephone-like descent would be the best thing that ever happened to my poetry. But I was beyond their help.

On the verge of dropping out, a perceptive professor recommended that I contact his spiritual teacher, Sri Mata Gayatri Devi, who lived less than an hour away. Meeting this fierce, down-to-earth, compassionate and supremely wise Indian woman was my first encounter with loving, conscious awareness embodied in female form. My relationship with her became a special container—a chalice—for my healing. Eventually, Jeff and I moved to be close to her and part of her spiritual community.

Thanks to Mataji and her community, the full-fledged crisis of that time was gentled. Over the course of our involvement with her, she welcomed and affirmed my mystical nature and encouraged me to meditate and continue my spiritual studies. She was also very clear about how to navigate the intermittent surfacing of those strange powers, which she called "siddhi powers." Far from their being the goal of spiritual development, she explained that these phenomena are sometimes prematurely awakened, but are best viewed as distractions along the way. She advised me to ignore them and predicted that they would eventually go away (and they did).

Jeff and I also learned to slow down and to establish a healthier and more intentional daily rhythm. Our sex life, which had become routinized and goal-directed in our efforts to conceive, grew enlivened again. Nevertheless, my heart still ached; I was afraid that our marriage would continue to falter because of me and my intrinsic flaws. My intense emotions and my ongoing struggle to find my life's work spilled into our shared life like too much rain on a newly planted garden.

Jeff: As you can tell by now, I lead with my mind and Diane leads with her heart. That's not to say she doesn't have a formidable intellect. She is intellectually powerful and extraordinarily eloquent, but her natural inclination is to live from her heart—generously, lovingly and passionately. Today I appreciate the beauty and mystery of how temperamentally different we are. Sadly, in the early stages of our marriage, I was so completely identified with my own intellect that I could not fully appreciate the richness of Diane's soul life and the gift it was to me and our relationship.

Diane: Although we were very grateful for the spiritual alignment we experienced during this time, I can see now that it was also true that something invasive and toxic remained hidden in us and between us. The roots of this insidious ailment grew down below the threshold of my awareness. The deeper I dug after them, the deeper down they dug, receding into the darkest crevices of the dark.

Section II: Ripening

Part 1: Learning to See in the Dark

The elements of our story so far—those we've included as well as those we've left out of this telling—converge at this threshold: seven years after our first meeting, five years into our marriage, we met Tom Yeomans who was giving a public lecture on Psychosynthesis. My first impression was that I was in the presence of someone of the kind Walt Whitman described in the Preface to *Leaves of Grass* as representing "a new order" of "priests" whose aim is "that every person shall be their own priest".

At one point, Tom was speaking about how to stay close to the soul, or Higher Self, by "staying close to the truth of one's experience in the moment." He wasn't simply talking about this. Right there, in a public school classroom with its fluorescent lights and metal desks, the space in the room where the thirty or so of us sat, listening intently, grew supercharged. As we continued to practice being present to our own immediate experience and to each other's, I became aware that something interior (to many of us, it turned out) was being quickened, generating a sense of warm, spacious excitement—not *about* anything, nor anything about to happen, but, the pure, potent excitement of being alive and being alive together, here and now. I learned later that this is what Tom called the soul force field of the group.

In this enlivened, relaxed state, I also sensed a deeper, cohering energy—an underlighting, overarching presence—permeating the atmosphere. Eventually, we came to speak of this as the soul of the group. Though it would be years before we understood what happened that evening, and how it happened, I was sure of two things: *this* is how I wanted to be and *this* is what I wanted to do.

Jeff: I too felt moved and inspired by Tom's presence and the promise of Psychosynthesis. Its embrace of the spiritual dimension filled the void in my academic, psychoanalytically-oriented training. Tom's message spoke to my heart and to my mind's need for understanding. I was stirred by the possibility of integrating the spiritual dimension more explicitly into my work and more fully into my life. I saw that psychosynthesis could be a bridge between my professional and spiritual selves. It was also exciting to find an approach that could be a bridge for Diane and me, a shared approach to our work and a shared framework for understanding ourselves and our relationship.

Diane: That fall, we both enrolled in Tom's three-year program, "Psychosynthesis for the Helping Professional," which became known as, "The Spiritual Psychology Training Program." Psychosynthesis is a marriage of the fields of psychology and spiritual or soul development—Jeff's field and mine. Not only did Spiritual Psychology "speak" to both of us, the conceptual framework offered us an elegant context for learning to recognize and appreciate each other's different orientations, interests and ways of being.

Now, as I reflect on the earnest young woman I was then, I am struck by how blind I was to what really ailed me and, by extension, our marriage. I had very few tools for making conscious the deeper aspects of my experience and found it excruciating to try to express them to Jeff. I often just cried.

Finding Tom and Psychosynthesis, and, later, Spiritual Psychology, marked the beginning of a long process of learning to see in the dark. Over the course of the first weekend training, he spoke in a language and introduced a conceptual framework that describes the spiritual dimension of human experience and recognizes the soul, or Higher Self, as the organizing principle of a human life. He also led us through guided imagery exercises and small-group work that enabled us to experience our own relationship to the material he had presented. His synthesis of didactic and experiential learning converged in a process that was a true expression of the verb "to educate," from the Latin "to bring forth." After many years of searching for my place in "higher" education, I felt I had, at last, come home.

Our deep connection to the other students in the program was an unexpected blessing. Not only did we bear witness to each other through intense, cathartic, individual and group work, we also laughed, danced, ate, sang, prayed, meditated, celebrated and wondered together. I am so grateful for the privilege of being a part of this beautiful community where I met some people who became my dearest and oldest friends. We have continued to learn together over the years as members of a community of practice.

In terms of the training content, one of the first steps toward developing insight was learning about and working with the concept of the "soul wound." That the failure to welcome and nurture the soul of a child can be harmful to her identity development, seems obvious; yet, I had never considered it before. It was extremely important to become aware of the inadvertent injury caused to my sense of self because I was seen primarily as a female physical body with a valuable mind and bothersome emotions, however loving, supportive and trustworthy my parents were (and they were).

I had intense feelings about this. And until then, I was unaware of exactly what those feelings were and where they came from. I began to realize how this original soul wound had given rise to long-standing emotional knots and limiting beliefs that negatively affected my relationship with myself and other people, especially Jeff. My habitual, irrational expectation that "he'll never understand me" grew out of my deep sadness and anger about having never felt fully "seen." Over time, my ambivalence about true self-disclosure slowly diminished, opening the space to see and be seen. Gradually our intimacy deepened.

Because of my particular soul wound, the practice of learning "to trust the truth of my experience" moment to moment and, concomitantly, to listen deeply to and respect the truth of the other's experience, was transformational. This was easier said than done. Both require the cultivation of Presence, a cornerstone of Spiritual Psychology.

Briefly, the practice of Presence involves grounding ourselves by bringing our attention to the breath, warmly noticing and allowing the sensations in the physical body, the emotions in the heart, and whatever thoughts are arising in the mind. Then still anchored in the breath, we extend our awareness to the particular space around us and the vastness of space beyond us. We also become aware of our particular historical time, remembering the context of the past and the future. Still aware of the breath, we bring ourselves into the present moment.

Jeff: Through our personal practice of Presence, we've enhanced our capacity to be present to each other and nourish the loving field between us. It gives us a safe space in which we continue to learn about and support one another.

Diane: With practice, Presence increasingly arises out of our intention. For many years, the first line of St. Francis's prayer, "Lord, make me an instrument of Thy peace," has been my mantra for invoking Presence. Being present enables us to tune into our own experience, moment to moment—as well as someone else's—without a lot of static. When we allow our attention to rest in the threshold between what we know and the not-yet-known, we are present to *what is* arising. This is where the soul resides; we miss it entirely when we are focused on the past or the future—though we may perceive its traces.

I have always been drawn to this edge; writing poetry is one expression of this. However, as a child, I learned early and well that my inclination toward the soul was considered unnatural, impractical and anti-social—evidence of being afflicted with over-sensitivity. I felt ashamed and mistrustful of my most enlivening and communing experiences. I didn't understand how my way of accessing deep connection could so utterly disconnect me from my parents and loved ones.

Working with these Spiritual Psychology practices led to a seismic psycho-spiritual shift: the double-binding belief that my natural way of being was wrong, was, to a large extent, released. This had a profound impact on my relationship with Jeff. As I became more relaxed and confident in my own way, I learned to better trust the truth of my experience. This helped me to speak from that place with more ease. Not surprisingly, I was able to be more appreciative of Jeff's way, and to listen more deeply to the truth of his experience. Being warmly seen, welcomed, heard and supported as the unique, multidimensional individual one is—no matter how quirky—would soon become the heart of my work in the world.

Jeff: Our growing appreciation for each other's unique ways of being has been fundamental to the health of our relationship. I was able to value Diane's feeling life without judging her for not being more rational. She learned to accept my rational approach to life and became less alienated by it. Spiritual Psychology has helped me to trust my deeper wisdom and loving nature and to bring more of my true self into my relationship with Diane. Learning about the nature of the self conceptually and experientially has provided a rich context in which I can become more fully who I am. As I do, I am better able to appreciate the beauty and complexity of who Diane is and who she is becoming.

Diane: While I was familiar with the idea that we have different parts of ourselves, learning about "subpersonalities" brought it to a whole new level. Identifying the distinct facets of the personality with their complementary qualities and functions illuminates how we all learned to cope with past difficulties and how adaptive each of us is. For example, I came to see that my "rebel without a cause" subpersonality emerged when, as an adolescent, I began to chafe against my parents' expectations, limits and beliefs. Working with this part of myself helped me to appreciate my need for freedom within the structure of our marriage and to work toward aligning with my inner authority. This had the effect, over time, of helping to balance the power dynamic between us.

Jeff: Likewise, when a conflict with Diane triggered my reactivity, recognizing the sub-personality in me that was activated was tremendously liberating. Understanding that my emotional reactions did not reflect the essence of who I was created a space in which I could compassionately work with my reactive parts. For example, learning to identify my "critic" sub-personality, the part of me that harshly judges myself and others, has been especially valuable. It has helped me have a more compassionate relationship with myself and be more respectful and appreciative, rather than critical, of Diane.

Diane: Flowing from the process of identifying the subpersonalities, the practice of disidentification opens the space for developing perspective and choice, and strengthens our capacity for conscious self-awareness. The more Jeff and I practiced this technique of noticing the activated part of ourselves (the subpersonality), and then stepping back from it to gain perspective, the more we strengthened the larger, clearer place in ourselves. In other words, as each of us became more aware of our "parts," we became more whole as individuals, and our marriage thrived. We spent considerable time practicing this in individual Spiritual Psychology-based counseling, training groups, and on our own. We still do.

Overall, the benefits of both learning and integrating these and other principles and practices of Spiritual Psychology exceeded anything we could have wished for. In addition to internalizing a comprehensive framework for understanding the multi-dimensionality of the human psyche and learning how to support the psycho-spiritual development of an individual, couples and groups, we found that—and I don't know a better way to say this—we were blossoming, together. Even our painful struggle with infertility became less consuming. Perhaps our intense focus on re-parenting our "inner children" took some of the urgency out of our longing to have a child.

I would add that the most surprising contribution to this "growth spurt" was the subtle, consistent increase in the vitality in my physical body: I felt more alive. I attributed this to Spiritual Psychology's emphasis on groundedness, the release of energy blocks and the effects of feeling more happily myself.

This was the substantially fortified and expanded field of our relationship when we moved to the Berkshires to work with a dear physician friend who was opening an alternative medical clinic in Great Barrington. We were overjoyed about the opportunity to live in the beauty of the rolling hills of western Massachusetts, where we had honeymooned. Jeff would bring his Spiritual Psychology training to his position as clinical psychologist and I accepted our friend's offer to hire me as a Spiritual Psychology counselor. Eventually, I became the one to whom the other practitioners referred patients suffering from life-threatening illnesses. I grew to love this work. I loved working with Jeff. I loved being a part of an integrated team of practitioners who were committed to an integrative approach to healing. Our life was taking root in this hospitable place.

Although we thought we had been prepared to be parents for many years, I see, in hindsight, we were only, at this point, finally ready. We needed to raise ourselves first. You might even say that our Spiritual Psychology training helped us to grow into the kind of parents we wanted to be. In January of 1991, we embarked on the arduous journey to Bucharest, Romania to adopt our son. His numinous entrance into our lives was a blessing that opened the way for many blessings. Four and a half years later, after 12 years of infertility, I gave birth to our daughter.

Being parents has brought out the best in us. Jeff was, and continues to be, a marvelous father—unflappable, patient, wise, funny and kind. In terms of a partner in the project of family life, I won the lottery. But, it was not luck: I recognized these qualities in Jeff all those years ago on the day we met. If the wellspring of joy I was born with was excavated over the course of my Spiritual Psychology training; then, becoming a mother connected me to its source. Put another way, operating out of the Mother archetype has enabled me to express many of my soul's core qualities.

I don't mean to imply that parenting has been only joyful or easy. It wasn't always and isn't always, but it always receives my wholehearted attention. Having internalized many of the principles of Spiritual Psychology has not only informed our personal development and ennobled our marriage, it has enriched the field in which we have raised our children. We can already see how both of our now adult children, having grown up in this field, are bringing many of the gifts of Spiritual Psychology into their relationships and into their work.

Jeff: As Diane mentioned, our personal psycho-spiritual work prepared us for our most important shared enterprise, raising our children. Although this book is about marriage, I want to briefly highlight the psycho-spiritual dimension of parenting, which has been central to our life together. One of the most beautiful gifts of parenting is the opportunity to heal the unloved parts of ourselves. In fact, our children have a remarkable capacity to shine light on our wounded parts. When we are conscious of this process and cooperate actively with it, we, ourselves, develop as we help our children to develop.

Raising our children allowed me to experience a profound, vicarious *re-parenting*, in which moments of connection with my children were simultaneously experienced by my adult self and my child self. For instance, when my son was being angry and rebellious, the angry and rebellious part of me inwardly resonated with his anger. As I endeavored to firmly and compassionately respond to my son's acting out, I was also tending to the inner rebel in me. In those moments, my rebel subpersonality felt understood and supported by the wise, patient, part of myself.

Similarly, when my daughter felt ashamed and upset with herself for making a minor mistake, the part of me that was often tyrannized by my own inner critic empathized with her shame. As I helped her deal with her harsh inner critic, I was inwardly healing the painful relationship between my inner critic and the part of me that didn't feel good enough.

Psychosynthesis, with its focus on psycho-spiritual evolution, offers a clear lens through which we can understand the inner work and healing that can happen as we raise our children. As we benefit from this often difficult inner work, so do our children. We become better parents—and partners—by consciously and lovingly integrating the previously unloved and neglected parts of ourselves.

For Diane and me, talking with each other about our feelings and reactions toward our children and watching each other parent was healing for both of us. For instance, I had identified very strongly with my calm, rational father and much less so with my very emotionally expressive mother. As a result, I tended to approach most situations, including parenting, with a calm, measured rationality. Parenting, with Diane as my partner, enabled me to integrate previously undervalued emotional parts of myself and become a more emotionally expressive father.

Applying spiritual psychology to parenting supports the process of transgenerational psychosynthesis as we integrate the rejected parts of ourselves and our lineage. The process of integrating heart and mind, which were polarized in my family of origin, supports the process of psychosynthesis in my children. Fortunately for us all, they (and their partners) are dedicated to their inner growth and development. They are committed to the work of healing what is unresolved in themselves, as well as the legacy of what was unresolved in us. I am excited and hopeful about the healing potential of Psychosynthesis for not only individuals and couples, but for families as well.

Part 2: Learning to "Let the Beauty We Love Be What We Do"[4]

Diane: The beauty of my relationship to Spiritual Psychology is that it names what I perceived intuitively. It describes the process by which a human life inexorably matures, and how we can learn to support that process in ourselves and in each other. I see it as an elegant map of how we evolve in the direction of greater complexity and, with the right resources, circumstances and guidance, greater coherence and beauty.

By extension, the principles and practices of Spiritual Psychology apply not only to the growth of the individual, but to a couple as well. I see our marriage (any committed, love relationship) as a shared, sacred ground, a "field," where we can grow together. Gradually, as each individual part becomes more integrated, the whole becomes increasingly transparent and the light of the soul of the marriage shines through. This is how I understand the words of Jesus: "Wherever two or more are gathered in love, there I am."

Over time, each part of us, *and* each of us as a part of the relationship—even those quirky, troublemaking, seemingly unlovable parts, those parts that have been traumatized, exiled or forgotten—can be identified, worked with and healed in the light of loving awareness, and restored to the whole. This dynamic, holographic inner picture reflects a breathtaking possibility.

I say "possibility" because, as we know, there are powerful forces that thwart the healthy evolution of every living system, from an individual to a couple and beyond. At the same time, there are forces that drive complexity and expansion so rapidly, that the process of integration can't keep up.

Jeff: In the past, societal norms and religious prescriptions defined the parameters of the institution of marriage. As these structures have broken down, marriages have become less stable and more likely to disintegrate. I see a tremendous need to replace outdated religious and societal prescriptions with an understanding of what it means to be human and what it means to be married in the context of conscious psycho-spiritual development.

Diane: So, how do we come to a living understanding of what it means to be human today? And how do we consciously develop ourselves and our relationships, psychologically and spiritually? Certainly, there are many teachers and paths. I have lived into these questions, in large part, through my practice of Spiritual Psychology, both in my own inner work and in my work as a counselor. In essence, this approach is about cultivating loving awareness which exists as a potential, or seed, inside of everyone.

I could say that Tom was my teacher and Psychosynthesis/ Spiritual Psychology my path, but that wouldn't be quite right. I did find my path and I have learned more than I can say from Tom. The truth is, I received something I consider even more valuable: the experience of my own soul quickening. There was something in the work that nourished and strengthened my connection to my deepest Self, and increased my capacity to call on this source of vitality in my work and in my personal and family life. This was true for Jeff as well. We found that we could then bring this energy to each other, to our children and loved ones, and offer it to our clients. In time, we realized that the path we were seeking was here in front of us and the teacher we were looking for was within. This exquisite alchemical process (known as "synthesis" in Psychosynthesis, "individuation" in Jungian psychology, and "the reconciliation of the opposites," in poetics and esoteric traditions) renders us more and more transparent to the light of the soul shining through us, illuminating our true nature. And this is mind-blowing: we realize the soul is not something *other;* it is who we are. Figure and ground shift. We are form and formless, body and soul, light and dark, masculine and feminine, verb and noun. We ripen into human beings who are learning to, in Rumi's words, "let the Beauty we love/Be what we do!"

This evolving, loving awareness has given me new eyes to navigate the deep dark where I can finally see the root of my personal ailment, an ailment that has also afflicted our marriage: the degradation of the feminine principle of life. By feminine, I mean those qualities (in males, females and those who identify as non-binary) that may be described as receptive, cooperative, empathic, sensitive, passionate, emotional, intuitive, gentle and nurturing.

Psychosynthesis/Spiritual Psychology as a practice and Tom as a gifted teacher, facilitator and guide have helped me to develop the power to see with loving eyes the most loathed, shamed and subjugated aspects of the self, and to shine this loving light on the forces that deemed them so. Holding and protecting the space where the work of lovingly restoring the parts to the Whole—in myself, my marriage, my counseling work and in all of my relationships—remains the primary project of my adult life.

This, and the many other gifts we've received from our work with Psychosynthesis and Spiritual Psychology over the years, are gifts that keep giving. Now that we're in our mid-sixties, I am amazed by the person Jeff has ripened into: he is who he has always been; he is the beautiful man I met when he was twenty-five. Yet, he is more *here* and more fun! I would say he is not only more embodied, he is more ensouled.

Jeff: Diane still exudes the beauty and intensity of the 21-year-old I met in Georgetown 44 years ago. It delights me that the wise, compassionate woman she has deepened into can still light up the room, and my heart, with her indomitable joie de vivre.

Diane and Jeff: We want you to know that we still struggle from time to time. And, thanks to the natural maturing process and our many years of practicing Psychosynthesis principles, we've come to see our difficulties not so much as problems to be solved or fixed, but as Rumi says, "where we are bravely working."[5] When one of us is dealing with a big issue that temporarily eclipses this perspective, mercifully the other has been able to hold it for us. Whether one of us is struggling to let go of something or someone, or laboring to birth something new—a skill, an understanding, a previously buried part of ourselves—Psychosynthesis continues to provide a framework and a perspective from which we can see our struggles as trials, even as opportunities, for deepening more fully into our living experience as souls on Earth.

It is in this field of warm acceptance, where the masculine and the feminine principles are more fully restored to each other— where body, heart, mind and soul are more synthesized—where we will continue to grow together as we enter the final phase of our lives. Our children, too, will partake of this field as they deepen into their own committed relationships. And, most poignant and promising, it will be this field into which we will welcome the souls of our grandchildren.

Chris and Judith

This is the captivating love story of two women who met in midlife, and who after two years of friendship, developed whilst working together, fell deeply in love. Their resounding Yes! to each other infuses their 30-year commitment to their personal healing, growth and their ability to navigate the challenges of being a cross-cultural, same-sex couple. This effervescent spirit also informs their approach to dealing with their blended family and the aging process.

CHAPTER FIVE

Saying Yes! Two Women, A Love Story

Chris Dennler and Judith Firman

Introduction

Judith: I am standing at the kitchen sink, looking out into our garden. Ahead of me there is a spacious lawn bordered on three sides. To the right is a mixed hedge, where holly, laurel, forsythia and privet huddle together to form a thick green wall. The narrow beds beneath are home to hosta, hydrangea, heuchera and a pottery buddha, whose head is nestled in a crown of flowers every spring. The soil here is damp most of the year round, in no small part thanks to Filou and Robbie, our Labradors, who just love to pee there when we're not looking.

At the end of the garden is a seating area, which enjoys the sun for most of the day and in the summer, when it is not too hot, we like to sit here and catch the last rays with a glass of something cool. The dogs will sprawl on the lawn and sometimes Truffle, our rescue cat, will decide to join us as we all bask in the warmth.

Behind this, there is a thick, high laurel hedge and a huge, graceful silver birch tree. The earth here is dry and dusty but I have managed, after several attempts, to persuade a few things to grow … just barely. I have to keep a watchful eye on it in summer and water when necessary. Now that the dogs have realized this, they like to help by "watering" up here, too.

I love this garden. It is the third we have renovated in the last 14 years and it's probably the last, given our advancing decrepitude. In some ways it mirrors our relationship. Chris and I have spent 30 years together and, like this garden with its varied aspects, we too have needed to nurture our relationship, adapt to changing climates and, yes, weather the odd storm—but thankfully not too many of those.

It's not unusual for couples with emotional/psychological wounds to be drawn to each other and we are no different in this respect. We have just had a long discussion about this in light of writing this chapter. Our relationship has been rich and rewarding and has given us much, but foremost and vitally, it has provided us with a crucible for healing. We have managed, through self-awareness and conscious choices, to avoid the mire of excessive co-dependency and have instead found individuality and interdependency. We have also been lucky enough to transfer the loving trust and respect we have for each other into our work and service, and for this we are humbled and grateful.

We are physically very different, Chris is tall, sporty, slender, olive skinned, brown eyed and with dark (now grey) curly hair. I am short, rounded, blue eyed with fair (now grey) straight hair, given to plumpness.

Emotionally, Chris is fiery and vivid in her expression while I am cool with a tendency to suppress. Mentally she is very sharp and loves to do things like sudoku and brain training—I do not. She loves red and black. I like muted greys and pale colors. I love to garden, paint and cook—she doesn't like any of these things, but does love walking for hours with the dogs and for several years had a horse that she rode every day. I like to coordinate my clothes (except when I do not) while she prefers jeans and a checked shirt. It won't take too much stretch of the imagination to realize that we might not always see eye to eye and there have definitely been bumps along the road, but, remarkably, we have always managed to find our way through to an agreeable solution. This has often included humor and often outright belly laughter.

Only once did I consider leaving the relationship. I had been to the hairdressers and had a change to a very short cut, bleached almost white-blonde. Chris hated it. She berated me. telling me that my decision to do this was selfish and she should have been consulted. In that moment, I was furious with her for attempting to inhibit my creative expression, and there was some very loud shouting and door banging. However, it didn't take long, before we were falling about laughing at our indignant reactions. I have never wanted to leave her since.

We first met in 1990, when I was in Vienna for a three-day Psychosynthesis teaching assignment. It was a new contract, my first time working in Austria and, according to Chris, it was also a full moon.

As was the usual procedure, I was collected at the airport by Aron, a man I had met before. He was Austrian and a former trainee in Switzerland where I had worked as a visiting trainer. He had excellent spoken English and would be my translator. As I came out of Arrivals, Aron greeted me with his broad grin. Alongside him was a tall, dark-haired young woman with an equally engaging smile. This was Chris, a Swiss woman, who was the Psychosynthesis group assistant, the person who was a constant for the group as trainers changed. She spoke little English, but she was there to support the group and to support me. Of course, I had no idea then how significant this unknown person would become.

We took the scenic route to the work venue, a sports center with conference facilities, restaurants and accommodations attached to it. After the usual kerfuffle of checking in, finding the room and unpacking, I settled myself to do some final preparation for the next three days' teaching. At some point during this planning, my thoughts began to wander and for some inexplicable reason I began to fantasize about Chris coming to my room and us having sex.

This was unusual for several reasons. Firstly, I was in a long-term, committed, heterosexual relationship and, while I was broad-minded, I had no conscious desire to explore a sexual relationship with a woman. Secondly, I had no conscious attraction to Chris, other than having noticed what a lovely body she had – the tall and willowy kind with long legs, of which I was slightly envious. In the middle of this reverie there was a knock on my door. I opened to find Chris standing there and asking me in broken English if there was anything I wanted. Inner gasp/gulp. "No, thank you! I am fine," I said, feeling flustered as I firmly closed the door.

Chris: I remember this so very well. I had enjoyed meeting Judith earlier, so when in the evening I went out for a walk on my own, I thought it would be lovely to end the day by having a drink together. With this in mind, I knocked on her door. I could only say the first sentence and bam! the door was closed in my face. In my native language we call this a "cold shower."

Judith: Over the next two years I would continue working in Vienna and Salzburg with this same group on roughly a monthly basis. Chris and I would spend most of the breaks together attempting to communicate, me with terrible French and even worse German and she with slightly improving English. We managed to understand each other (we think) with the help of a small hand-held translating machine. How different this might have been if we had had access to today's translating technology—nowadays it is possible to use an app on your phone to speak in full sentences. Back then our conversations were agonizingly slow, but we used simple words, hand gestures and laughed a great deal. In fact, I think, maybe we ended up understanding each other better as a result. Why? Because people who speak the same language make so many more assumptions about what's being said, imagining that they know what the other person means. I liked her a lot and enjoyed our chats together. I had no idea that she was in a relationship with a woman. She would talk about her partner and I mine, but it was not until 1992 when we met at a conference that she introduced me to her.

Two years later I was back in Salzburg to run a final five-day course, teaching "The Practice of Psychosynthesis." This would be my last time working with this group and, for all intents and purposes, my last time teaching in Austria. On the first morning, I was picked up by taxi and taken to the venue where I dumped my things into the seminar room before heading out to stock up on provisions I would need for my stay.

While meandering through the aisles of the supermarket I thought about this being the last event and perhaps the last time I would see Chris and Aron. With this musing I began to feel sad and slightly bereft. I had grown to enjoy the trainees in the group and I really loved being with Chris. Simply put, I enjoyed our friendship.

I was thinking just this when suddenly I felt a sense of dismay as it occurred to me that perhaps she was so nice to me only because it was her job to be. At that very moment I turned the corner and there was Chris, shopping basket in hand. As we hugged hello, I felt a great sense of warmth and affection at seeing her again.

Chris: This moment is still so vivid for me. I am standing in the shop seeing Judith with her shopping basket and then saying hello. I felt a very warm wave of feeling wash over me. I realized it would mean a lot to me if she liked me as much as I liked her.

Judith: Like many long-term couples, we often think the same things at the same time without the other realizing it. Sometimes when we are together, I might mention an idea quite out of the blue and she will say, "I was just thinking exactly the same thing," or vice versa. There have been so many incidents of this kind of synchronicity that we now take them for granted, rather than being surprised by them. In fact, we'd find their absence to be more unusual.

It was the Saturday evening of the very last seminar when my relationship with Chris began to shift. We found ourselves flirting with each other, surfacing a deep attraction and fascination, which some hours later led us to making love. The lovemaking was deep and profound and amazing—a whole new experience. Being with this woman was like two clouds melting together in a sunlit sky. My heart was bursting at the deep connection with her. Not only was it Self to Self but it was passionate and familiar. It was like nothing I had ever experienced before. I had had my fair share of heterosexual experiences, but those encounters were nothing like this.

Chris: Our love grew without us noticing. Being alongside each other over the two years we were working in Austria, we spent every evening together talking and talking. I felt deeply seen and felt I was seeing her, despite the language barrier. Our times together were effortless and warm. On the final evening of the last seminar we became lovers. Even though, at first, we filed it away as a beautiful but unique experience, I knew deep inside that I had arrived, that I had found my soulmate. It was like swimming in lava without getting burnt. My senses were sharpened, my mind open and awake, my heart singing the most beautiful song I had ever heard. Nothing would stop me from standing up for this love. Now, 28 years later, this love is still growing.

Recently, someone asked me what I saw as the biggest success in my life. My answer was immediate and clear: it is our partnership, the fact that Judith and I have built a deep, happy and enriching relationship. The lava flows and is always there, especially in moments when I look at her as she plays with our grandson; as she works in the garden turning it into an oasis, as she embellishes our home with her amazing eye for beauty; as she walks towards me when I wait for her somewhere.

From the beginning, there was trust, even in conflicts; there never has been a fear of loss. This feeling is indescribably wonderful. I believe this is one of the most important foundations of a relationship: unbreakable commitment.

Over the next few months, we went through the painful process of leaving our respective partners and Judith telling her adored daughter Catharine, then just 14 years old, about our relationship. This was not an easy transition for her—she found the whole thing painful and traumatizing. With an extraordinary amount of persistence, she refused to speak to Chris for the first five years. To Catharine it must have felt like her mother was leaving her (as her father had done when she was less than a year old). It dug at old wordless wounds, so hard and so painful.

Chris: These years when Catharine refused to talk to me were very challenging. However, in a strange way I also admired her for being so free and authentic.

One day, in a Psychodrama training it was my turn to be the client so that my colleagues could practice. My topic was my relationship with Catharine. It was an intense process for me, with the outcome that I decided to stop "withdrawing" with a book when she was around, but instead to engage with her. I set this intention for my next trip to England and then something amazing happened. When I knocked on the door and Catharine opened it, she said a friendly hello and asked me if I would like a tea. All the tension was gone and from this moment on it was easy between us.

Over the following years I learned to become a stepmother, which became a big gift for me. I love Catharine deeply and I would do everything to protect her. I am incredibly proud of how she manages her life, how she acts in her relationship and how she is as a mother.

We learned that being a step-parent to a teenager requires great tenacity and goodwill (as most step-parents will tell you). To manage the kind of resistance that Catharine put up required endurance from all parties. However, even she in the end let go and now we all have a healthy loving relationship. We are proud of ourselves that we found a way through a really difficult time and now she loves having two mothers, and two grandmothers for her son.

For the most part Judith found that, whilst many of her close friends and family were supportive of the relationship, she also encountered ignorance and intolerance. This was both shocking and illuminating and a good lesson for a white, middle-class, privileged woman. She was in therapy, and very grateful for it, too.

Judith: Despite all of this I felt deeply secure with Chris; I knew, perhaps for the first time in a relationship, that I was not going to be abandoned. In time this allowed me to stop projecting my sense of security onto Chris and to find it within myself. I am speaking of that indestructible place or space in myself that I can always count on, that place of deep calm, wisdom and love. Some would call it Higher Self, or Soul—the label really doesn't matter, it's the experience and deep knowing that underpins our lives together. I know that our relationship created the ground for me to blossom, grow, deepen my sense of self, become a more fully realized and self-expressed person.

Chris: I like how Judith describes this. The experience of being indestructible as a couple has given me the trust and energy to dive in to the highest and deepest areas of myself. I would say that, as a consequence, I have become a much more independent and a stronger me.

Judith: The fact is that despite our differences, we also share a love of so many things. Our lived values are rooted in a deep commitment to Psychosynthesis and "peace work" as Chris would call it. In the early years of our relationship, as mentioned before, we worked together in Austria, Germany and Holland. For me it was the first time I had a co-leader, which presented some interesting challenges for both of us. Delivering courses alone for so many years meant she was unused to collaborating and sharing my thinking, but we overcame this and learned to work with groups in a way that we found remarkable. We danced very well together—literally as in moving to music, but also metaphorically in how we worked when we were teaching together.

Chris and Judith: For the first 14 years of our time together we were living in different countries, Judith in the UK and Chris in Switzerland. Judith was teaching Psychosynthesis in London but had also begun to work as a business coach. Meanwhile, Chris was rebuilding her private practice after leaving the organization she had worked with for some years.

In 1995 we began to think about starting our own Psychosynthesis center in Switzerland. We experienced a huge surge of energy at the thought of creating a new kind of training, based on an adult system of learning. We felt inspired as we began to play with a name and quickly settled on "Zentrum fur Psychosynthese, Bern" (Center for Psychosynthesis, Bern). The name was concise, and it clearly communicated our intention. How we worked with our trainees was crucial for both of us. We did our best to be respectful, kind and authentic teachers, operating with clear boundaries, doing our best to keep our egos in check.

To kick the whole thing off, we went on a retreat together, to not only celebrate our love but also to envision and create our training program in Psychosynthesis. A year later, in August 1996, we opened the Center and in January 1997 we started the first group with 20 trainees.

Understanding how much this retreat had helped us, we knew we wanted to build this into the way we worked together. Each year we would choose a beautiful place, in Switzerland or in the UK, and made sure we had time to both enjoy ourselves and to look at what was working and what had to be changed in the training. We remember those times as being very productive. It felt like putting the energy of our passion and love for each other into a form that was serving something larger, something more complete, more whole. Often, we inspired each other with new ideas and, even though Judith had 12 years' more experience in Psychosynthesis, she was always open to the new ideas Chris brought in. We respected and admired each other. We still do.

The training we designed would focus the first two years on "self-experience," that is, experientially learning all the tools and techniques of Psychosynthesis, with personal psychosynthesis being the main outcome. The second part of the training would be a repeat of the first two years, plus the addition of deeper theory and an exploration as to how to apply this in whichever field of work the trainee chose. We ran some successful five-day, basic courses and then took a leap of faith by renting a building, shared with other therapists. This was the physical birth of the The Psychosynthesis Center, Bern, where our dream was becoming a reality—although, at this point, we couldn't guarantee we would have enough participants to cover costs. For many years we have lived by an old Sufi saying, "Trust in the Goddess (or God) and tie up your camel." On the one hand surrender your fate to the higher, and on the other hand, make damn sure that you are also taking the practical steps to lower risk. In this case, we decided that, should our venture fail to thrive, we could move into the center and use it as our home.

Judith: Chris had an admirable, impressive willingness to grasp this endeavor with both hands; it involved learning new administration skills as well as how to run the training programs. She has been passionate and enduring in her love for Psychosynthesis ever since first encountering it in 1987 when she was a teacher of psychiatric nursing.

Chris: In 2004, Judith decided to make a change and work as a business coach full time in the UK. This decision was hard for me and everybody else at the Center, but we understood her desire to move on and do other things. Luckily, while the Center was growing, we had found some wonderful colleagues, and thanks to this dream team, I was happy to lead without her and continue to build on what we had started. This took courage and an ability to adapt, flex, hang in there and, where necessary, have difficult conversations.

Growing Together

Chris and Judith: We are two women who fell deeply in love. We have said yes to each other and we are committed to service. From our early days of learning about, and then working with, Psychosynthesis, it seemed to us that (in the past) there had been a real absence of acknowledging the feminine principle and all that goes with it, or perhaps we should say there was an over-emphasis on the masculine principle. By this we mean there is a propensity to see emotions as irrational or second-class citizens, when in fact they are just non-rational. Additionally, there is a tendency to give primacy to mental functioning and an overuse of hierarchy. We should stress that *both* are vital in human self-expression and one cannot exist without the other (bear in mind too this has little to do with physical gender identification).

The list below indicates some differences and contrasts between the feminine and masculine principles, although it is necessarily a simplification of a large matter.

Feminine Principle	**Masculine Principle**
Yin	Yang
Earth (depth)	Sky (height)
Emotions and Feelings	Thinking and ideas
Darkness	Light
Moon	Sun
Stillness	Activity
Absorption	Penetration
Curves and circles	Lines, levels, columns

This tendency to favor the masculine ideals is not surprising, as Psychosynthesis has its roots in the early part of the 20th century—before women even got the vote. It is also a reflection of our wider western society. Negation and oppression of the "feminine" is not a new topic and we will not go further into this here. However, as a reaction to this, and maybe even an overreaction at times, we have found ourselves with a need to soften, curve, round, spiralize and make into circles, that which appears to be linear in the progression of the development of the human psyche. Equally, we see and experience the Divine to be both within and without, above and below. We have been delighted to see in recent years the emergence and wide acceptance of the concept of "emotional intelligence"; it is a welcome development and validates what has been so important to us over the years.

Getting Married (Civil Partnership)

In 2006 we decided to marry, because we could. At first, we just wanted to change Chris's legal status so that she could live permanently in England, but we quickly realized that this step actually meant a lot more to us; it felt profoundly significant. Consequently, we planned our wedding very carefully and created a real celebration. It was deeply touching to share our commitment to each other in front of friends and family.

What has Helped Make our Relationship Work

In writing this chapter we asked ourselves: "What are the most important things for us to share about what makes our relationship work?" Here they are:

- Learning how to deal with misunderstandings, arguments and aggression.

- Learning how to be independent and interdependent at the same time.

- Having projects together and apart.

- Setting time aside for each other for fun, joy and play.

- Choosing to have difficult conversations.

Arguments and Disagreements

In the first 14 years before Chris moved to England, we had three lives: together in Bern, together in London, and each alone in London and Berne. On average, we were together for 10 to 14 days every month and, when we were, it was nonstop and intense.

Early on in our relationship we became aware that each time we met after being apart for a week or so, within the first 10 minutes we would find ourselves arguing, and usually this was about silly, picky things. In attempting to understand why, we looked deeper at what this could be about. We figured out that unconsciously we were angry with the other one, because we had missed each other so much. From then on, we started each reunion with this awareness. Through deliberate and conscious acknowledgment of this fact, the problem was solved.

Shared Interests

We are so fortunate to have the gift of sharing a vision, which has informed both our lives and our work. We believe that if a couple has a shared passion, or even a hobby, it gives them something extra. We were blessed that for us this was Psychosynthesis. This idea/philosophy has infused our relationship at every level. We were able to teach, create and serve. We were able to grow a great deal and we continue to do so even at this age and stage, although some of the challenges are very different. These days another one of our passions is Thomas, our grandson, who brings us huge amounts of joy and reminds us how to play.

Tips and Tools

Here are some of the practical tools we use or have used in our relationship to "make it work." We adapted models from Psychosynthesis to support us in our process and these are examples of our commonly used strategies:

- Basic communication and interpersonal skills, like active listening.

- Using "I" statements, for example I feel … I think … I believe … I want … etc.; this helps to distinguish I from the other. Avoid sentences that start with "you made me feel…".

- Replaying a situation or starting again by leaving the room and coming back in, this evokes a change of inner identification.

- Meditations, such as the disidentification exercise.

- Swapping arguments: Chris becomes Judith and Judith becomes Chris and we continue the discussion from this new perspective.

- Meditating alone to figure out what are the wants and deeper needs, as well as meditating together.

- Naming each other's subpersonalities or reminding each other of them.

- Stating when you are grumpy and allowing each other to be grumpy—this helps a lot and lowers expectations of the other.

Before we learned all of this, we had some difficult times. Chris thinks she put a lot of pressure on Judith, who then tried to cover up her frustrations with love and smiling. This would activate Chris' aggression, which in turn would activate Judith being even more kind. We could say that Chris was acting out the emotions and Judith the calmness. When we both understood that this dynamic wasn't working, we started to look at other ways of "being" together. It would be a fair summary to say that Judith learned from Chris how to argue in a more open and direct way, by risking being much more explicit about what she was feeling about a situation. Chris learned from Judith how to be more forgiving and more accepting. We both have had to work hard on these areas.

If one of us has a challenge that isn't connected to our relationship, we support each other by:

- Asking questions to help the other describe clearly what is happening. Offer advice only if asked for, often just listening helps.

- Asking which subpersonality is being evoked in the situation.

- Reminding each other about the Wise Being.

- Guided imagery – reminding each other of the tools and technique we can use with ourselves. Or sometimes we will guide the other. For example, when Judith was really anxious about going for an MRI (she is slightly claustrophobic) Chris worked with her to overcome the anxiety by finding an image for that part of herself that would support her through the process. It worked wonderfully well and subsequent MRIs have been managed without the anxiety.

Time Together, Playing and Laughter

We laugh often and we dance with each other, occasionally we sing. This has been a theme all through our years together. We both delight in making the other giggle. In our training we used to run an exercise called "the eyes of wonder"—these being the eyes of a child who can see the world in all its wondrous, magical and majestic glory. It is this place or lens in us that can marvel at simple things, like a twig, a stone or the fallen petals of a flower, as if seeing them for the first time. For years Judith had on her notice board two fairy wings (others may have thought them the pressed petals of a rose), but she knew differently. Lovely.

In the early days we used to play a game of subpersonalities role-play. Each of us decided who she wanted to be. For example, sometimes we pretended to meet for the first time and make up a whole new persona. One day Chris pretended to be a university professor, as she did this, she noticed that she became totally calm and peaceful with a feeling of competence and a clear sense of certainty. This newly discovered part became something that she could call upon when teaching.

It's with some hilarity that we recall a celebration at the end of a course. This group decided that each person should turn up as a subpersonality nobody had seen before. Judith came as a porn director and Chris as a porn actress. Judith wore a man's pink suit jacket and a three-day stubble, and Chris was in a black miniskirt, silver bustier, lots of makeup and big hair. It was very funny, but strangely empowering and freeing (go figure!). We feel the need to let you know that neither of us have aspirations to be either a porn director or porn star—but who knows what may come about in the future.

These days being grannies brings us a lot of fun. Thomas, who at the time of this writing, is now five years old, provides us with even more opportunities for play and to bring out our "inner child." We each feel happiness in a very pure and wonderful way. We are delighted to be grandparents, our gratitude for the time we have with him fills us with joy. To watch him become absorbed in an activity or work out how to put something together, or to giggle with him about something silly, or read him a story is just special. This last year we have had very limited contact with him, and we have missed out on nearly 12 months of his development, a sad and inevitable consequence of COVID-19. Our two Labradors are another perhaps unsurprising source of joy, walking, playing or just cuddling with them.

Creating Things Together

Sharing projects together has always been important to us. We make a great team and when our energy is aligned, we can accomplish a great deal—and have done so. We experience that wonderful thing called synthesis, where the whole is greater than the sum of the parts. We can count on each other to come up with what's needed, be it something practical or psychological.

At the same time, each of us has her own interests. Judith has the garden, cooking and painting and some occasional work, Chris has her gundog training, her long daily walks and a private practice, where she undertakes Psychosynthesis one-to-one sessions on the internet with clients from all over the UK and Europe.

Choosing to Have Difficult Conversations

We have long discussed death and dying and what will happen when one of us dies before the other, which is likely. This was especially true after Chris moved to the UK. It was a topic that we talked about with some regularity and we undertook these conversations quite lightly. It was the death of some of our close friends that prompted us to make the decision to live together after all those years of living in two countries.

Of the two of us, Judith has had more health issues: two total knee replacements, breast cancer (thankfully now in remission) and two operations on her neck and cheek to remove non-cancerous lumps. Of all of these, breast cancer was the most frightening. After the initial shock of diagnosis and a lot of hand-holding and hugging, we found ourselves gradually not speaking to each other about how we really felt about it all. Sitting together, in silence, on the top deck of a bus on the way to hospital one of us, we don't recall who, said how afraid they were feeling and how scary it was to acknowledge this, let alone share it for fear of upsetting the other. This broke the dam and suddenly we could both allow ourselves to talk about the heaviness and the deep-seated helplessness we were feeling, along with the stark realization that although the prognosis was good, Judith might not recover. She was lucky; the cancer was caught early and had not spread, so she made a full recovery. It was a humbling experience for both of us.

We are not alone in finding ourselves making some big life decisions in the face of this kind of health crisis. In our case, we determined that Judith should reduce stress as much as possible by limiting her work hours considerably, where possible, stopping traveling and doing as much work from home as possible. Although we had recently moved house, we made a momentous decision to move yet again in order to be closer to Catharine and family. Within the next 12 months, we had found a wonderful home in the countryside just outside of Leeds in West Yorkshire.

In Conclusion

Writing this chapter has prompted so many wonderful memories and thoughts of our story, alongside the challenges of capturing what we think is essential to our relationship. We believe that any couple, or indeed any kind of loving relationship, can thrive, blossom and grow given the right conditions, which include choice, commitment, shared values, respect and love.

In the Judith and Chris world, there is little to distinguish sexuality from spirituality because we experience it more as a continuum. Therefore, it is important to state what is obvious to us—that heterosexual couples don't have the sole rights to successful long-term committed relationships. We are lucky to live in the UK, a country that celebrates difference and allows same-sex couples to marry and to be an accepted part of society. I wish this were true for others in so many other places in the world. Elsewhere we could be imprisoned or even killed because same-sex love is considered to be a sin/evil/abnormal/abomination. Also, at the time of writing, it is very disturbing to observe in the USA a retrograde movement, born of ignorance and fear, where there is an attempt to deny rights that have been so hard fought for not only for same-sex couples but for women.

It is our belief that the Self or Soul is non-gendered. If Psychosynthesis teaches that the soul infuses the personality, it makes complete sense to us that Self or Soul will have a multiplicity of expressions of sexuality. We are an example of one of these multiplicities. For many years now Chris has refused labels such as lesbian or bi-sexual; she has always described herself as a sexual being. We do not identify as heteronormative.[1]

Today it is the last day of December 2020 and it is grey and cold. We have just spent almost a year in lockdown due to COVID-19. It has coincided with Judith moving into reduced working and consequently she is spending more time than ever pottering in the garden. This autumn she has spent many hours reorganizing, transplanting, and planning for things that will either bloom next year or mature in the future. Last night there was a frost which put paid to the dahlias and geranium. What is left are some seed heads that we leave for the birds. The vegetable plot has been given a new covering of manure and last year's garden compost, so mostly it's bare earth and it looks wintery. Chris has been able to continue her private practice work, as she was working mostly online before the pandemic. In February 2022, she retired from all therapeutic work.

Another change: our much loved, 15-year-old cat, Truffle was "put to sleep" after a short but terminal illness. Together we made the hard decision to end her life before her suffering became too great. We miss her graceful feline presence in our lives and household.

Cut off from family for most of this last year, we have spent even more time with each other. Despite the obvious challenges it has been joyful, touching and enriching. We are so grateful to have each other, our living situation and general circumstances. We are acutely aware that this is not true for everyone and many people will have suffered greatly during this lockdown period.

While it is very unlikely that we will have another 28 years together, there is a certainty ahead that we will face when it comes. It is our intention and hope that what we have nurtured together over these years will not only sustain us but will continue to grow.

Ahmed and Shamai

Shamai's chapter describes an intense soul love, a journey
of differences, and a deepening understanding of death and
loss. She writes sensitively about the path of caregiving,
walked with love, joy and a growing awareness of self.

CHAPTER SIX

Love and Loss

Shamai Currim

My first marriage lasted 30 years. We were teenagers who met in high school and rushed into the relationship to fill an attachment need. Both of us came from dysfunctional families where we never felt that we belonged or were loved, so we searched outside of our family of origin to fulfill that need. Faulty childhood attachments, according to Dr. Marni Feurman, affect future relationships:

> We tend to recreate unhealthy relationship patterns from our childhood in our adulthood. As much as people may dislike it, the familiarity is comforting. You may even confuse the feelings of relationship chemistry with what is the familiarity of your early life experience.[1]

The recreation of familiar but unhealthy life patterns is usually an unconscious act that, while making us feel good, can also create insecurity and feelings of distrust. My first husband and I both came from abusive backgrounds so, in accepting abusive patterns of behavior from each other, we never got that real sense of belonging, even in the family that we were creating. In looking back, it's as if the foundation of the relationship never got an authentic start and we both came out of that marriage feeling battered, as if we were fighting for our lives. The fact that I had found Psychosynthesis, which allowed me to look inside of myself and the world that I was creating, increased my longing to live a more authentic life. Years of therapy, undertaken as part of my Psychosynthesis training, helped me move farther from the abusive patterns of my life and into a healthier self-love.

Dr. Roberto Assagioli, the founder of Psychosynthesis, tells us that we possess both psychic as well as physical energy and that these energies can be converted by means of a psychological process. He tells us that we have internal subpersonalities formed from life experiences that determine how we integrate ourselves into the world. Subpersonalities may conflict with one another and create considerable chaos in our lives. As we become more aware of these internal forces, we can learn to befriend them and eventually learn to create some internal balance. With these inner changes the subpersonalities may cease to be the dominant forces in our lives and the conflicts between them may be mitigated. As we become aware, our subpersonalities start to take other subpersonalities into account. These changes and discoveries make it easier for all aspects within us to work together.[2]

As I worked on integrating my subpersonalities, I became the coordinator of my life story and, in living more authentically, became consciously aware of how my life in my marriage was lacking in joy, acceptance, and respect. Eventually the marriage crumbled and the vows we had spoken no longer held the essence of truth. I had outgrown my need for an attachment that included abuse and was ready to move forward on my life's path, so I separated from my husband.

Assagioli reminds us that in the human psyche there is a fundamental tendency towards union, or synthesis, but that it is not enough to put two people in contact with each other, for they will just lie inert. We must light a fire or even a spark in order to create change. Since I had moved out of the marriage relationship, a spark between us was no longer possible, and I truly believe that if we had stayed together we would have stagnated and eventually lost a primary purpose of life, which is the ability to find ourselves. Assagioli sums this up well when he talks about the two major phases of psychological growth. In marriage, as in personal growth, there is first the development of the "I", or the center of the personality, and then there are subpersonalities within an individual, the internal structures that are formed through conflicts of normal human experience.[3] When the various elements of our being are in conflict, our energy becomes blocked, and this causes pain. Each time that a synthesis of two or more parts of our personality occurs, energy is freed and we experience a sense of profound well-being. The harmonious integration of all our component parts around a unifying center simply unblocks and stimulates a process that is more closely allied to us than any other: becoming who we are.[4]

Towards the end of my first marriage, I had an experience that showed me that life was more intricate, more involved, and could be more conscious than what I had known. In a moment of awakening I was able to see life through different eyes. As I walked home from work one day I heard a beautiful high-pitched sound and was told, by an inner voice, that this was the sound of my soulmate. In that transpersonal experience I came to find out about Psychosynthesis and the psychology energies. I had started my training at Psychosynthesis Pathways of Montreal, as well as studying and training in 12 other alternative modalities while completing a BA in Applied Social Science at Concordia University in Montreal, Canada. It was around this time that I also became an initiate of a Sikh guru from India who was part of a lineage of masters teaching Surat Shabd Yoga, or the Path of Truth. Little did I know that not only would this path change my life, it would also lead me to my soul mate and second husband.

Shortly after my experience with the inner voice, I traveled to Chicago to see my guru. While seated at a luncheon with a group of initiates, a friend came along and introduced me to Dr. Ahmed Currim, suggesting that, because we both had backgrounds in healing work, we might want to sit together and talk. The physical attraction between us was strong, and the psychic attraction even stronger. Ahmed recognized and voiced the sadness he saw in my eyes, something no one else had ever noticed or spoken of, and he promised me a remedy (he was a homeopathic physician). He gave me his business card and he told me he would send me the remedy in the mail. It never arrived. I put his card in my wallet, where it sat for five years.

In 1997 I traveled to Bangladesh to work as a teacher trainer. Bangladesh is a predominately Muslim country, so this Jewish girl had the unique experience of living with Muslims in the Indian tradition. I returned to Canada in 1998 to present at the Association for the Advancement of Psychosynthesis conference in Pohenegamook and immediately began divorce proceedings. (I later learned that Ahmed was also going through his own horrible divorce at this time.)

In August of 2000, a friend and I took a summer journey through areas of Quebec I had never seen and just before leaving I found Ahmed's business card in my wallet. Recognizing that the card wouldn't bring him into my life even though I knew that he was my soulmate, I threw the card away, letting go and surrendering to life's fate. The next day, upon arrival at our destination, and even before we checked into the bed-and-breakfast inn, we stopped in at a palm reader, just for fun. As I entered, the woman looked up from a reading she was currently doing and, looking directly at me said, "You are supposed to be with a dark-skinned man and you have already met him. Will you just get on with your life!" and she went back to her reading. Having let go of the card and the memory, I didn't connect to what she had just told me. Her words were profound, and yet I couldn't place her prediction with my earlier experience.

Only one month after this episode with the palm reader, I again found myself visiting my guru, where I once again met up with my husband-to-be. Ahmed was of Indian, Muslim descent and I found that my experience in Bangladesh (formerly a part of India), living among Muslims, was a profound synchronicity. Since we were both single now we were able to move into our relationship, and within six months we were married.

I left my family, my country of origin, and my professional life to live with my soulmate. Never in the past could I have believed that I, coming from a Jewish family, would marry a man born in India with a Muslim background. As we embraced each other, we were also able to embrace our families of origin and our common spiritual path. Not only was there acceptance, there was also an enrichment and a higher attainment of understanding. Our coming together as a couple brought together both ethnicities and religions.

An important part of the Islamic religion is the month-long fast of Ramadan. Having practiced this with my Bangladeshi family, I was able to bring this into our relationship, a respect for

Ahmed's family of birth. When both festivals of light came around (Chanuka and Diwali) we happily celebrated both. Ahmed's strong connection to his parents, both of whom he lost when he was very young, became a tradition of sitting in front of their pictures on birthdays and anniversaries and sharing our lives with them. I spoke of my gratitude for having such a fine man as a husband and how he would make them proud today. This helped Ahmed to feel supported and helped to build up his self-esteem.

Our age difference of 12 years was at first difficult. Coming from different generations I would dance around the house to a fast beat, and he would suggest we waltz to classical music. I think it was easier for me to adapt to his needs, perhaps because I was younger, or perhaps because I had learnt to be more pliable, more giving. While Ahmed preferred the quiet life, perhaps because he was surrounded by patients all day, I loved the social life, so we compromised by inviting friends over often for meals. These friends were people we knew through our guru, so our social life was shared with people of like mind. I began my therapy practice in Ahmed's office. So much of our time was spent together, social and professional, which we found very rewarding and enriching.

It also became quite enmeshing: his need for mothering, and mine for acceptance. Reluctantly, Ahmed began work with a Psychosynthesis practitioner. While willingly engaged in the process, the pain proved to be too much and, while trying to skirt the pain, he eventually stopped going to sessions.

Assagioli views marriage as a work of art, a canvas where the husband and wife can learn to alternate in a variety of roles. He believes that psychosynthesis of the couple is fundamental to achieving psychosynthesis of humanity.[5] He used triangles to represent the synthesis of polar opposites. In his discussion of marriage, he put Husband on the left hand side, Wife on the right, and the higher guiding principal at the triangle's apex, indicating that the synthesized couple forms a third entity—the couple itself. In this way, the couple can be energetically strong, especially when the two persons and the couple itself are all connected to a higher source. He stated that couples who model this spiritual strength are rarely found in our society, because the spiritual and erotic energy is so difficult for most people to live with. Through the repression of this highly elevated degree of moral or spiritual purity or excellence, society's tendency is—often unconsciously—to belittle, defuse, or destroy the couple.[6]

My marriage with Ahmed began on a spiritual level. Our mutual respect, through chastity and the laws of purity that we learned in our common spiritual path, brought us to a place of mature love, respect, and growth. With every step we took together, our experiences and lived wisdom continued to grow. We faced our love, as well as our demons, together. Our family of origin patterns were shared and faced together. Long talks, tears, and even silence informed our mutual growth. Our talks helped us to become more conscious and more supportive of each other. We were able to travel the world and study under advanced homeopathic mentors together. Our mutual understanding of the world supported our relationship and gave us many positive experiences. On our wedding invitation we had used the words, "as two souls become one," and we were truly living that experience.

If we put this into the synthesis of polar opposites framework provided by Assagioli, Ahmed on the left was encouraging my growth as I was doing the same on the right through mutual understanding of our spiritual path. We meditated together, kept to a vegetarian diet, and visited often with our guru. As we progressed we became mirrors for each other, moving through the stages to self and God realization. We took turns being the most vulnerable and, in living authentically, we moved together to the higher point of the triangle, to a lived experience of higher source as a couple, moving as one, in sync with each other. We shared psychic experiences together at higher levels of consciousness and moved forward from them.

And then, life hit us with cold water. Two years into our marriage Ahmed began to show symptoms of severe cognitive and physical impairment. At first it manifested as difficulty in walking. Every night Ahmed and I had walked along the beach together, arm in arm, without a care in the world. Now, Ahmed was living as if his head was leading his body, bent over and running, and he could not stop. I would try to keep up and eventually stand in front of him to stop the flow of his body. He began to confuse words and his loss of short-term memory was apparent. We would have discussions, make decisions together, and by the next day he would argue that I was trying to control and confuse him. His inner boundaries were slowly eroding, as were his social skills. Eventually we stopped going to restaurants because he would have fights with the waiters over trivialities that became monumental to him. Friendships disintegrated and, not understanding the pattern of illness, many people lost respect for Ahmed and avoided any contact with him. His medical practice dwindled because he could no longer provide the professional care so demanded of a physician. What followed was brain surgery to attempt to correct the excess of cerebral spinal fluid (normal pressure hydrocephalus) that was causing damage to his brain, and then other surgeries that continued to erode not only his physical health, but also his mental capacity and his ability to be in the world. His ability to care for himself became erratic, until I finally had to move into a full time caregiver role. Now our polarity of opposites triangle was eroding as Ahmed became more and more in need of my physical, emotional, cognitive, and spiritual support.

Love flows from love, so, for me, sacrifice in the name of love was no stranger. When we first got married I had given up my family and country of origin, as well as my career, and over the years together I had filled these in with our new family which we created, and career possibilities. Now I felt very alone, with many tasks which felt overwhelming, and for which I felt I had no training or understanding of what to do. Many times it felt like I was running on an empty tank and, as I cried out in pain, I learnt how to open my heart to receive more. With Ahmed's decline there came a change in my role that oscillated between partner and caregiver, a delicate balance of give and take. That role could change many times a day, or take weeks to manifest. My caregiving tasks included personal and home care, food preparation, health care, mobility support, supervision, transportation, emotional support, health monitoring, as well as trying to help him to feel oriented or grounded. Anxiety and irritability became the norm and I found myself losing my sense of balance and equipoise. I found it difficult to know how to help my husband as he slipped from the reality we shared to one only he could enter. It was a role for which there really is no training. Few people are prepared for the role of caregiving for a loved one, and when it's our spouse we no longer have any partner support. I attended many caregiver training programs over the years, trying to learn how I could make things better for Ahmed, as well as for myself.

Love became caregiving, which became a priority in my life. My sense of self became identified with the role of caregiver. This took both a physical and emotional toll on me, as well as on our relationship, and many times I felt very lost with little support from the outside world. I lost a sense of privacy; I no longer had a viable social or professional life. I found myself living moment to moment, unable to see or plan for the future, and eventually I developed physical problems that manifested from the stress.

Assagioli clearly states that individuals should not lose themselves completely in the couple. He wrote that we need to resist the tendency to throw ourselves completely into the task, as it may be a form of evasion from individual responsibility to one's Soul. But the needs of my situation overwhelmed my awareness of this need for self-restraint.

As in everything in life, maintaining the right proportions is key.[7] My approach to life has always been to do the best I can, to make things better than when I found them. I think, for this reason, and probably others that I was not aware of, I didn't know how to stop giving. When a loved one is in pain or confusion, for most of us the first reaction is to help in whatever way possible. Each day and night was filled with caretaking tasks. I was lucky if I got a couple of hours of sleep a night because Ahmed's cycle of day and night became confused. He would walk the halls all night and I was concerned that he would hurt himself or, even worse, do something that could hurt others. I was constantly on guard, and this eventually took a toll on my body. The couple entity as I knew it was gone, as well as my sense of self.

I truly understand, now, why people say caregivers die before the people they are caring for. It got to a point where I clearly said to myself that I would give up my life for this husband that I loved so dearly. I thought I shouldn't, and yet every fiber of my being allowed itself to let go in order to maintain the caregiving role. My goal in life has always been to do the best in whatever endeavor I engage myself, and that is exactly what I did—my best, a total surrender to whatever I felt was needed. I barely slept, I watched over my husband to keep him safe and out of harm's way. In this technical world that meant I even had to keep him safe from predators on the Internet. In his weakened cognitive state, he fell prey to emails asking for money, and he even responded to emails, suggesting remedies for their purposed maladies. He sensed my difficulty in caretaking and emailed to women asking them to move into our house. He feared that I would leave him and he knew he couldn't take care of himself. My husband had no family or siblings in North America who could step into a caregiving role and give me some respite. I depended on the government Medicare system to provide me some much-needed time away, to regroup and regather the needed energy and sustenance to continue in this role. It was the most difficult work I have ever done.

Ahmed's decline was irregular and sporadic. He could appear to be high functioning one day and low the next. This sporadic up-down decline was particularly brutal for me to endure. One day my hopes would be lifted, and dashed the next, until I not only began to mistrust my emotions, I thought I was going insane, thinking perhaps that I was the one that was sick, and not my husband.

One of the things that was lost in my life was what Roberto Assagioli has described as marriage as a work of art, where the husband and wife can alternate in a variety of roles. Ahmed and I seemed to have become frozen in two roles: an ill person and a caregiver. The attachment between us had become equally frozen into survival mode, and I felt myself drawn irresistibly into an identification that saw all the growth and harmony between us slowly slip away. The "couple entity" was still there, but the energies and dynamics of it were no longer synthetic.

Assagioli tells us that every art has its specific techniques; likewise, the art of living has its own techniques, and mastering them is indispensable in practicing it successfully. One such technique is to consider life as a game and stage performance. He reminds us that "To act a part or role in life, in fact several ones, constitutes a psychosynthetic technique of fundamental importance".[8]

Elsewhere he says:

> Individuals are interwoven into an intricate network of vital, psychological and spiritual relations, involving mutual exchange and interactions with many other individuals. Without an adequate psychological knowledge, understanding, and conscious use of the methods of psychosynthesis, there is abundant evidence that conflicts and dramas can jeopardize and break up marriage relationships.[9]

My part in our relationship, which in the end did not feel much like a game, had been nearly reduced to one role, and then "the performance" was over.

Ahmed died in March, 2017, 16 years after we had gotten married. On his deathbed, when he was no longer able to do most anything, he reached over and put his arm around me, and touched his other hand to his heart, to let me know he loved me. He closed his eyes, and left his body.

The companionship, the feeling of being needed and wanted, and the love between us had kept me going in my role as his caregiver. Being able to find the positives in a caregiving role was part of what allowed me to be satisfied and find pride in what I started to call "my life." Separating the work from the emotional attachment helped me to continue. Giving back to someone else is gratifying, and it gave my life meaning. Ahmed and I breathed as one unit, moved as one unit, and it wasn't until the day I suddenly felt a disconnect of our souls that I understood how far down the rabbit hole I had gone. It was like I got my self back but didn't know how to be in that self.

At first, my grieving took the form of giving back to the community. All those long, caretaking years allowed me to share, to support others going through similar circumstances. I began to provide volunteer services at a local palliative care hospital and to do home visits for seniors who are isolated. I continued in my caregiving role for a full year after I threw my husband's ashes to the wind. I couldn't stop. I couldn't let go of the role.

My body finally forced me to remember that I was *alive*, by forcing me to acknowledge my vulnerability. I began to have episodes of blacking out, and eventually lived through the experience of my heart stopping. With the emergency placement of a pacemaker, I no longer have blackouts, and am reminded that being present to my personal self is just as important as the service that I perform. I have no choice but to slow down now and to surrender to my life. I've learned how to take it easy, to enjoy every moment, and to relish the memories of the past years—and am discovering that there are more good memories than I thought there would be. I am alive, I am present, and the way I express my role in life has changed. I have rediscovered the other life-roles that had been shunted aside for years, and found new ones as well. I use my experiences to enliven my paintings, sharing my life through color and words, expressing my soul journey on a canvas of love. I am slowly letting go of our shared photo albums, remembering the past, and allowing myself to move into the future, while being in the present.

This has been my hero's journey. It was as if I had walked into battle, was almost devoured by the disease, and came out trium-

phant. My experiences have taught me that love—true unconditional love, compassion, and commitment—can help us to endure,
to grow, and to find peace within ourselves. Our marriage *was* a
work of art after all, and much more happened than I had realized.
I learned that I am stronger than I knew I was, and much more
courageous. I learned I could bend with difficulties, and hold the
strength when my life needed to be grounded. I was able to allow,
and to surrender, and to come back more alive than when I started.
I engaged in a constant friction and delved into the unknown. I
drowned, pulled myself up, and continued. I gave my all and came
out victorious.

Our souls merged and I saw death from the other side. In an
inner experience I walked with him as far as I was allowed to walk,
and then encouraged Ahmed to go forward. He came to visit me in
visionary experiences, first three months after his passing, then
after one year, and then a year later, each time showing me that
he was no longer in pain, no longer held down by the illusions of
life that had been created during his experiences in this life. He
was pure light, fully joyous and effervescent. I was comforted in
knowing that he had finally found the happiness and belonging
he so longed for during his life journey. He was able to dance with
joy and even sang spiritual *Shabds* in honor of creation.

Ahmed's physical body may be gone, but he is never far away
from me. Memories have a way of living on, the good even more
than the bad. I see him in the crescent moon, and feel him on the
wind. I talk and laugh with him, and continue to enjoy the companionship once provided by our love. The synthesis is permanent.

Vincent and Judith

This chapter tells the story of this couple's relationship, begun with an intentional focus on forming bonds of trust, after both had left previous relationships with broken trust. Judith and Vincent narrate their story together, covering the arc from their early relationship to full maturity. They reference concepts from attachment theory and treatment and offer insight and guidance from their lived experience, as they each grow individually, while gradually opening to deeper levels of emotional closeness.

CHAPTER SEVEN

Navigating Relationships

Judith Broadus and Vincent Dummer

Kindness and compassion are among the principal things that make our lives meaningful. They are a source of lasting happiness and joy. They are a foundation of a good heart. Through kindness, and thus through affection, honesty, truth and justice toward everyone else, we assure our own benefit. This is a matter of common sense. Consideration for others is worthwhile because your happiness is inextricably bound up with the happiness of others.
—*H.H. the Dalai Lama[1]*

Judith: Our relationship began in 1983 at the Kentucky Center of Psychosynthesis, where Vincent had just arrived from the Netherlands to become a trainer and I had been studying as a trainee. This made it easy to get to know each other as people, gradually developing trust, since there was a professional distance between us. We easily became friends and would have lunch or dinner together to discuss Psychosynthesis theory and application questions. When Vincent gave me a training opportunity to co-lead a trauma support group, we had many good opportunities for learning about each other's understanding of Psychosynthesis. As we spent more time together, we also began to share on a more personal level, with some caution to keep it from getting into psychological process issues.

Vincent: Yes, we had been co-leading that trauma support group weekly for many months, having great discussions afterwards reflecting on challenges and new ideas to try out for next time. Judith was great on "group process," how participants were feeling and not expressing their feelings directly. That was a good way to get to know each other.

Judith: For several years, we continued the friendship and began to also share with each other our individual trials in each of our personal issues and relationships. One thing I had realized in therapy was my strong identification with my emotions as being truly "me." With Vincent, who was more identified mentally, I began to appreciate the value of sharing ideas and my ability to think. Even though for years I had evaluated myself as being not adequate intellectually, he seemed to value knowing what I thought about this or that. I continued with training and my personal therapy, and he continued in his role as a trainer. It was the container of Psychosynthesis that provided continuity to grow trust.

I returned to school in 1984, and earned my Master's in Psychology in 1985. My program had given me a research assistantship so I now had some small income of my own, but that felt huge to me. As well, the emotional support I got from the women teaching in my department helped me to move forward with what was becoming an obvious next step for my development towards more independence. In 1986, on the day I defended my Master's thesis, I got a call from a woman who had been having an affair with my husband. I won't go into details about that marriage here, but it had certainly not been a satisfying relationship for me. I filed for a divorce very soon after that call confirmed his infidelity. I felt like I was jumping off a cliff, but not taking that leap would have seemed wrong to me and my children. I was afraid, but determined to move beyond my fears to find a more genuine way to live my life. It was never part of my vision of life to have a divorce, especially since I had honored my marriage vows. I had also been inspired by reading Gandhi and his emphasis on *ahimsa* (non-violence). I wanted to find the most genuine way to live my life, sharing my values with my children, not to separate them from their father.

In 1986, the same year I filed for divorce, my oldest son suffered a serious head injury when a semi-truck ran into the side of the car in which he was a passenger, leaving him with a frontal lobe injury. My two younger children, a boy and a girl, were confused and fearful as they experienced the changes in their older brother, from being a sweet, smart person they could emulate, to being irascible and impulsively aggressive. I felt crushed and despairing. He suffered a second head injury in 1989, when he left a moving vehicle his father was driving, and this time the injury involved his right temporal lobe. It became a confusing time, especially for my first son, but of course, it was also true for the rest of us as well – disorienting, unsettled, and frightened, so easily angered.

Vincent: When I moved to the United States from the Netherlands in 1983, leaving my family, home and country behind, I was looking for enrichment and deeper support. I had experienced that during my first stay in Kentucky in 1977, when I attended the University of Kentucky for an internship. I remembered that time with a profound sense of liberation, getting for the first time direct clinical experience. That training experience was in cognitive therapy, very effective for many people, but it also brought up many questions. I thought of myself as someone who had received adequate emotional care growing up, but during my adolescence and young adulthood I felt a lack of support and guidance in my understanding of life and the world. I turned to psychology as my new home base, where I hoped to find better answers. I didn't get any help from my mother. I was frustrated with her sense of inferiority, and my inability to convince her to change that attitude. Perhaps resulting from this sense of helplessness, I began a search to better understand the concept of self and ways to increase self-acceptance. It dominated my graduate study and dissertation topic and got me interested in Psychosynthesis. Through Psychosynthesis training, I found that the distinctions between "sub-personalities," "I," and "higher Self" validated my own understandings. I turned away from cognitive behavior therapy and embraced Psychosynthesis training as my new path and community.

I deliberated on the choice between an academic career and a clinical career. In Rotterdam, Marco De Vries was doing exciting cancer research at Erasmus University using Psychosynthesis but I also had been in contact with the directors of the Kentucky Psychosynthesis Center, and they were interested in recruiting me as a trainer. Once I completed the Psychosynthesis training with the London Institute and obtained my doctorate in psychology, I began to explore ways to get a visa, work permit, and license to practice psychology in Kentucky. Any reasonable person would have given up, seeing the obstacles on the path, but somehow I persevered and managed to gain legal and professional entry to the USA.

I decided to immigrate to the U.S. based on my sense that it would be a richer experience and more aligned with my sense of purpose, a continuation of a path I had been on. However, those first five years in Kentucky were really challenging. I spent considerable time second-guessing myself, wondering if my hopes were realistic, questioning my decision to move, commit to a spiritual path and pursue my sense of liberation. I had also expected to be in a romantic relationship, but encountered rejection. This culminated in a crisis, when a major rift developed at the Center related to "perceived taking sides" with victims and perpetrators of abuse. The atmosphere of growing distrust made it apparent that I could no longer stay with the Center.

While this was going on, Judith and I had both been looking forward to going to Europe and the Psychosynthesis conference in 1988. When the conflict at the Center made it no longer realistic to follow the original plan of attending as a Center group, we either had to go separately or not go. I had become aware that the intimate relationship I was in was no longer mutual, and when this conflict developed, it ended my trust and commitment to my prior relationship. I really was in a crisis, questioning why I had moved to the U.S., rethinking my sense of purpose, and feeling very alone, but unable to identify where I had gone wrong. So, I concluded that there must be a next step that I just was not seeing.

Judith and I really could not justify the financial expenses of a trip to Europe, certainly not if we were to do it the "American way," with everything preplanned and reservations made in advance. Together, we had less than $2,000 to spend on this trip of 15 days in Europe, after paying for a charter flight from Baltimore and prepaying for the conference. Having grown up in Europe and traveled on a shoestring before, I made the bold statement that an average budget of $100 a day would be all we would need. This opened the door to an adventurous, magical mystery tour.

We visited my family, borrowed a station wagon from my brother-in-law and set course to Paris, sleeping in the car in the parking lot of Chartres Cathedral. I am pretty sure it was not the jet lag, but rather some other source of energy at play that prevented us from getting much sleep. We both knew that something had changed in only a few days and we were telling each other how amazing it was. There was a sense of magic, an opening up, and coming out of a painful and dark period of time, a beginning to restore a sense of trust and commitment. We immediately agreed on the ground rules of our relationship. We both knew what we didn't want and what values guided our lives. What stood out was how comfortable we were with each other. It was easy to be genuine and authentic and easy to see when we would get identified and old subpersonality patterns took over. It was a joyous transition to something new, filled with humor and tenderness.

Judith: We drove from the Netherlands via Paris, down through France to the Mediterranean Sea. It was my first trip to Europe, and the ancient architecture was such a mind-opening experience. I was enchanted by the sights and sounds of foreign names, and loved eating new-to-me delicious foods. When we arrived on the Mediterranean coast, it almost didn't seem real on that beach in Toulon. Standing together in the full moonlight by the Mediterranean was so romantic, and so much fun, yet we were still both being very cautious about becoming sexually intimate with each other. My sense of trusting the institution of marriage was completely gone. Earlier in my life I had believed that a marriage could be a safe and secure haven. Now I saw that as magical thinking. Vincent and I both had knowledge and training in general semantics (a system of linguistic philosophy, developed by Alfred Korzybski, that explores the arbitrary nature of words and symbols and attempts to refine ways of using language), and this helped me trust him. But, given my recent experiences, I was in a vulnerable state, and it felt way too risky to venture into a new relationship at anything but a snail's pace.

We arrived in Venice, a magical place if ever there was one, where the opening of the conference took place; then the conference continued in Sesto, in the Italian Alps, so we went on there. Our time together did not remain without a reminder of the conflict we had left behind in the US. There was a difficult encounter once we reached Sesto, since sleeping arrangements had not been settled, so I had to choose between sharing a room with the dissatisfied contingency from our local Center or sharing a room with Vincent. As you may guess, I chose to stay with Vincent even though it meant publicly sharing a room, and appearing to take sides in the Center conflict.

In Italy we visited Assisi and encountered the elegant simplicity and beauty of the crypt of the chapel of St. Francis, with its simple white-plastered walls and floors contrasting with a profusion of ferns, mounds of sensual red anthuriums and white baby's breath. In my joyful heart, I felt we were married there in spirit, if not legally.

Without fanfare, we hopped on a ferry to Greece. Cows roamed wild on the roads, impeding our progress as we traveled. Camping in our borrowed station wagon, we woke to sheep bleating near our campsite as they were herded to drink from the water of the lake where we had parked. Our relationship was a constant delight, with a changing background of scenery and exotic names, with a soundtrack playing on our portable stereo.

It was a rough re-entry for me when we came back to the States, since we needed to handle the situation with my children delicately. They were still adjusting to the divorce and did not accept Vincent. We decided to see each other mostly on the weekends, letting the children warm up to Vincent more slowly. Meanwhile, I had to figure out how to continue working to support myself and the children while remaining in graduate school and caring for my disabled son. These were big concerns with long-range implications, in sharp contrast with the immediacy of the experience I had had in Europe with Vincent.

I was just grateful my son was alive and that I would have the chance to be with him as we went down his bumpy path to learn together, with lots of help from the Universe and many generous, skilled people. Initially, Vincent and I tried to manage his rehabilitation ourselves. We bought a building suitable to become a residential rehab facility and began recruiting staff. Realizing the daunting magnitude of our undertaking, it was a great blessing when we were able to access assistance from the Kentucky Brain Injury Association, who helped provide us with a case manager for his care, to coordinate the services for the next decade.

Vincent remained a steady and guiding support during these most difficult years. My parents were available to help with childcare and, as usual, were part of my primary emotional support. Emotional support, as well as considerate advice, also came from Vincent and my psychosynthesis therapist. I also needed intellectual guidance, as my confidence in my judgment was low. I had strong faith in the goodness of God to protect us but I was still projecting God as external to my own being. This fundamental split in my own consciousness remains in the process of healing into wholeness, as I slowly regain the confidence that "I" am distinct but not separate from the source of being.

Vincent: Looking back on our relationship, it seems that the first two decades were primarily about healing the injuries we had sustained before we met. We really dove into the trauma literature, with Judith finishing her dissertation on the long-term effects of trauma. What really stands out for me was my difficulty in directly asking for what I needed. When I experienced insecurities, I believed that I had to be more mature and not dependent on reassurance or empathy from someone else; I thought I should somehow be able to do it all by myself. This self-sufficiency pattern was rooted in my childhood experience of available, but ineffective, parenting. I received care that did not resolve my needs (but probably did meet my parents' needs), and this made me feel misunderstood. In my previous relationships, I would express my feelings and areas of confusion or inner conflict, but continued to get the message that it was "my issue." Sometimes the message was subtle and other times very overt, but the sense of having a secure base where I could take my feelings and have them unconditionally accepted—let alone receive an emotionally empathic response—was foreign to me. What I received instead was something like, "if you resolved your underlying issue, you would not have this problem, so let's try to identify your underlying issue." Eagerly I would go along, hoping that it would lead to higher self-sufficiency; but I was actually continuing to dismiss my feelings and the interpersonal context of them, and to excuse others for not giving me a more empathic and caring response. In time, I actually became more needy and demanding as I felt more depressed and misunderstood, while my misdirected anger became a source of further alienation. My attachment insecurity was of the dismissive type, causing me to become even more mentally identified and judgmental of people who were caught up in feelings of inferiority. I looked at myself as being fairly independent and autonomous and not needing other people for my well-being.

However, experiences with Judith opened up completely new aspects of love that I could not dismiss, which made me do a 180-degree turn around. I remember telling her that she was my "love guru," something that made her very uncomfortable, but it reflected that I had abandoned the pursuit of autonomy in favor of a form of interdependence. For this change I had to really work on restoring my trust in people. Relating to Judith became my path of awakening, working with my dislike of emotions that didn't make sense to me. Instead of distancing myself from these experiences, I embraced them and looked for the truth and wisdom, as well as the distortions in them, so that these experiences became more meaningful and trustworthy. My belief that I had a better grasp and understanding of things made room for ideas like: "I better figure out where Judith is coming from," and: "Judith is right." I did not discount my own understanding of issues, but I reminded myself that often it would be incomplete.

I found a compassionate and caring attitude from Judith, who was aware of the conflicts I had with others but refused to take sides and just wanted to be there for me. She was simply present, not trying to explain my situation as the result of a deeper issue that I had. She allowed me to grieve and find my inner truth while comforting and validating my feelings—unconditionally. I remember thinking at the time, "I just need to be loved and understood genuinely." In that healing environment, I started to address my anger and began to be willing to be available for others and reciprocate what I had received, which in turn, benefited the development of our relationship. It has now become a stable attitude that, whenever I have an emotional injury, I feel safe to bring it to Judith. Even if she could easily question me and point out how I contributed to the problem, she will trust and support me in processing the event, by staying supportive and caring. What is more important, I have learned to ask for what I need, and know when I get it.

Judith: It is only in reading Vincent's thinking in our chapter that I realize he was intending to heal the injuries which had occurred prior to our relationship. I knew he thought I had problems with trust, but he had not been so forthcoming with his own part, so that is one reason I am grateful he found a way to help our relationship become more a matter of common ground. I didn't know until I read it here that he found me to be so genuinely loving towards him—I had intended that, but didn't know it was being received as it was. As for me, I was grateful to be with a kind, respectful and patient man. I did still carry some pain related to my children rejecting Vincent, and my biggest heartache continued to be the injury of my eldest son. I also felt anger toward my ex-husband for his betrayal of our family and lack of help in dealing with the aftermath of the accident. I had navigated being a single parent for the twenty years we were married, and my ex was now more like a rebellious teenager. I felt I had failed as a parent and didn't know how to repair that. I was constantly anxious that Vincent would also find me inadequate and find reasons to leave me.

Vincent: I believe another way of describing those years would be in terms of our connectedness. We would have these close connections and then the connectedness would diminish when life responsibilities took over and a serious argument would bring the focus back to how we got disconnected. We worked with our subpersonalities and owned our triggers, and were able to restore and reaffirm our intention for closeness. Whenever we could take some time off and be together for some extended time, we were able to reestablish our sense of "being at home." We basically each had a sense of security, but when triggered we still had our old ways of dealing with this breach of vulnerability. As I had a mental identification, a dismissive style of dealing with emotions, Judith insisted I confront my tendency to withdraw and be defensive, and she encouraged me to share my feelings in order to get a better understanding of what was happening.

Judith: My pattern of defensiveness was more related to my emotional identification. I had finally started to realize how much fear and anxiety had dominated my life, and I wanted my life to be guided by love, not fear. It became an ongoing dance of recognizing the pattern, making time and space for meditation, and then choosing a better way, allowing a view of the "conflict" as seen with the eyes of love, which seemed to provide an open door to better communication and understanding. For example, if my fear of Vincent leaving me was triggered, quiet time alone in meditation provided the space and perspective for me to dis-identify. I would regain a connection to being in my body and instead of adding insult to injury by criticizing or judging myself, I would allow recognition and acceptance to replace emotional turmoil. Then I could find a way to put it all in words, which gave me more mental distance from the tumult of feelings so I could regain a sense of emotional balance.

Vincent: For me, meditation served the function of intellectually clarifying the distinction between subpersonality and "I" or "non-self" in Buddhist terms. I already was pretty good at dis-identifying from my emotional reactions, but meditation practices fostered my ability to claim and cultivate wisdom and compassion as my natural state of being. Further, the meditation practices helped us to connect with a new community of people. A leftover feeling from the conflict at the Psychosynthesis center was that we had to somehow justify our relationship, whereas with the new meditation community acceptance of our relationship was never in question. For our relationship, it was really helpful to have another community where we could be of service and receive another way of understanding our challenges with life. The Buddhist view and Psychosynthesis theory were very much aligned and offered a type of cross-fertilization.

Judith: That cross-fertilization led us to take Psychosynthesis training to a Shambhala Meditation community in Santiago, Chile, where we had been invited to teach at a regional university. One of the primary Shambhala teachers from South America, who attended our workshop asked us to "Please bring Psychosynthesis to Shambhala!" This period of encouragement to coordinate Shambhala meditation practice with Psychosynthesis, coupled with the "causes and conditions" of having a critical number of people in Lexington who wanted Psychosynthesis training, led to us offer a three-year training program called "Mindfulness-based Psychosynthesis." It was stimulating and challenging to learn how to teach together. It was a bit stressful for me, since I had a strong tendency to defer to Vincent, combined with an urge to find my own voice. Yet it was satisfying to feel an emerging sense of shared purpose.

Vincent: That training may have been a transition from the healing decades to beginning to express our own truth. We refreshed so much of what we had learned in Psychosynthesis and brought in new research. We also worked with letting the participants guide us where we needed to go. As we taught together, our differences were frequently on display and we modeled how to be honest and non-defensive, agreeing to disagree as we reached for higher ground and, at times, "synthesis." It was very alive, and, as we videotaped all meetings, we were able to continue to do virtual online teaching as we completed the three-year cycle. This training gave a new impetus for the training Center to continue as a community of like-minded souls who care about each other. We continue to meet on a regular basis, primarily supporting each other in being of service in our world.

In this training, we had a weekend where we discussed Adverse Childhood Experiences research and used the Adult Attachment Interview[2] as a guided meditation, to explore early attachment experiences and the manifestations in intimate friendships. Everyone confirmed the continuity of how these early patterns continue to influence every new relationship, with the hope of creating a more secure relationship. In preparing for that weekend, I recalled being so moved by John Bowlby's works[3] during my graduate program, and revisited the literature with great interest. The material offered a beautiful explanation for my experience growing up: my parents offered a secure and loving environment growing up, but were completely unavailable for my spiritual growth during my adolescence, forcing me to figure out things on my own. This steered me into the field of psychology, rather than engineering, which would have been a natural fit for me.

Judith: In the *now* of this moment, as we type the conclusion, thus far, of our journey together, I want to emphasize the importance of learning to be grounded in my body and breath, including both my tender, gentle feelings as well as those of impatience and discouragement. I have learned that my mind can help comfort my feelings, and that altogether, I can trust the process of Life (or God, or my higher power, or the Holy Spirit, or my Soul). It is this ground of goodness that offers security for us to continue together into the great mystery of the unknown. I trust my companion to continue to be kind, respectful, and supportive; in fact, by 2019, I had developed sufficient trust in "the process" for us to take the step of becoming formally, legally married, as recommended by my attorney.

I still want to improve by discarding the unnecessary clutter in our house, and to make better friends with time. I want to continue to stay open to learning to improve my therapy skills, to be available for my children, and to cultivate the garden and house plants. I have a friend who is also interested in Healing Social Justice related to racial issues with African Americans and

Native Americans, so I notice my energy is available to support that. It is also an unknown how my relationship with Vincent may yet continue to grow. I do trust that an ongoing intention to grow love will produce fruit not yet realized, as our souls share this path towards greater wholeness and beauty.

Vincent: If I were to identify a main difference in our relationship in the past 10 years versus the previous 20 years, it would be in the degree that we are involved in "cheerleading" for each other. The attachment literature on promoting secure child-parent relations [4] identifies three components that increase the security in a relationship:

1. The "safe haven principle": being available to nurture the other person's feelings and injuries.

2. The "lighthouse principle": being a cheerleader to encourage the other person in their ongoing growth and really seeing and supporting that potential.

3. Just "showing up" as the situation calls for it, doing what needs to be done unselfishly.

Judith and I had many opportunities to be nurturing to each other as we were dealing with the emotional injuries from prior relationships. We had to focus first on dealing with the challenges of providing help for Judith's brain-injured son. But somehow it seems that we had been holding back on encouraging each other to claim and pursue our passions and potential. This holding back was like an unconscious bias, a subtle fear that fully encouraging the other person's potential could be detrimental and lead to abandonment.

It is this increased "cheerleading" that has further stabilized the "I—Thou" aspect of our relationship. Instead of being concerned about failure, we see the potential for success and offer support and encouragement to go for it. It helps that we are both basically careful, and receiving the extra encouragement makes all the difference in learning to leap. Knowingly taking these calculated risks would not result in a blame fight if something were to fail. We would simply deal with the consequence and move on.

Judith has encouraged me to play with my engineering side. I built a tiny house for personal retreats, that is completely energy-independent. I also improved the sound system at home, allowing for high-quality sound reproduction to enjoy together. This opened up a tremendous amount of creativity and satisfaction in me. There is something special about bringing into existence something that is dearly held. Meeting the challenge and bringing all the capabilities to the table at times results in this wonderful experience of "flow." This is the sense of liberation that I had been looking for all these years. I'm now at peace, if I were to die today.

Judith encouraged us to take greater responsibility for our living situation and address the climate impact. So I worked out a plan to shrink our carbon footprint by 75%. We built a solar system for our office and home that replaced our "dirty" electricity with "clean" electricity, switched to electric heat pumps to cut the gas use in half, and installed hookups for future electric cars. Our transportation needs were also drastically reduced through teleconferencing. Everything proceeded as planned until the electric inspection took place and we discovered that the electric service to the house was out of compliance and would require a complete overhaul—an expensive set back. In the past, my taking on such an ambitious project would have caused concern and tension in Judith, as she had lived with a person who could be hypomanic and threaten the family security. The setback of having to redo the electric service to the house would have been a confirmation of her fears. Now, she just takes delight in the progress we are making and the obstacles we are tackling to get there.

Of course, there are many other factors that supported this transition from healing to thriving, including fewer worries about the children, good health, financial security, and living life as an ongoing work-vacation, where the work offers tremendous meaning and benefit to others. The vacation aspect gives us permission to enjoy the moment and to extend generosity to self and others.

We each, in our own way, are taking a more active role towards our communities, realizing our inter-dependence. We recognize each other's strengths: Judith may draw attention to feelings of disconnection between us or between us and others, while I might best articulate how we could go forward, after we have discussed the issue.

Judith: I want to close by honoring the ground of goodness, our secure and safe harbor which shows up in many unexpected ways, and with gratitude for the fullness of our life together. I am grateful that two of my children, my daughter and my oldest son, have both benefited from and recognized Vincent's generosity and good will. I am looking forward to the possibility of grandchildren, to future travel plans as well as a revitalization of our shared professional paths. I pray to continue to grow in the practice of the "three Ps," as Vincent has called these virtues: patience, persistence, and perseverance."[5]

Ed and Ilene

Ilene's chapter looks at the stages of relationship through the familiar analogy of the 24-hour day: dawn, daylight, dusk, and darkness. Drawing on her marriage of three decades, she explains how the ongoing development of awareness and will has played a key role in deepening their relationship. Ilene addresses many issues, including finances, stepchildren, and health crises, but it is especially moving when she shares how she prepares for her husband's death and supports him in this process.

CHAPTER EIGHT

Our Marriage: Enriched by Awareness and Will

Ilene Val-Essen

A secure partnership offers us the promise of an exquisite array of gifts. It serves as an elixir to loneliness: we're lucky, no worries about a date for the weekend! It's also an extraordinary affirmation of self: someone we love has chosen to share their life with us for decades and remains delighted with that choice. And, my favorite gift, partnership provides an opportunity to explore uncharted territory: we become more courageous and resilient when we travel together with open hearts.

Since most of us choose partners who complement us, we're exposed daily to different ways of thinking and being in the world. Love can help us become curious and eager to enter our partner's passions. Love can also ease the challenge of difference, helping us become more open to acknowledging and accepting diverse aspects of the world and alternative points of view. Through a loving relationship, we become less limited by our natural biases and prejudices and better prepared to embrace a wide spectrum of life's varied offerings.

We receive another blessing of relationship by living with a beloved witness, a steady partner who remains present as our daily lives unfold. Witnesses play many powerful roles. They serve as sounding boards offering feedback, suggesting creative solutions, or contributing practical skills. They may provide emotional support or a second pair of hands. In a loving collaboration, we discover that we're more effective than we would have been alone. Our lights often burn brighter; our gifts may touch more lives.

This certainly has been true in my more-than-thirty-year marriage with Ed Schuman. Without my husband's writing skills, my life's work—my books for parents and the Quality Parenting programs—would not be as accessible as they are. He taught me how to share complex ideas using simple, clear language. As a filmmaker, he taught me the power of storytelling and the use of visuals to engage an audience. As a kind and encouraging partner, he modeled what parents and children deserve: a safe, supportive environment for learning.

Even with the best intentions, even in the healthiest of relationships, these gifts may not always be evident. Every relationship that prevails for decades goes through rough spots, rough patches, and for some, rough years. We all face trials and tribulations.

Relationships have a life of their own. They unfold and reinvent themselves, often without our permission or our full awareness. Changes in the relationship may surprise, delight, disappoint, or agitate us. Just as human beings cannot control life, we cannot control the evolution of a relationship. Our deep connection with each other may offer clues to the enigmatic nature of our relationship, but not always. When two unique individuals live together over time in this volatile world, change is inevitable.

How Can Psychosynthesis Support Our Partnerships?

How can this magnificent transpersonal theory contribute in helping us strengthen the mysterious magnet that keeps us together through both sunny and stormy times and support us in deepening our bonds?

Simple answers delight me; through them layers of depth become accessible. My simple answer for sustaining successful relationships involves the ability of both partners to develop and enhance two key aspects in Psychosynthesis: awareness and will. Drawing on my marriage of three decades, I will illuminate how awareness and will have strengthened our relationship. These illustrations represent my perspective only; I did not consult with my husband in their selection. Analyzing our marriage would not be Ed's cup of tea, but he has read this chapter and has given it his blessings.

Psychosynthesis is a process that is present in every human being's life, including those who have never heard the word. Relationships that work throughout the world demonstrate awareness of one's own needs and one's partner's needs and engage the will to meet them.

To create a framework for this chapter, I'll offer my definitions of these fundamental concepts. Then we'll examine them by looking at the stages of relationships through a familiar analogy: the 24-hour day.

The story of a long-term partnership begins before dawn when, as two separate individuals, we open ourselves to the possibility of relationship. At dawn, we focus our awareness and will towards making a wise choice.

Once we become a committed couple, we enter daylight. During this extended period, we focus our awareness and will towards sustaining our relationship. The formula for success is simple, though a challenge to carry out: we dedicate ourselves to reasserting our commitment and to resolving our issues. Our hard work often rewards us with greater harmony, love, and joy.

In dusk, we acknowledge our mortality. Existential questions may surface, leading us to focus our awareness and will on reviewing our individual lives and our relationship. We may establish goals to maximize the light that still glows. Uncertain of who will first enter the final stage of darkness, we may also attempt to prepare for the inevitable: one of us will come full circle and find ourselves as a separate individual once again—separate, yet transformed by the life we lived together.

Definitions

Awareness: What we allow into our consciousness physically, emotionally, mentally, and spiritually.

Will: Intelligent energy to act, especially when needed, often involving courage and integrity.

Stages of Relationship

Dawn: The new light signals the birth of the relationship.

Daylight: In the full light, the relationship matures, experiencing the full spectrum of weather.

Dusk: The diminishing light reveals the physical, and often the emotional and mental fragility of the partners.

Darkness: The physical relationship ends when one partner passes into the depth of night.

We'll look at the first three stages through the lens of *awareness* and *will*. Fortunately, my husband and I are alive and together, sparing either of us from experiencing the heartbreaking death of a partner and the final stage: darkness.

DAWN

Awareness

Awareness is especially important in the sunrise stage of a relationship. In my previous marriage, I was quite aware of powerful insights that provided important cues to the problems that would lie ahead, but I ignored them. The truth bell rang, but I didn't listen.

In his book, *Divorce Won't Help*,[1] Edmund Bergler writes that we learn everything we need to know about our partners in our first three encounters. Struck by his daring statement, I decided to consider his premise. Looking back on my past marriage, I discovered that the author's understanding rang true. Early in our dating, I learned that when this man made a commitment, his promise didn't hold up over time. With little affect, he explained that his wife had been shocked when he left. He had initiated little discussion and invested little energy in trying to work out their differences. This was particularly poignant to me because their daughter was only eighteen months old.

Although I registered these facts, they paled compared to the thrill of our chemistry—and I allowed this fire-engine red flag to recede into the recesses of my mind. Youth and naivete blinded me from imagining that I would be treated similarly. "I am special. We are special," I told myself.

But as Bergler's book suggests, divorce won't keep us from experiencing another disappointing relationship unless we recognize and heal our old patterns. I had engaged in therapy after my previous marriage and felt I had done the deep work that was needed. But clearly, I hadn't completed it. Following my ex's pattern in his past relationship, he ended our relationship similarly, with little conversation and little commitment to trying to resolve our issues. One evening, out of the blue, at least for me, he simply asked me for a divorce, adding, "This may be the biggest mistake I'll ever make in my life."

Stunned, hurt to the core, and completely disoriented, two questions weighed heavily on my mind: "What happened? What part did I play?" In a dream-like state in the wee hours one morning, the phrase "the peacemaker's error" popped into my mind. I adopted these words as the title of a paper that I began writing, which then became the centerpiece of my life. Although I focused on clarity and eloquence in my obsessive revisions, my primary dedication was to the truth. I had to understand my error. After fifteen months and 50 highly-polished pages, the truth was revealed: I had sold my soul in the hope of peace.

Journaling: An Effective Tool to Strengthen Awareness

As a psychotherapist, I discovered that it's commonplace for people, when dating, to ignore disturbing information, especially when it interferes with their yearning to be in relationship. I've repeatedly witnessed clients close their eyes, numb initial concerns, and turn off their minds when "love hormones" race through their bodies. To alert us to the potential harmful effects of this dizzying joy, I invite clients to journal. I share openly that when I first met my husband, journaling proved to be invaluable and suggest that they begin to use this powerful tool as soon as they meet someone of interest. Most clients willingly engage, comforted by my encouragement to write in their journals about both positive qualities and those that may raise red flags.

As we spend more time in the relationship and continue the ritual of journaling, additional positive qualities may surface and those we initially recognized may deepen. To help us evaluate potential red flags, we can intentionally initiate conversations with thoughtful questions to gain more understanding and clarity.

Identifying Positive Qualities

After dating Ed for a short while, I discovered that he was responsible, thoughtful, and bright. I also learned that he loved to teach me, fought fair, and cared about my happiness. These examples highlight a few of the discoveries I noted in my journal:

- When Ed called to make our first date, he asked if I liked Italian food. I understood then that he wasn't just pleasing his own palette, that he wanted me to enjoy the meal as well. Sadly, his thoughtfulness felt foreign, yet deliciously appealing.

- My journal entry after our first clash was clear: "That was the cleanest fight I've ever had! Ed took responsibility for his part and created a safe space for me to admit mine."

- When I learned that Ed had won the DuPont award for journalism, it wasn't the prestige associated with the award that intrigued me most, but the fact that Ed had achieved excellence. Having dreams of writing my own book, I imagined that he would understand my yearning for excellence and would support my efforts.

- Even though my father had never been identified as having a drinking problem, I knew that he had had blackouts. When I smelled alcohol on Ed's breath after he'd had a cocktail at dinner, I accused him of being an alcoholic. Calmly, he offered, "I won't drink when I'm around you if you're uncomfortable." His non-defensiveness and willingness to stop allowed me to recognize that these were unlikely signs of a man abusing alcohol.

- I was raised in a culture where appearance was everything. When Ed commented early in our relationship— "I'll always see you as the youthful woman I first met"—it became a salve for my soul.

These vignettes from my journal indicate a person of character, which I saw clearly in Ed.

Recognizing Potential Red Flags

Ed raised a flaming red flag when he confessed: "I've had difficulty making commitments." Wanting to remarry, I found this unsettling. Fortunately, months later, Ed explained that he had been tying loose ends together and was now available to date someone seriously. To my delight, he added, "I'm interested in marrying again." We had a similar vision for our lives. Only time would tell if we could fulfill our dreams.

Two other issues concerned me: 1) Ed's age: he's eleven years older than I am, and 2) Ed's physique: he's quite thin and bony, which often caused me pain when our bodies touched.

Ed's physique was easier for me to address, especially when he and his coach agreed that despite grueling efforts, no change was present—and was unlikely in the future with Ed's body type. Their work ended—to Ed's great relief. Soon, I was able to laugh at myself, "I can handle his thin frame; my body type is a female version of his!"

Our age difference took more thought: Should I continue in a relationship where this issue didn't seem to matter presently, but would likely catch up with us in the future? At that point Ed was robust, could climb up a hill like a goat, and swam several times a week. Often, he had more energy than I did. But I was aware this could change easily. Could I be there for him when I was more energetic physically and far more ambitious professionally? The truth is: I didn't know. But in time it became clear that I loved him and wanted to stand by him his whole life. I told my therapist, "Ed isn't perfect, but he's perfect for me." Ed has infinite love, patience, and devotion. I imagined that if we'd have twenty years together, they'd likely be the best years of my life.

Looking for red flags in a potential partner is valuable. Equally important is looking honestly at one's limitations. Even before I started dating, I had doubts about myself. I felt I was damaged goods, a high-risk investment with plenty of clean-up to address before I'd consider myself a good candidate for a new relationship.

I promised myself that this time around I would place a high value on my awareness and dedicate my will to further my healing.

Will

Setting an Intention

After completing my paper, "The Peacemaker's Error," I wanted to date—more as an opportunity to practice refining old patterns than to find a partner. Having denied and dismissed my needs in the past, I pledged to be authentic. Having been hurt profoundly, I promised to be kind to others. After each date I'd journal, grading myself for authenticity and kindness. (I used to be a schoolteacher and couldn't help myself!) I also noted whether I wanted to see this person again, checking off a Y (yes), N (no), or NEI, (not enough information).

This story illustrates my process:

> I'm sitting at a Chinese restaurant and order a cup
> of wonton soup and cashew chicken. My date frowns,
> "That's too much food for you. Skip the soup." With
> calm, I asserted: "I love this soup and I'm quite hungry."
> I looked to the waitress and said simply, "Please include
> the soup in my order." Although this interaction
> dampened my feelings, I didn't withdraw, which I would
> have done in the past. Instead, I stayed engaged in
> conversation hoping that my date would enjoy himself.
> In my journal, I marked an A for both authenticity and
> kindness—and an N for no second date. As I fell asleep
> that evening, I was delighted that I had followed my
> course.

Deliberate Actions

Life taught me two powerful lessons that I wanted to make use
of as I moved forward in dating: First, insights fade quickly when
I'm entangled in strong emotions. Second, only when I'm calm can
I count on the strength of my clear mind.

Thinking about these discoveries, I posed a practical question:
"What can I do to ensure access to my mind during this first stage
of dawn?" Looking back on my history, I clearly saw that when
I had sex with a new partner, my mind floated into la-la land. To
avoid poor judgment, I set a clear boundary: no sex until I'd had
at least six dates! I calculated that was a decent amount of time
to get to know someone. Once, I almost faltered, but convinced
myself that I must hold on tight, having placed my trust in that
guideline. On that sixth date, something happened that was a
game breaker. Asserting my will wasn't easy, but it proved to be
invaluable and strengthened my confidence. When Ed and I did

have sex, I allow myself to "lose my mind." Why not? I had done my homework—and he had proven to be a good man! This golden "six-date rule" may not be fool-proof, but it worked for me and has benefitted many of my clients.

DAYLIGHT

Awareness

In the period of extended light when little is hidden, emotional challenges inevitably surface. Each person in this newly committed relationship might revisit the perennial question, "Who am I?" and ponder a new question, "Who are we?"

If as a couple we choose to become parents, the scope of our questioning only widens:

- What expectations do I have of myself, my partner, my children? What is the source of these expectations? Are they mine? Our culture's? Our family's? Are they realistic?

- What are my needs versus wants? My partner's? My children's?

- Can I recognize when I'm reacting from a subpersonality, that part of each of us that responds automatically to a situation—generally aggressively or nonassertively? Can I shift to the centered self, a more capable part that's able to think before we act? Can I help family members make that shift as well?

These provocative questions provide a useful starting point, but they're not easy to answer. In the unchartered territory of parenthood, our own childhood experiences inescapably surface: those we cherished and those that caused us pain. Ideas about right

177

and wrong were imposed on us when we were youthful sponges unable to think for ourselves, making it difficult to distinguish our adult values from those of our family's culture.

Often, our personal challenges become entangled with those of our partner. Finding common ground may be time-consuming and painstakingly difficult—adding considerable stress to the partnership. Additional issues add to the mix: work requirements, grandparents, scheduling, finances, and career ambitions. Quite simply: Children dramatically complicate and can enormously enrich the marital life cycle.

Will

As we increase awareness, how do we implement change in order to meet our realistic expectations and needs, as well as to support those we love? As we move forward, how do we deal with frustration and disappointment? A simple, reliable answer is found in the familiar expression, "Where there's a will there's a way." To exercise our will is by no means a simple task. Success relies on the strength of our determination and the depth of our commitment to our relationship and our family.

If we have the passion, do we also have the skills? Can we, with a modicum of ease, shift from a knee-jerk reaction of a subpersonality to the calm, clear response of the centered self? When we face extraordinary stress and discover the limitations of the centered self, can we shift to the higher self and address the situation with wisdom and compassion? Can we lovingly accept our own vulnerability, knowing that self-acceptance helps us accept others?

Without awareness, our blind spots can lead us down dark alleys. Without will, our upsets can turn into wounds. Wounds can turn into scars that may never heal, limiting who we are as individuals, and who we become as a couple and family.

Strengthening both awareness and will to ensure the success of the relationship becomes particularly important in this extended period of daylight when the couple often becomes a family. For couples who have had previous marriages, facing challenges brings additional layers of complexity.

Finances

Ed and I faced many challenges during this extended period. Our first test occurred soon after our marriage when Ed lost his job and secure salary. To my surprise, and with relative ease, I offered to support us both until he planted new roots. It felt good to be there for Ed financially and it strengthened my self-image as an equal partner. Inequality of earnings had been a source of contention in past relationships; being a willing breadwinner helped me heal. After some time, however, my comfort with Ed's lack of income diminished. Respectfully I announced: "It's time for you to contribute." Ed agreed and soon afterwards developed films for prisons that proved to be successful both creatively and financially. Fortunately, throughout the rest of our marriage, money has never become a contentious issue.

Subpersonality Behavior

My habit of clamming up when I felt hurt, however, was problematic and frustrated Ed terribly. My bubbling personality would lose its fizz and I would become mute—often unable or unwilling to speak for hours, sometimes for days. In time I became aware of the source of my behavior and explained to Ed: "In my family talking could be dangerous. If I shared my thoughts or feelings, they often became ammunition to be used against me." Silence became my safe space—clearly a limited coping style, especially when relating to Ed, a remarkably accepting man.

Initially, in response to my withdrawal, Ed kept his distance. His family had been intrusive and giving me space was his noble attempt to respect me. But it backfired. In response to his distance, I imagined that he didn't notice my feelings, or worse, that he didn't care. It wasn't easy for us to break this pattern.

Our commitment to change helped. We learned that we could address difficult issues best when we felt close. During a lovely hike in the Santa Monica mountains, I revealed another reason for my reactions, "I felt invisible as a child. When you give me space when I clam up, you unknowingly pour salt on an old wound." In time, Ed learned to be more assertive, insisting that we talk—and I found the courage to crack my hermetic seal of silence.

Stepchildren

Figuring out how to relate to Ed's children was a daunting challenge for me. Ed's oldest son was estranged from his mother and had zero interest in having a stepmom. His younger son made it clear to his dad that he was uncomfortable with my personality. More salt on my family wounds!

Fortunately, my son Derek, soon off to college, welcomed Ed. Derek felt relieved that Ed would take care of me, lifting an emotional burden Derek didn't want to carry. Derek also recognized that Ed and I shared similar values and that we were good for each other.

To give you a taste of the initial dynamics with Ed's children, I'll share a repetitive scene that I refer to as "Sunday Morning Heartbreak":

Our dining room table is set for the five of us: Ed and me, Ed's two sons and my son. Brunch is spread out on the sideboard. As we gather around the table, one chair remains empty. Ed's oldest son hasn't shown up and no explanation has been offered. This has happened many times and I take his absence personally. My complexes race rampantly: "What's wrong with me?" I like his son and have been kind to him. "What have I done that could account for him making it so glaringly obvious that he has absolutely no interest in being with me? I try so hard. Why must I experience so much pain?" His youngest son, although present, basically ignores me throughout the meal, never looking in my direction when he speaks. I'm invisible in Ed's family, just as I had been in my own family growing up!

The arduous task of creating relationships with my stepsons involved many iterations. First, I projected my upset onto Ed, demanding, "Why don't you stand up for me and shape up your adult sons?" When no progress occurred, I threatened a harsh stance: "I'm not going to invite the boys to our home anymore." Thankfully, after letting off steam, I came to my senses and quieted my hurt subpersonalities.

In time, Ed shared more about his boys' lives and eventually convinced me that they had no malice toward me. This helped. Able to step back a bit, I stopped taking their absence or lack of interest so personally and continued to welcome them in our home.

As the years passed, I developed richer, more meaningful relationships with friends and colleagues. This change had a huge impact on my relationships with my stepsons. With joy and purpose in my life, I became less attached to my image of family and let go of my unrealistic demands and expectations. Instead, I focused on being as present as possible in the moment, making the most of our time together. My new approach with his boys helped Ed relax. Freer, he became more responsive to my needs and actively included me in conversations. I no longer felt invisible in the presence of family—an extraordinary blessing!

Ultimately the greatest transformation occurred as I was working to develop a higher-self character named Faithful for my book *Parenting with Wisdom and Compassion: Bring Out the Best in Your Family.*[2] It took at least twenty versions to finally clarify Faithful's mindset: "When we value relationship more than our upset, growth is possible for everyone involved." Once I grasped the power of Faithful's gift, something switched inside me: I understood that in order for me to be able to reliably place the family's well-being as the highest priority, I needed further healing.

I began by examining the stories I told myself that fueled my upset and re-opened my wounds—and consciously chose to revise them to embrace a more compassionate understanding of the boys and myself.

Next, I followed my own favorite advice from my first book, *Bring Out the Best in Your Child and Your Self*[3]: "Water the flowers not the weeds." When I thought about the boys, I focused on their many fine qualities: their unwavering love and dedication to their dad, their generosity with friends and family, and their integrity in living their lives. It became crystal clear that they had grown and matured over the years and had rightfully earned the title *mensch*!

When I was with Ed's sons, I acknowledged comments they made or actions they took that I appreciated, such as sharing an interesting point of view or offering helpful advice. I also openly took pleasure in their joys and passions and initiated conversations that resonated with their interests. Eventually, I felt comfortable enough to share experiences that touched me.

Becoming a part of the family conversation pleased me, but it was no longer essential. Attending to the well-being of the whole family became my highest priority: supporting authentic peace, harmony, and goodwill among us. Ease and acceptance grew.

Change is inevitable—and the winds of good fortune blew our way. When Ed's younger son found the love of his life and they married, family engagements became more frequent. Our new intimacy was unexpected and fully embraced. Awareness of our limited and shallow interactions in the past only makes me relish the richness of the present even more. Often when we part, I find my eyes flowing with tears of bliss.

My relationship with Ed's oldest son, who became an attorney, changed as well. When I needed legal expertise and asked for his help, he gave it without hesitation. He even complimented the letter I had written, which blew my mind. His praise still reverberates in my heart today. He, too, found a new love in his life and brings a happier, more engaged spirit whenever we're together.

At some point, I decided that I would not allow anything that happened between Ed and me to shed doubt on our lifetime commitment. I realized that if my son Derek and I had a dispute, nothing would sever our relationship. We were blood. I would always be his mother and would do everything within my power to resolve our differences. I would never "divorce" my child. I decided to place Ed in the same sacred category as my son—and view him as blood. As blood, we were family. As family, we were bonded for life.

This one decision profoundly solidified our vows and added stability to our marriage. Challenges were now faced with constructive questions: How can I experience more personal joy? How can I support Ed's quality of life? How can our relationship benefit each of us as individuals and help us grow stronger each year as we add another ring to our marital tree?

Toward the end of this period, I realized that, with persistence and extensive discussion, Ed and I would always resolve our issues and find our way back into calmer water. Although I appreciated our dedication and success, it was time-consuming and emotionally draining. I wanted to find another way.

Daylight, by definition, is filled with light. I wondered, "How can I use that light to offset the dark?" As I asked the question, a different part of my mind lit up. Intuitively, I sensed that talking or problem-solving may be overrated or greatly overused when far less complicated and less stressful options may be equally, or even more, effective. I experimented.

One day when I didn't feel I was getting enough attention, instead of complaining, I focused on times when I felt full. I remember consciously commenting to Ed, "I've always loved when you'd find interesting plays or lectures for us to attend. I felt special, as if you wanted to please me." Inevitably within days, Ed would email or mention an event in town that he thought we might enjoy. Shedding light on past light brought light into the present. It seemed as if I had hit the jackpot. So simple. I was blown away.

Another example: When the chaos in our home unnerved me, I'd comment when I'd find Ed creating order. As he was cleaning the kitchen counters, I'd explain how my body relaxes when our home is clean and uncluttered. Hours later, I noticed the rocking chair, the waystation for his clothes, had been cleared.

I've shared this discovery of affirming what we want with many couples. I am delighted when they tell me, "It works!"

DUSK

When do we determine that we've entered this phase? In a marriage, the fading light could indicate the fading of love, yet in a strong marriage love prevails, though it may be expressed differently. Many elements may signify entry into dusk. The United States government identifies us as senior citizens at the age of 65 and offers the safety nets of Medicare and Social Security. With these support systems in place, retirement becomes a consideration. Reduced energy and health challenges, often bringing discomfort and limitations, insist that we acknowledge the obvious: we won't live forever. Family members, friends, peers, and colleagues who have passed away make it impossible for us to turn our eyes away from this truth.

Although I've painted the passage into dusk with a broad brush, there are many exceptions. Unfortunately, some people enter dusk before they reach 65. On the other hand, some people who have reached 65 don't identify themselves as being in dusk; they enjoy robust lives. Spouses, of course, don't always pass into dusk at the same time.

But whenever we enter dusk and live there a while, we discover a world of possibilities and limitations, contradictions and extremes, feelings of joy and sadness, hope and despair, aliveness and boredom, courage and fear—and all the shades in between. We know this stage will end. Guided by awareness and will, we can work together to affect the quality of our final stage in partnership.

For those of us who have embraced Psychosynthesis, recognizing our mortality at dusk often elicits a resurgence of existential questions: Have we lived the life we've wanted? Have we accomplished our goals? Are family relationships and friendships strong and loving? Have we helped to make the world a better place?

Provocative questions may lead us to consider taking action. Do we want to apologize for past behavior? Forgive those who have hurt us? Or express love and appreciation to deserving people in our lives? Or consider new ways to serve our community? Our planet? Or check off items on our bucket lists?

Addressing unfinished business can be daunting, but it can also free us of burdens that we've carried for decades. It takes courage to face ongoing pain in our lives, and persistence when the road proves to be rocky and the promise of success cannot be guaranteed. Rather than removing suffering, attention to it may stir up more discomfort.

Yet intention often finds its resolution. When we succeed, although we walk in the same shoes, our gait changes forever. In dusk, as we learn to let go of heavy burdens, our hearts and minds open and expand. Although we continue to age and our bodies show those effects, our approach to life often becomes more flexible and resilient, allowing us to experience a different kind of light.

There's no precise prescription for healing unfinished business. We may decide to approach this process in a formal manner with a therapist, through a spiritual practice, or by addressing specific issues as they unfold. Hopefully, we'll ultimately find a modicum of inner peace before we take our last breath and enter the final stage of darkness.

Awareness: Ed Moves Toward Dusk

Ed knocked on dusk's door when he was diagnosed with prostate cancer. The frightful "C" word jolted me into accepting Ed's mortality—and the painful truth that I couldn't manage without him. From that moment on, I prepared for his death with the goal of developing the confidence that I could live alone when he was no longer by my side.

Financially, I could support myself. And I had practical skills to take care of basic tasks required to live on this planet. But I felt that I couldn't survive emotionally on my own: I didn't have enough friends or a social life that would sustain me.

Will

I geared up my will and got to work immediately. I started a women's book club, joined a supervision group, and accepted an invitation to a couple's book group. I also created "tea time" with neighborhood women, with the intention that we'd take care of each other in times of need. In addition, I courted women friends whom I loved, hoping to increase our social time together. Often this involved creating rituals that involved our spouses: we'd buy season theatre tickets to matinee performances and enjoy animated discussions over dinner.

Wanting to be involved in a spiritual community, I joined a weekly sangha that studies the teachings of Thich Nhat Hanh. Since this group attracts a wide age range of people with diverse backgrounds, it also naturally feeds my interest in getting to know people from all walks of life.

Joining groups that meet regularly—filling my calendar with ongoing events and predictable connections—assured me that my life would be meaningful and rich. I could look forward to being with people I loved in my life without much effort or planning.

I also found ways to enrich my time alone: deepening my meditation practice, listening to fascinating podcasts, engaging in passion projects that lasted for years, appreciating time in nature, and visiting museums and cultural events on my own.

Awareness: Ed Enters Dusk

Dusk deepened for Ed when he experienced an aortic dissection, requiring open heart surgery. During this grueling procedure, he had a stroke. My vital husband came home, after weeks in the hospital and an extended stay in rehab, wearing diapers and functioning mentally with a fraction of his previous capacity.

Life changed dramatically. And these changes happened weeks after the publication of my first book, which had taken a decade to write. Ilene the author vanished, replaced by Ilene the caretaker. I stepped into this new role with vigor and love; every inch of me wanted to be there for Ed. Fortunately, our pagra—a relationship's emotional bank account—was well-endowed. Years of goodwill had prepared me for the outpouring of devotion he needed and deserved.

Will

During rough times, access to a strong will becomes crucial. But when ongoing stress persists, and our aging bodies and brains slow down, our emotional resolve can easily weaken.

As I mourned Ed's regressed state and the lost opportunity to promote my beloved book, life as I had known it—and imagined it—disappeared. My new life now included the loss of my hubby as my best friend and partner, and a plethora of responsibilities in uncharted territory with inadequate support. Such extreme stress became fertile soil for aggressive lower-self behavior. And soon I lost it!

My Confession

When Ed cursed before the stroke, I disliked it. When his cursing increased after the stroke, I detested it. The story I told myself that fueled my fire was this: anyone who cursed with abandon had little self-respect. Then I convoluted the story even further: choosing a man with little self-respect meant that I had little respect for myself. I surmised: we're both losers!

I rarely get angry. However, creating and believing this crippling tale sapped my psyche. Enraged, I found myself yelling at Ed—and feeling good about it. Despite my harsh approach, I imagined that I was actually helping him gain control over what I had always thought was a terrible habit. My antics slowed down Ed's cursing, but didn't stop it.

When I admitted to a most loving friend that I was at my wit's end and described my behavior, she was appalled. Her reaction helped me face the dark side of my lower self. As a nurse, she explained that cursing was a common result of a stroke: Ed had little control and no intentionality. With this new perspective, I could dis-identify from my awful story, empathize with Ed, and allow my heart to open again.

Redemption

When I look back at this time, I'm able to forgive myself. Both our lives had been turned upside down. Ed's cursing, which had always triggered a strong reaction in me, had become extreme. When I was able to change the statement, "We're all human beings doing the best that we can," from a platitude to a humble acceptance of our frailty, it became easy to feel compassion for Ed and for me.

A favorite quote expressing this truth comes from the classic play "A Raisin in the Sun" by Lorraine Hansberry. Mama preached unconditional love when her son Walter destroyed his sister's personal dreams, as well as those of the family: "Child, when do you think is the time to love somebody the most? When they done good and made things easy for everybody? ... that ain't the time at all.

It's when he's at his lowest and can't believe in hisself 'cause the world done whipped him so!" Mama's expression of pure love took my breath away. She has become my muse.

Awareness: I Face Dusk

I moved toward dusk when I was diagnosed with Mycobacterium avium complex, a chronic lung disease. I entered dusk years later when I was also diagnosed with chronic inflammation response syndrome, commonly known as mold illness. Exhaustion became the keynote of my life. At my worst, I'd find enough strength to leave the bed for fifteen minutes, only to return again for fifteen minutes to recoup. I spent my limited energy with doctors who offered little help at exorbitant expense. While my husband and I experienced little vitality, our quiet, insular life suited us both.

Some years later, as I began to glimpse renewed health and vigor, Ed faced another health challenge. With his skin ashen for days, his energy depleted, and no return calls from doctors, I called 911.

When I heard the sirens outside our door for the umpteenth time, my heart sank. No part of me wanted to go to the hospital again. The timing sucked: while Ed was coping with an emergency, I wanted to party. My dancing shoes had gathered dust during my years of fatigue, and I was eager to rock and roll, spread my wings, and enjoy my new-found glimmer of health. I couldn't imagine that I'd be able to sit for hours in a dismal hospital room and be as fully "present" as I had been in the past.

At first, as I feared that his diminishing grip on life and my renewed zest for life would turn into a crisis.

Will

Fortunately, it didn't. I was able to honor both my strong personal wishes and my commitment to my husband's well-being. Ed and I spoke openly and honestly. Crossing this bridge together actually brought us closer.

Once Ed's acute abdominal issues had been addressed successfully, heart valve issues took center stage. His hospital stay led to an extended stay at rehab. During these weeks, Ed seemed content with whatever time and energy I had to give. He encouraged me to do my own thing and assured me he was okay.

We have always respected our differences. But it felt alien to me to experience a strong urge to follow the beat of my own drum when Ed's health was compromised. In the past, I'd spend most of my free time happily visiting him in the hospital and helping him in any way I could.

My sense of urgency was palpable. Even Ed's sons sensed it. They too encouraged me to take time for myself. And I did. I read, walked in the early morning light, meditated, wrote, cooked, danced in front of the mirror, and hung out with family and friends—once until 1 a.m. I loved my freedom, my open schedule, and an incredibly clean and organized home with no signs of a senior occupant. Friends commented on how happy I looked. It seemed as if life's challenges had weighed me down for years and I needed a break. Now I was having a love affair with myself!

Even though I spent less clock time with Ed than I had during previous illnesses, my heart and soul felt fully connected when we were physically together, on the phone, or when I was thinking about him.

Awareness: Living in Different Shades of Dusk

I wondered, "Can we make it work?" My excitement in being alone still scared me. What would happen when Ed returned home? I feared it would be difficult to maintain my aliveness and provide the support Ed needed during his recuperation.

As I reflected on Ed's resilience in the confines of the hospital and in rehab, I realized that he could easily manage emotionally in the comfort of our home. Frankly, I had never fully registered how self-contained he is: masterful in engaging himself with a plethora of resources on the radio, audiobooks, podcasts, and movies. I then trusted that if we made certain his physical needs were met, he'd be fine.

Love Deepens

Comforted by this awareness, permission to express my independence came more easily. Having lifted the burden I had imposed on myself, I stopped fretting over Ed or feeling the need to entertain him. Enjoying a new sense of freedom allowed me to recognize the magnitude of his generous heart, not only now, but all throughout the years we've been together. A simple truth became overwhelmingly apparent: Ed has supported me unfailingly for thirty years. As I absorbed my extraordinarily good fortune, my aura expanded, radiating with light. At that moment, I understood that I'd be able to love Ed unconditionally for the rest of our lives.

New Strength

Through the trials and tribulations of dusk, I transformed, recognizing that I'm more capable of being alone than I had thought. A fullness exists within me that hadn't been present in earlier years. I enjoy a larger circle of friends who love me dearly and family holds a more secure place in my heart. Self-acceptance has replaced a strong critical voice. In my new paradigm, the world holds more beauty and trust, I face darkness with greater understanding and compassion, and peace walks with me as a more present companion.

I'm not naïve. When Ed leaves this world, if he goes before I do, the loss will be enormous. But I am more confident that I'll be okay. I'm more resilient than I had imagined and more passionate about and skilled in living a robust and meaningful life.

Will

As I've enjoyed a stronger sense of self, my mission for our final years as a couple has become clearer: I wish to make the end of Ed's life as rich as possible. In practical terms, this means:

- appreciating Ed's goodness and devotion each time I experience these fine qualities.

- acknowledging his talents and contributions to better our world as an outstanding filmmaker and through his ongoing generosity.

- traveling down memory lane as often as possible, delighting in our good times and laughing at our foibles.

- living consciously to maximize our present.

- creating more memories.

- apologizing when I'm less than who I want to be and making up quickly.

- affirming his importance in my life frequently.

When Ed closes his eyes for the last time, I want him to know without a doubt that he has been loved and cherished deeply.

Lying in bed together several weeks ago, Ed commented: "I think we're in a honeymoon phase." With his sweet words, I am hopeful that we're on the right track. Nothing could make me happier.

POSTSCRIPT: DARKNESS

I completed my chapter several years ago. Then new authors came aboard, and time moved forward. During this period Ed passed away. I asked the group if they thought I should write about this final stage, and they encouraged me to do so.

Ed returns home from another stay at the hospital. At this point, the doctor explains that he requires 24-hour care and advises us to enroll him in hospice.

Awareness

In Ed's weakened state, he remains confined to the bed for approximately 23 ½ hours per day. I'm now responsible for everything. Ed's emotional state has deteriorated, with the worst of his sub-personalities taking center stage much of the time: he's irritable and angry. I feel physically exhausted and emotionally beaten. If this weren't enough, I'm blindsided, discovering that I face a serious medical diagnosis myself. The man who has always had my back, has disappeared emotionally. I'm raw and alone with my frightening news. At the same time, I must try to wrap my head around the idea that my husband is soon to die.

Will

In *The Tibetan Book of Living and Dying,* Sogyal Rinpoche claims that the experience of death is even more significant than that of birth, holding the potential for growth and transformation, suggesting that it could affect the quality of the person's transition and even their next incarnation. Of course, everyone doesn't hold these beliefs, but since I hold them close to my heart, they became a powerful motivator and inspired me to act, to create an environment to maximize Ed's opportunity at the end of his life.

As I mentioned in the section on Dusk, our pagra had always been well-endowed and we understood that we could readily draw upon it. With the weight of our current issues, coupled with the worldwide trauma of Covid, our pagra had been sorely depleted. To act now to realize the vision I held for Ed, I had to embody the directive contained in our book's title, *Willing to Love*. I recognized readily that Ed, as a human being and my husband of 32 years, deserved to have the best passage possible. But I, as a personality, didn't have the resources. So, I called upon my higher self to step forward, to fill his final weeks with meaning, love, kindness, and caring—to make his passing a beautiful experience.

I believed this vision was possible because years ago a colleague of mine casually told me that the months before her husband died, they had intentionally engaged in rich and intimate experiences: reading poetry, looking at art, listening to music, and reminiscing about their long life together. Their experience became my ideal model—and I attempted to emulate it.

Friends had doubts, believing the process of dying itself would preclude this. They also feared my idealism would be shattered and worried about my well-being.

But in truth, I had planted seeds to enhance his isolated experience long before these final months. These are a few examples:

- When we had dinner with one of Ed's cherished friends, I

mentioned privately that Ed truly loved him and was quite lonely. And suggested that if he'd consider calling Ed periodically, it would be meaningful to him. This dear friend seemed moved that I had asked and said that he'd mark his calendar to call Ed monthly, which he did without a prompt.

- When I had ongoing events, such as teatime with my girlfriends, I'd invite them to visit Ed while he was quite weak and mostly confined to bed. With love in their hearts, these dear women would let Ed know what a treat it was to be with him and said that they wanted to do this each time we met.

- Before Covid, Ed and I and two women friends had season tickets to go to the Fountain Theatre. To fill the void, we initiated the "Fountain Four": we'd select movies to watch prior to an online meeting when we'd discuss them. Ed wasn't always eager to watch their selections, so they encouraged him to choose something that engaged him, and we agreed to discuss his choice first. Once he tired and slipped back into the bed, we gals would savor each other's company. Ed felt moved that we honored his minimal energy and was always happy to see me joyous.

Enriching Ed's Final Months

When Ed was officially in hospice, my goal was to make each day special and to demonstrate to him physically and verbally that he was loved and always in my thoughts. Much of what I did was quite simple.

I let him know how special it was to me that we'd share as many meals together as possible. Often, during these times, I intentionally went down memory lane: talking about good times, the many ways he has made our house a home, the beautiful qualities he possesses, and his many talents. I remind him that he has always had my back, sacrificing his time and energy to support my dreams.

Each day I let Ed know when I was available for us to have a "date" and how much I looked forward to these. Sometimes our date consisted of looking at a magnificent art book that a friend sent as a gift. Other times, I brought down the iPad and we'd watch a movie. I also offered him my beloved noise-canceling headphones to listen to a Beethoven symphony.

Reading this chapter to him (minus the stage of darkness, of course) proved to be one of our most memorable experiences. Ed took in each word and at the end remarked, "I guess I was a good husband!" Tears well in my eyes as I write. I wanted Ed to accept this truth and when it became clear that he had, I felt a sense of completion—and elation.

Just a sweet sidenote. True to form and in a loving manner, Ed made an editing suggestion for the opening paragraph of this chapter, which I had never felt was quite right. He nailed it! Even in his last days, Ed's keen ear improved my sentences, making me laugh with sheer delight.

Building Community

When trapped in his hospital bed, Ed often became weary and listless. In response, I'd call or send emails to friends and family, saying "Hi, I've discovered that Ed really perks up when he has visitors. He thanks them profusely and says how much he has enjoyed their company. If that's something you may want to consider, he and I would be most grateful." People readily responded.

As Ed's body became weaker and death crept closer, I looked even more carefully through his contacts and reached out to other people I thought he'd like to connect with to say goodbye. We then calendared more Zoom meetings or FaceTime, and in-person experiences when possible. At one point, Ed caught on to what I had been doing and expressed his gratitude with warmth and a sparkle in his eyes.

As people offered their gifts of love and presence, Ed gained a new picture of himself, learning that people admired him, found him witty, creative, generous, courageous, and talented—and he transformed in front of my eyes. Even when his body weakened and his breathing became more constrained, still he was able to embrace each person who entered his world, whether the care-givers and nurses or cherished friends and family. He thanked everyone for their caring and expressed his gratitude. Observing his outpouring of loving kindness, filled my soul. I felt uplifted, believing that he had positioned himself to experience a beautiful passage, that my dreams for his final moment were unfolding as I had hoped.

A few days before Ed died, I gently explained, "If there is any truth in the beliefs that I cherish, you might want to consider investing some energy in just one practice. You believe the brain simply decays. But if there is more to death than the end of the physical body, I've read that as you are going through the transition, you can make it much easier if you focus your full attention on following the light." Ed listened. I continued, "Since you're resting a great deal, you might want to spend a few moments practicing, because if this idea has merit, you'd be better prepared."

We had also discussed previously that a dear friend of mine has helped many people pass. Ed knew that I wanted her to help me when my time came. In the early hours of the morning on the day that Ed died, he stated calmly, "I'm ready." I asked, "Do you want me to call my friend?" He said "Yes," and I promised that I would. He was quiet most of the morning, but when he spoke, he uttered only two words, "light" and my friend's name.

Ed passed into darkness peacefully three minutes after she arrived. She and I felt beautiful energy in the room as we remained with him in quiet.

Knowing that I was able to support Ed's peaceful transition satisfied me deeply. Still, I felt a sense of heaviness, clear that I hadn't fully forgiven him for his anger and irritability towards me. When I shared this truth aloud with a friend, I understood it was time.

That night I "talked" with Ed, and in our dialogue, I sensed that it was likely that a lack of oxygen throughout his difficult times may have affected his brain and consequently his behavior. We talked a long time, covering a great deal of territory. At the end of our deep sharing, my body felt light and vibrated with joy. I had forgiven him.

In the morning, I felt alive, flooded with beautiful memories of him and of our marriage. In the days that followed, I experienced more energy than I had felt in years. And, I have come to believe that my own healing is possible.

I'd like to think that Ed entered the stage of darkness by consciously following the light. And that I supported his passage into darkness by summoning the light of my own soul—being *Willing to Love* and to forgive, even when it wasn't always easy.

Emmanuel and Urs

In this thought-provoking chapter, Urs presents his life partnership with Emmanuel as a kind of gay vocation, a chosen purpose, of offering love and support to others in lieu of raising children. Urs writes about their marriage, intertwined with their life of service to others, using knowledge of Psychosynthesis and their own inner gifts.

CHAPTER NINE

Synthesis and Service: Living Our Gifts in a Same-Sex Partnership

Urs Mattmann

In this chapter I will focus on what we in Psychosynthesis call transpersonal qualities. I will explore how they can be discovered, nurtured, and enhanced in and through a same-sex relationship, which, for us, is a relationship in service to the world. At the heart of those transpersonal qualities is an understanding of Love and Will.

The context for this exploration is my relationship with my life partner of 35 years, Emmanuel Grassi. Emmanuel grew up in the Italian-speaking part of Switzerland and we met on May 4, 1986, in the German-speaking part of Switzerland, where I grew up. A year later we moved in together, and on October 8, 1988, we had a service of blessings. Though we met in Switzerland, we currently live in England.

It is only now in the 21st century that legal recognition of same-sex couple partnerships has become a reality in Switzerland and as well in the United Kingdom. In 2006 we were finally able to get our civil partnership agreement in London. Switzerland has now accepted by popular vote same-sex marriage, which became law on July 1, 2022, as Great Britain did a few years ago. Emmanuel and I are considering transferring our civil partnership to marriage status.

Both of us come from a religious upbringing (mine is evangelical and Emmanuel's is Roman Catholic). Our religious backgrounds have brought us both gifts and challenges. Religion awakened a deep interest in spirituality in each of us from an early age, but at the same time we had the challenge of reconciling faith, spirituality and our homosexual orientation.

Finding Psychosynthesis

The concepts and teachings of Psychosynthesis have been with us from the early part of our partnership, offering us both guidance and inspiration and playing a significant part in our life together.

I was trained as a Psychosynthesis therapist in Switzerland from 1997 to 2002, and in 2008 to 2009 I studied Transpersonal and Integrative Supervision at the University of East London and the Psychosynthesis Trust in the UK. Psychosynthesis has influenced not just my private life, but it is also the foundation of my therapy work. What was it about Psychosynthesis that drew me to it like a needle to a magnet?

In my training to be a social worker from 1985–1988, a major focus was psychology. While C.G. Jung was briefly mentioned, most of our training was based on the teachings that originated with Sigmund Freud. I missed the awareness of a spiritual dimension. The lower unconscious was important, but I knew that it wasn't all there is. As a progressive Christian I was very interested in spiritual life, of both Christianity and other religions. In my three-year social work training, I felt I had to split myself. I believed in a divine aspect in every human being, but that idea was not recognized in the psychological traditions I was studying. In Psychosynthesis I found a framework and a language that acknowledged both the psychological and the spiritual aspects of human beings. When I discovered the concept of the Higher Self my approach to my work felt so much more complete and holistic.

The Process of Synthesis Within Our Relationship

While both Emmanuel and I needed to discover our own individual spiritual paths, it was a journey we undertook together. We encouraged and supported each other in expressing our potential and becoming more fully who we each are. This process is always ongoing; it is something we will work on for the rest of our lives.

Though we share so much on a deep level, we are actually very different in our personalities. Psychosynthesis has given us a way to think about the power and the process of the synthesis of opposites in our relationship. When we met we realized that, while we were both gay, white European males, we were quite different in personality and character. Emmanuel comes from the Italian-speaking south of Switzerland with some ancestors in Northern Italy, while I am from the German-speaking north of Switzerland. I grew up Protestant, he Roman Catholic. He is more than ten years older than I am. He is extroverted, with a more southern, Latin temper, while I am an introvert and have more of a northern European temperament. Generally speaking, I am more the intellectual, abstract type, while he is more the pragmatic type, great at housekeeping, cooking and all technical matters. In general, I make friends more easily with males, he makes friends more easily with females. I am an Aquarian, Emmanuel is a Cancer. All these differences have brought up plenty of material for the process of synthesis, but have also given us the challenge of accepting and appreciating our differences and in doing so, finding fulfillment.

While our relationship has included hard work, the spark was there when we met for the first time in 1986 at a Gay and Lesbian Christian Conference, which was held at a Franciscan Centre in Lucerne, Switzerland. I still remember how I felt when I entered the large dining room and saw Emmanuel sitting with others. His table was full, so I sat close by at another table. Although we were engaged in conversations at our own tables, there were glances between us and a touch of "some enchanted evening" magic in the air. Maybe there was already the attraction of opposites at work.

Roberto Assagioli, founder of Psychosynthesis, wrote little about sexuality; the small commentary he wrote about homosexuality is not helpful at all. One of the historical criticisms of homosexuality is that this orientation does not conform to the concept of opposite sexes, which has been one of the foundations of heterosexual marriage in patriarchal cultures for the last 5,000 years or so. The complementarity and binary nature of the sexes was completely misunderstood, implying that two men or two women could not fully complement each other. The thinking of the dominant culture has been as the Yin needs the Yang, so the female needs the male to form a couple. Thankfully, this way of thinking has been seriously challenged in the last few decades.

So how does a transpersonal understanding help us to get to a deeper appreciation of male to male and female to female complementarity? How is synthesis at work here? How can Love and Will evolve through this same-sex complementation? An important starting point for Emmanuel and me is the understanding and conviction that same-sex attraction is not an accident that happened in the course of human evolution, but that human evolution included this because it serves a purpose and has potential.

To approach homosexuality in this way is in line with the orientation of Psychosynthesis, which does not just focus on what went wrong in our lives but also acknowledges the existence of our strengths and our potential.

The Potential of Homosexuality

We would suggest that the time to question how homosexuality developed is over, and more important is the question: "What is the purpose of being gay or lesbian"?

In answer, I will begin with some personal impressions from my own life experience and development. Until a couple of years ago I had always thought that my homosexuality became apparent to me when I was about 13 years old and discovered my sexual impulses and romantic feelings for the male sex. However, at one point I realized that my being gay had been with me as far back in my childhood as I can remember. My earliest memories are from November 1963, when I was less than four years old. Even then my gay orientation was present! Of course, not in the sense that I had sexual desires, but in the sense that already in my early childhood I had a feeling of being different and that I had a different outlook towards the environment around me.

At the age of six, when I entered kindergarten, I had a special sensitivity and a sharp sense of justice. I felt an intuitive connectedness with everything that was rare or threatened with extinction or exclusion. This perception extended beyond children and adults to plants, animals and even cultural objects. My awareness and my senses were less attuned to what was considered normal or according to popular fashions. I was interested in what was conspicuous, different or queer in the non-sexual sense of the word.

In the years to come, I experienced myself having a different point of view toward the sexes and gender roles. I realized that my perception of the two sexes was different from that of many other people. I had no drive to mix with boys in competitive games or fights or to share their thinking patterns. I was not interested in typically masculine sports. In contrast to most of my male peers in school and in my neighborhood, I enjoyed playing with girls at least as much as with boys.

David Philbedge, a gay Buddhist living in England, tells about his memories from his own youth:

> I'd felt from an very early age an outsider, which I think is a common experience for gay men – as you grow up you feel somewhat out of synch from the other people around you. It shifted my perspective, my attitude to life in general, which basically manifested itself in me being incredibly discontented and difficult. If you have a sense that you are different from what's around you, you're not going to get sucked in without thinking, you're not going to accept received wisdom. All worthwhile spiritual paths involve asking questions: it's that sense of being an outsider that maybe begins that process. Spirituality is about realising your place in the world: if you're lesbian and gay, your position in the world is going to be different from what other people tell you, and from their position in the world.[1]

In pointing out the giftedness and sensitivity of lesbian, gay and bisexual (LGB) people I am not saying that heterosexual men and women or transgender people are not capable of being sensitive or gifted. I am saying that instead of looking at homosexuality as an obstacle, I believe we need to look at it as a gift to humanity; gay men often express the qualities of sensitivity, intuition and nurture. While that might not be equally true for all cultures on this planet, in the cultures I know, LGB people are very well represented in the arts, the caring professions, in the priesthood, and as therapists.

Consciousness and Homosexuality

The evolution of human consciousness is ongoing. This view is supported by important writers and spiritual leaders of the last hundred years such as Sri Aurobindo, Jean Gebser, Pierre Teilhard de Chardin and Ken Wilber. I see homosexuality in the larger context of the evolution of human consciousness: I believe it is a step as important in the growth of humanity as the abolition of slavery, the dismantling of racist structures, and the battle for the full integrity and equality of women. In that sense, I see it as a contribution to a wider and more mature consciousness of humanity, and I believe this has to happen as part of the ongoing unfolding of creation. A global dimension of synthesis in the process of evolution of consciousness, with the overall goal being unity in diversity. As humanity we are experiencing what Ken Wilber would describe as "a transition from mental and fragmented consciousness to integrative consciousness."[2] Others like Teilhard de Chardin or Jean Gebser also pointed in this direction.

This process has its painful side and phases of chaos and disorientation, which is what we are experiencing currently. However, I believe these changes are necessary. After separation must come integration, if we are to survive. Sascha Donges and Catherine Brunner-Dubey have developed a model of Psychosynthesis for humanity in their milestone Psychosynthesis book *Psychosynthese für die Praxis*.[3]

Transpersonal Qualities and Service

In my book *Coming In – Gays and Lesbians Reclaiming the Spiritual Journey*,[4] I made a list of the transpersonal qualities I believe are often present among LGB people, including:

1. Spiritual and religious openness

2. Sensibility/sensitivity

3. Improved same-sex interaction/same-sex completion

4. Alternative sex roles for men and women

5. Sense of justice

6. Healers and shamans

7. Gift of offering hospitality

8. Consciousness scouts/agents of change

9. Artist, creator of beauty

10. Called to mysticism

11. Reconciliation of sexuality and spirituality

12. Inner authority

13. Teaching and mentoring

14. New ways of being prolific

The book explores all this in detail; as Richard Rohr writes in the foreword to *Coming In*:

> Addressing the unique gifts that gays and lesbians have to offer to the rest of us – 'queer' gifts not only for personal development but also for service in and to the world – this book shows how a relevant and liberating

spirituality can enrich the lives of gay and lesbian people on a practical level.

So what are the transpersonal qualities that are so important in Psychosynthesis? They exist, of course, beyond sexual orientation. In her milestone book *The Unfolding Self,*[5] Molly Young Brown lists 52 transpersonal qualities. Here I will focus on the core qualities of Will and Love, as well as the qualities of beauty, compassion, service, and creativity.

Spiritual Children

Sometimes Emmanuel and I use the metaphor that our couple synthesis creates "spiritual children." Because a same-sex couple cannot generate physical children through intercourse, the power of being together in service to others makes it possible to give birth to spiritual offspring to be fruitful and productive in the work for the universal good in this world. Practically this means that the couple can offer hospitality, providing warmth and security to others. Because LGB people often experience the prejudice of being seen as outsiders and mavericks, we believe that they have the call to be merciful in a special way with other outcasts. As sexually different people, they are acutely affected by the dogmatic and repressive sexual morality that connects sexuality with dirt, sin, lower urges, etc., still prevalent to this day in fundamentalist religions. On the other extreme we see the "worldly" tendency to see sexuality as a place of consumerism and egoistic gratification.

For Emmanuel and me, our relationship is about trusting and sharing our spirituality, finding a common vision as a couple, learning to listen to each other, and finding the Divine or Universal will (for the two of us it connects us to God) both personally and as a couple. In Psychosynthesis terms it means that Emmanuel and I, as a couple, have a practice where we consciously connect to the

Higher Self. Emmanuel does so in creativity and beauty. He is a passionate cook and his number one hobby is Ikebana, a Japanese meditative flower arrangement art. I have a daily silent meditation practice and use guided imagination exercises such as the ones listed in Piero Ferrucci's classic book *What We May Be.*[6] I also love to listen to spiritual teachers such as Marianne Williamson or James Finley. Reading and music are other ways we reconnect to our Higher Self. For Emmanuel this includes biographies (recently he read about the Dalai Lama); for me it is literature from the mystic and contemplative tradition, for example, Julian of Norwich, Thomas Merton, Richard Rohr, and Cynthia Bourgeault. We also attend inspiring and moving services of worship and liturgies together, and we say a prayer before dinner. We both gain strength from the awe of beautiful architecture and from being in nature; we like walking along the sea. We both are enchanted by the "Great American Songbook" and are excited to go to the theater. The Higher Self also manifests itself in our communication and even in our dreams.

We express the Higher Self and transpersonal qualities in communion with others. We are blessed to be connected with many wise men and women. These connections are very important and help guide and nurture us. I personally have a problem when sexually unfaithful relationships are called "open relationships." I think all mature relationships need to be truly open, but in the sense of interacting with others, finding energy, inspiration and joy beyond the immediate and intimate partnership of the couple.

Love and Will

The two core qualities of Love and Will, as Roberto Assagioli wrote of them, were the organizing principles for us in our wedding service. When Emmanuel and I celebrated the consecration and blessing of our partnership in Basel, Switzerland, we prepared this service with a pastor of the Reformed Church but with an ecumenical outlook. In this special worship service we made a vow to each other where we expressed individually the intention and focus of our relationship; this was our expression of Will. Our vows also included the language of love, and also of course some religious references since this was not a Psychosynthesis ritual but a service within a progressive and mystic Christian tradition, reflecting our spiritual background and involving a minister. Taken together, our words to each other embodied a higher synthesis: the loving will.

Emmanuel: "Urs, I promise to love you, respect you, to support you in your work, to sustain you in prayer. I promise to stand by you in difficult times and to rejoice with you in good times, with the help of our Lord Jesus Christ."

Urs: "Emmanuel, I want to share my life with you, to be on the way with you, to set off to new frontiers. I will do my best to see and live our relationship always from my central relationship to Christ: to accept and love you, also in dark times. I want to give you space to develop your abilities to the full and to shower you over and over again with my gifts."

Our partnership is in service to the world, as we try to express and live the qualities of compassion and service. First, we want to shape our life partnership as a gay couple in a way that we support each other. This happens through our talks, including arguments, comforting each other and common prayer or meditation.

Our vow to each other is rooted in Will and Love. Love as compassion, kindness, good intentions and trust. Will demonstrated as strong commitment, faithfulness and the ability not just to look at each other, but also to look in the same direction in life. With the latter, we share similar core values and an openness for what the world "out there" calls us to do. In our partnership, we can reveal ourselves to each other in every way, as we are. With this attitude, we strive to accept and love both ourselves and each other. This unconditional love strengthens and nourishes us. It would never be possible in a casual camaraderie.

Beyond this focus on each other, we also want to live our partnership in a way that radiates our zest of life outward to the world beyond us. We believe this happens through our heartfelt profound connection and in our growing more whole through overcoming our mutual challenges.

Although our sexuality is not related to procreation, we nevertheless experience tenderness and sexual intimacy as a life-enhancing force. In our erotic embrace we gain energy. We want to put this energy into service for our fellow human beings and for creation.

Practically, the following core experiences are close to our hearts:

- Hospitality: offering to others acceptance and security.

- Being attentive to outcasts.

- Engaging in social matters and spirituality.

- While this is less important now at this stage in our lives than it used to be when we were very active in Christian LGB organizations from the 1980s to the early 2000s, we are still committed to finding an integration of spirituality and sexuality, engagement with other queer people and their friends for justice, respect and full acceptance for gays and lesbians in church and society.

- For Emmanuel, by expressing practical forms of hospitality such as being a pastoral presence and spreading beauty by creating Ikebana arrangements.

- For myself, through fulfilling various roles as a healer in my ministry, as a psychotherapist, as a spiritual director and also by facilitating or co-facilitating retreats.

Through the power of our relationship we experience a greater availability and freedom. We understand our partnership is also in service to our neighbors, community and all creation. We want to live and radiate spirituality as a couple. Through our common journey we have developed a spirituality that is more than just the spirituality of each of us individually. We want the commonly lived culture of our relationship to be infectious. In that way our partnership can be an inspiration for other lesbians and gays and may inspire heterosexual couples as well.

What I have said here about completion and challenge in our relationship is a process where we grow personally and continue to learn. We trust that whatever comes our way helps us to develop, with the result that new life can grow in us and through us. At times this includes conflicts and misunderstandings that we need to address, which is not always easy. We also need to accept our limitations.

This Modern Age

Life is growth and while the body ages, we want to stay young in spirit. Recently both of us started a new decade: Emmanuel turned 70 in July 2019, and I turned 60 in February 2020. We were able to celebrate with many friends with different day trips, just in time before the Covid crisis struck. There have been many big changes for us in this time of Covid. As I started writing this chapter and discussing the content with Emmanuel, we left our beloved London after over 15 amazing years and moved to North Yorkshire. So much is different; in leaving London we also left wonderful theaters, concert halls and sophisticated cabaret venues, which we used to enjoy on a regular basis every month. The center where I worked with Psychosynthesis clients shut down, and all of my work moved online. No more traveling every day by train, enjoying the journey, meditation on a prayer or affirmation, and walking through beautiful Pimlico to my office. The churches closed and when they reopened things were much different, with social distancing, no singing, no handshake, hug or kiss of peace, with communion in a restricted form. While we were confident that life would eventually return to a healthy normal, now new steps were needed.

And in fact, something new was waiting for us. We were drawn to an ecumenical Healing and Retreat center, Holy Rood House, in Thirsk (North Yorkshire) as a next step in our lives. At Holy Rood House I gained a new employment as a Senior Therapist, Spiritual Director, and Chaplain, and my life partner Emmanuel is working as a volunteer.

Roberto Assagioli often said: "There is no certainty, there is only adventure." It was that way for us: things fell apart during Covid, and yet a new synthesis appeared. In this new context our relationship was tested. We needed to evaluate how our very different personality types fit together in this new, non-urban world. Which transpersonal qualities are being called for now? Are we aligned with our Higher Self?

Emmanuel and I felt that another change in our lives was due. Until 2005, we had lived in a community for many years, which gave space to disadvantaged people (major mental health issues, substance use problems, learning disabilities). We felt we were coming full circle in the call to join a new community.[7] Holy Rood House differs from our old one as it connects many different aspects under one umbrella: retreat center, healing center, theology center, therapy, counseling, and spiritual direction. And we live in our own apartment. I quote from the introductory text of Holy Rood House on a flyer:

> Our main focus is on health and well-being. We are a community of healing and we find ourselves working at the cutting edge of society and the Church, breaking down prejudices and fears, and welcoming many different kinds of people of all ages and backgrounds. Our holistic and sensitive approach to different traditions is reflected in our accompaniment towards the transformation of people's lives.

Our relationship has found a new vessel to serve the world. We are more animated, challenged and inspired to adapt and grow, while new aspects of synthesis are required and revealed. Once again it is not just about the two of us; we are integrating into a team, into a community and into action with others as we evolve into new pastures.

I often share about being guided by what is called, in Psychosynthesis, the Higher Self (what 12-step people might call the Higher Power, religious people may call the Holy Spirit, the Christ within, Atman, or Buddha nature). An exercise originating from Roberto Assagioli has helped and guided me over the years. I have found it helpful in my work not just in the context of therapy but also in my relationship with Emmanuel. We are both familiar with this exercise, which I adapted it for LGB individuals, including same-sex couples.

I will end this chapter with this classic Psychosynthesis exercise. In our relationships, we sometimes have to climb mountains in order to move forward in life or to make important decisions. But

215

it is all worth it as we center into the wisdom and guidance of the Higher Self.

Psychosynthesis Exercise of Inner Dialogue[8]

- Sit yourself upright and comfortably or lie on the floor. Close your eyes and become aware for a moment of your breathing.

- Now imagine that you are in a valley full of flowers on a warm and sunny morning. You are in a wonderful place. Gradually become aware of your environment: the valley with the flowers, the sky intensely blue, the clean air, and the morning breeze gently caressing your cheeks. Feel the contact of your feet with the ground and be aware of what clothing you are wearing.

- You feel a sense of readiness and expectancy. As you look around, you see a mountain. It towers close to you and looking at the summit gives you a sense of elevation.

- You see a path leading towards the mountain. You decide to follow it. The path takes you inside a forest. You can smell the pleasant aroma of the pine trees and sense the cool and dark atmosphere.

- Now you see the path leading out of the forest and becoming steeper. Walking uphill, you can feel the muscular effort demanded of your body and the energy that pleasantly animates it. The path becomes steeper and steeper; perhaps you have to use your hands.

- The air is getting fresher. You feel a sense of elevation and notice the silent surroundings. Your climb brings you into a cloud. Everything is whitish and misty. You proceed carefully and cautiously. Now the cloud dissolves and you can see the sunny sky again above you.

• Up here, everything is much brighter and clearer. The air is clean, the colors of the surroundings are vivid, and the sun is shining. Climbing is easier now. You seem to weigh less, and you feel attracted to the top and you are eager to reach it.

• You are now on top of the mountain, on a plateau. Far off, you see someone. It is a wise and loving person. You feel his/her readiness to listen to what you have to say and to answer your questions. You have noticed each other. You are walking toward each other. You feel more and more the presence of this wise person. You feel an emanation of joy, holiness, power and love.

• Now you are facing each other. You have the chance to ask this wise and loving person questions and share your concerns. Ask him/her the following questions and allow yourself some time before becoming aware of the answer:

  • Where does the potential of homosexuality lie?

  • What gifts and talents are trying to emerge in my life and as part of being in a same-sex relationship? What transpersonal qualities are needed in this stage of my life?

  • What is a concrete step that I can take in my life that will allow me to grow as part of a couple? Possibly the answers come through words, but pay attention to any symbols or gestures. Whatever the answer, try to respect it rather than judge or devalue it. You may want to ask more questions or perhaps you may prolong the dialogue. In any case, notice the answers.

- Show gratitude in whatever form you prefer and say goodbye to this wise person, knowing that you can come back anytime to the top of this mountain.

- Now, in your own speed and time, walk all the way back until you get to the valley covered with flowers, the place where you started your journey. Then slowly open your eyes, get up, stretch, drink something and write down notes About this inner journey, paying particular attention to the responses the wise being gave to your questions.

- Discuss the experience with your partner and reflect on what it could mean practically for your relationship and your lives.

- While we grow older, life continues to unfold and gratitude and presence deepen. We have been guided by wisdom indeed.

Amy and Randall

The wedding vows that Amy and her husband Randall wrote at the start of their journey together serve as a powerful touchstone in this chapter. In their story of shared international adventures, she shows how the concept of marriage as a "spiritual grinding stone" encouraged them to embrace the personal and interpersonal growth that marriage demands. Recognizing the presence of the soul of the relationship, they learned to trust this sacred container that guided and supported their journey together.

CHAPTER TEN

Marriage as a Crucible of Transformation

Amy Spalding-Fecher

When we speak of marriage in spiritual terms, we are inviting
ourselves into it at a much higher level. To participate in a marriage of this kind is not only to enter into it as the estate that
will bring us happiness, but to see it also as the spiritual crucible of transformation, of suffering, and also of great joy.
—*Daphne Rose Kingma*[1]

The roadmap that my husband and I laid out for ourselves
on our wedding day was the start of a spiritual adventure
that took us to places we could not have dared to imagine.
Had I known of the peaks and valleys between then and now, I
wonder if my younger self who spoke our vows would have been
willing to take the leap. When I revisit our wedding vows, I recognize that they were written from a place of profound wisdom
connecting us. I now appreciate that we were called into marriage
by something vaster than the two of us, to do the work of a lifetime. Through our vows, we aligned ourselves with the "soul" of
our relationship. Over time, this soul has been the container that

has held, encouraged and directed us. Our partnership has been our spiritual crucible of transformation.

Responding to the Call

We had been married 20 years before Psychosynthesis came into our lives. I write this chapter in hindsight, and with the knowledge of how, in the past seven years, Psychosynthesis sped up and deepened the growth already occurring in our relationship. This chapter is also written strictly from my point of view. My husband, Randall, has reviewed it and remarked that he thinks he comes across as far more patient than he really is. I disagree, for without his patience and perseverance, I do not think I would be writing this chapter.

When Randall and I met in San Francisco, I was a year into my first job in architecture after graduate school. Virtually all my focus and intention were directed towards my budding career. Randall was years away from settling into his career in international environmental policy. There did not appear to be a lot of common ground between us, and there was an age difference of more than five years. After a few casual conversations, Randall's impromptu invitation to join him on a trip to Mexico ignited a spark that led to a lifetime commitment, not just to each other, but to our own growth. A few weeks after we met, I traded in 80 hours of overtime for a ten-day "first date" to the Yucatan peninsula, where we rented an old VW Bug and set off on a road trip.

After a spectacular time amidst the temples, cities, and beaches of the Yucatan, I announced on the flight home that, while this had been a wonderful trip, I really thought it would be best to end the relationship before it got too serious. Randall, crestfallen and perplexed, convinced me to give it more time. We were at different points in our lives, and I didn't see how we could each evolve in the way I pictured by staying together. But what I didn't realize then is that the soul evolves in the way it needs to, not necessarily in the way that one imagines. The quietest of invitations (and a great deal of persistence on Randall's part) called to me, asking me to linger a while and engage with this mysterious attraction. We enjoyed each other's lively company and our deep conversations, yet as we drew closer my delight and my fears rose up in equal measure. Like a wary cat, I was fascinated by the hand reaching towards me, but was prepared to run at the slightest feeling of my own vulnerability.

There was something in Randall and in our relationship that drew me closer as the months went by. I alternately acknowledged the potential and then did my best to resist both the call and the relationship. It was hard work navigating this roller coaster. My resistance was partly my logical brain thinking our partnership was impractical, with each of us being at different stages of our lives, and partly my very scared, wounded self, not wanting to risk caring deeply and getting hurt. Guided by my intuition, I chose over time to trust the possibility that there was something here to embrace. Now I understand that this was the relationship that would help me do the work of deep healing and connection necessary to grow. I trusted enough to gingerly take one step, and another, and another as our path unfolded in front of us.

From the start, we embarked on explorations of nature, travel, friendship and culture. I found myself doing things that I thought I had put aside permanently in order to develop my career in architecture, such as living and working in New Zealand and backpacking in Asia. It felt both reckless and exhilarating to pursue these adventures, as if a part of me was waking up and stepping into a potential I had never envisioned within a relationship. Perhaps it is not just what we love in another that attracts us to someone else, but what we fall in love with in ourselves as a result of being with another person. Our growing relationship led me to experience more of my passionate, curious, adventurous self, which awaited me beyond my life experience and the limited stories by which I defined myself.

From that first trip to the Yucatan, to hiking together in Yosemite and following bear tracks on cross-country skis, to meditation retreats and Sunday morning bike rides across the Golden Gate Bridge, we found something in one another that thrilled, stretched, and nurtured us. Those early adventures annealed us, forging our relationship into a true partnership. A core of respect and resourcefulness grew between us, providing both inspiration and refuge. We could sense not just what each of us brought to the relationship, but the ways in which the relationship itself gradually began to transform and nourish us.

Commitment to the Call

By the time Randall asked me to marry him, I was all in. We openly acknowledged our appreciation and regard for one another and experienced a certain amount of awe at the life we were creating. We set about writing our own wedding service, one which reflected our unique beliefs and aspirations. We started with our deepest belief:

> We give thanks to the Divine, who has brought our souls together so that we may inspire one another to seek the highest truth. It is our intention that in one another's presence we will nurture the unfolding of our true selves.

We didn't really know what "highest truths" meant back then, but it reflected our thirst for both inner and outer knowledge and commitment to spiritual and personal growth. This was consistent with our aspiration to support one another on the journey to become our best selves. At the time, we were involved in a spiritual community, which influenced our attitudes and the language we used in our vows. Our spiritual practice reminded us that we were connected to a larger whole and encouraged us to orient towards the higher aspects of ourselves. Although we left that particular spiritual path after a few years, I am grateful for its influence while we were planning our wedding, for it raised our aspirations and the quality of our commitment to one another. From the point of view of Psychosynthesis, we were orienting our relationship towards qualities of the higher unconscious, thereby committing to our journey of knowing and expressing our transpersonal Selves through our relationship.

In planning our wedding ceremony, we were intent on creating a rite of passage marking the transition from "I" to "we." As we wrote our vows, we were able to give words to our longings for ourselves and for each other. We unknowingly tapped into the soul that united us, articulating the vision that bound us together. The fact that we listened and wrote and spoke our vows in front of dear friends and family is part of what has kept us on the path together. We unknowingly created an "Ideal Model"[2] for our relationship, one that reflected the deep call we both felt in embarking on our marriage. Roberto Assagioli, the founder of Psychosynthesis, saw the Ideal Model as "an essential method for Self-realization, of hearing and responding to Self's invitation to move or grow in a particular direction."[3] Randall and I did not know that this was what we were doing at the time, but we certainly articulated and committed to what we thought was possible in our life together. It is clear nearly three decades later that the image we created for our marriage has been a light guiding us through all the twists and turns of our endeavors.

An Ideal Model helps us to distinguish between which beliefs are part of us, and which might be false stories. Many of us have fairy tales about what a marriage can be; we romanticize ourselves and our partners, and we have doubts and insecurities about how we show up in a relationship. Many of these internalized scripts are unconscious. They may be stories we inherit from our family and our culture, from movies, and from what we see around us. Randall and I knew that we were creating a new model for ourselves that was unique to us. Planning our ceremony was an opportunity to recognize, acknowledge and shake off old stories and models, and hone in on an inspired picture, or the highest realistic vision, of what was possible in our relationship.

On the day of our wedding, we stood under stately old oak trees at the edge of the ocean surrounded by dear family and friends. As I looked at my beloved and spoke my vows, witnessed by so many who loved and believed in us, I experienced unspeakable joy at the alignment of two hearts, minds and souls. No other "call of Self" in my life has been this profound and this transformative, and to this day I feel the deep resonance and truth of that moment.

Through our vows we committed to growing towards authenticity and to bringing our best self to the partnership:

> It is our highest intention that in one another's presence we may unflinchingly become more of who we are and commit ourselves to bringing peace, love, and joy into our lives.

Individually, we committed to supporting the potential we saw in each other:

> I want for you that which brings you the greatest fulfillment and promise to encourage and support you as you strive to attain the finest of which you are capable.

Loving someone over time has taught me that encouraging my partner to fulfill his potential necessarily required me to "unflinchingly become more" of who I am. Sometimes that process was not conducive to peace, love, and joy. I have flinched many times in the course of our relationship, but I have been persistent in my commitment to my own growth as well as the growth of our relationship.

Living up to our Aspirations

For marriage is the spiritual grinding stone that will hone you to your brightest brilliance. It will cause you to become not only who you wanted to be, but also the person whom you have no choice but to be. In marriage you will be reformed, for in choosing this particular person to love and make your whole life with, you are choosing to be affected.
—*Daphne Rose Kingma*[4]

When planning our ceremony, we came across this concept of marriage as the spiritual grinding stone and asked our wise friend marrying us to weave it into her address. We embarked on our married life knowing and accepting that our commitment would bring us opportunities and challenges to address our limitations and grow in ways that would bring us closer to our potential.

We found this analogy quite poetic until life demanded that we soften some rough edges. The analogy of the spiritual grinding stone has often helped us to make sense of our journey together when things got tough. This idea, that marriage hones you to your finest brilliance, is a potent reminder to lean into the work in order to uncover what lies within. When I was young, I thought a soul mate was someone with whom you felt completely at ease and at home with, and that your partnership would be a constant source of love and support. This is a relatively static view of how relationships unfold. I am grateful to have come to understand that a soulmate is someone who requests, encourages, occasionally demands, and supports you in looking at your rough edges and in committing to refining them in order to evolve and express yourself fully in the world. In our case, I believe it was our marriage, the "crucible of transformation," that held and supported us through the years in submitting to the spiritual grinding stone. Some of the more painful periods of our marriage were when we resisted the process of transformation.

It has taken years for me to fully appreciate that, in coming together, Randall and I were the perfect instigators of change for one another. Our relationship aspired to the heights of spiritual union, and yet, we chose just the person who would take us to our deepest wounding and into our darkest places. Like most people, we came into the relationship with unconscious longings for our partner to fill unmet needs and heal wounds at the heart of our experience. I came into the relationship with what I viewed as an unacceptable need to be seen, to know that I mattered, and know that I would not be left alone in my darkest times. How I behaved, when that need was not met by Randall, triggered his core needs. Our interactions were often a dance of protest and retreat as we circled around our own and each other's tender parts, often stepping on toes and occasionally being painfully out of step with each other.

> We will aspire to bring forward the best in one another and to remember to bring qualities of forgiveness, compassion and integrity to our relationship.

Over the years, this intention was one of the noblest and most difficult commitments to fulfill, and there were many times when I could not find the part of myself that made that commitment.

In the midst of reactivity, petty squabbles or deep inner despair, I could not see over the horizon of my own confusion and pain to glimpse the bigger picture, the one with the power to remind me of my purpose. Soon after our beautiful wedding we put our aspiration to the test, as we set out to backpack through Asia and eastern Africa for ten months on an extended "honeymoon."

Listening to Randall enthusiastically share his previous experiences of traveling on a shoestring with just a backpack and a Lonely Planet guidebook encouraged me to consider such a radical departure from my professional trajectory. Six weeks into our extended trip, I realized that this was no honeymoon. It was certainly an exciting and enriching time. We both enjoyed the cultures, people, and landscapes we encountered. The experiences we had during our travels nurtured us spiritually, emotionally, and intellectually. They also exhausted us physically and challenged our fledgling relationship. Trekking for 21 days in the Himalayas was challenging and rewarding, whereas long rides on crowded trains and exiting train or bus stations to a deluge of hawkers and jostling crowds just about sent me packing to go home. The trip exposed the fault lines in our psychological states that occasionally made the journey very arduous. On the one hand, I delighted in our adventures and in being together. On the other, I sometimes felt overwhelmed, anxious, and on high alert as we arrived somewhere new, which was every few days. When that anxious part became activated, I reacted. I became angry that Randall could not protect me from the uncertainty. This was my "fight or flight" response. Randall had no idea what to do with this part of me, and, in search of his own safety, would stay very still lest he make the situation worse—the "freeze" response of his nervous system. I felt alone in my panic, and Randall didn't know how to reach me. Thus the cycle would begin, and within minutes we would find ourselves alienated from ourselves and from one another.

I have a memory of the two of us huddled on a street in New Delhi, arguing intensely over how to tie a knot in the string around a package we were sending back to the States. It seemed that the whole world depended on this knot being the perfect knot. At the time I was not able to recognize that this contracted, controlling behavior was only a part of me, one with a very narrow perspective. Being in unfamiliar situations frequently threw us back into identification with subpersonalities seeking safety or certainty. As Assagioli wrote: "We are dominated by everything with which our self becomes identified. We can dominate and control everything from which we disidentify ourselves. The normal mistake we all make is to identify ourselves with some content of consciousness rather than with consciousness itself."[5]

We still laugh at our petty tussle over that knot, recognizing how we were so identified with the limiting parts of ourselves insisting that the correct knot would give us the security and control we sought. A few weeks later I experienced the antidote to such identification as I meditated early one morning with a view of the Himalayas. Observing the vastness of Annapurna touched by the gentle light of dawn and knowing that I too was vaster than I could comprehend, I identified with the core of my being, the Self. One of Assagioli's sayings is to "see things from the aspect of eternity." This high-altitude experience helped put things in perspective and is one I often return to when I want to connect with a deeper, timeless aspect of myself.

When I was not identified with these scared and anxious parts, I was able to bring resourcefulness, compassion, and creativity to our relationship. We navigated and celebrated numerous moments of joy and complexity during our trip. After six months of traveling, we spent a few weeks near Dharamsala in India. We were there to attend the Dalai Lama's annual public teaching to a large gathering of Tibetan monks. We also were able to take classes in Buddhism, taught in English by experienced Tibetan teachers. After a few days, Randall became very sick. We were holed up in a guesthouse in a small village, and in the middle of the night I grew very concerned about him. I knew there was a 24-hour clinic staffed by medical students from all over the world nearby. I raced down through the dark empty forest to find help. Through tears of gratitude at finding help, I was able to identify with a very capable part of myself focused on getting Randall the help he needed. I got the medicine, ran back up the hill, and tended to Randall with calm, reassuring clarity. No doubt I still had a scared vulnerable part inside somewhere, but it wasn't driving my behavior. Instead, I identified with a more functional and focused part that served that situation well.

Thanks to Psychosynthesis I now understand that we all have the capacity within us to choose what we identify with, and, more importantly, to Self-identify, choosing behavior in service of our highest good. The power of choice, a function of our will, gives us the option to disidentify from behaviors and beliefs which are not serving us. Assagioli wrote that in the principle of disidentification "lies the secret of our enslavement or of our liberty".[6] I could choose to be a slave to my fearful thoughts, or I could pause, disidentify, and choose wisely. What this example helps me to understand is how automatic and unconscious our behavior can be. Through the practice of self-reflection, we can bring our automatic behaviors to conscious awareness and begin to transform them.

As the trip went on, I grew to take refuge in Randall's steady demeanor, learning to trust our ability to navigate what came our way as we went along. His calm presence was an example of the power of what Psychosynthesis calls an "external unifying center." When I became anxious and afraid, I learned to trust Randall to be a safe container in which I could find my way back to equilibrium. Our relationships thrive to the degree that we can securely attach and find safety in our partners. When we are not able to identify with our own compassionate regulating center, another empathic being, or other influences such as nature, poetry, images, music, and art can be unifying influences in turbulent times. This is a profoundly healing gift of committed relationships. That Randall provided this empathic environment allowed my nervous system to calm and return to a place of safety. I began to develop more trust that the world was not such a scary place. At the same time, this was also a double-edged sword. For many years neither of us knew how to consistently stay engaged with each other when the volume went up in our interactions. We knew it was possible to be a refuge for one another, yet we repeatedly and inadvertently reactivated wounds rooted in our early childhoods, perpetuating the belief that no one could tolerate us if they truly knew us.

These wildly different experiences reflected the polarities not just of our trip, but of our relationship, as we oscillated between the highs of spiritual connectedness and the lows of psychological and emotional isolation. Overcoming or bridging this split has been the work of our marriage. At times we veered towards "spiritual bypass," thinking that if we meditated enough or were disciplined enough, we could rise above the polarized interactions. These practices did indeed bring insight and perspective to our situation, but only when we were conscious of not relying on them as an escape from our discomfort. At other times we fell into psychological collapse, where all we could see was the pain of being hurt and hurting each other. It was only when we came across Psychosynthesis, years into our marriage, that we learned that there was a way to synthesize these polarities.

Losing Connection

After our trip, we returned to Boston, in 1995, where Randall attended graduate school and I found work as an architect. Our respective pursuits demanded a lot of our time, including one summer when Randall worked in India. We were supported by our commitment to a daily meditation practice as well as by attending several meditation retreats and personal growth workshops over the two years in Boston. These laid an invisible foundation to the life we would live as a married couple—a commitment to understanding and nurturing our relationship, and a commitment to spiritual practice.

After graduation, when Randall was offered a three-year contract with the University of Cape Town, we once again jumped at the chance to live and work abroad. We packed up two boxes with some pots and pans and our camping gear, happily rid ourselves of all our winter clothes, and set off into the unknown. I remember sitting in the little tin box of the airplane somewhere over the Atlantic feeling suspended between the past that we had lived in the U.S. and what we had yet to create in South Africa. Anything was possible in our new life far from home.

Moving overseas reflected a shared desire to simplify our lives and step back from the culture of overwork and over-identification with professionalism so prevalent in our experience in the U.S. We knew we wanted to start a family in a calm and relaxed environment. This desire formed the heart of our vision. Our family life began in a very basic three-room wooden cottage on a smallholding surrounded by mountains and close to the ocean. Our first child was born at home in a bathtub flooded with sunlight. We happily benefited from hand-me-down baby clothes and well-loved but outgrown toys passed on by new friends. For entertainment we conversed with the large tortoise next door who patrolled the fence, played in a nearby brook, or picnicked in the stunning Kirstenbosch Botanical Gardens. Outwardly our life was more basic than that of our peers, and we cherished the simplicity and honesty of it. We had a happy, active one-year-old who rarely slept. When the sleep exhaustion got the better of us and our parenting skills, a generous friend offered to take our daughter for a walk regularly so I could sleep. It took a while to adjust to the ever-present safety concerns of living in South Africa, such as burglar bars on the windows and steering locks on the car. But we found a balance between the vigilance required to be safe and the inspiration we enjoyed in living in such a beautiful place. We lived in a happy little bubble—so happy that our initial three-year contract extended into a 16-year sojourn in South Africa.

It is almost impossible to describe our years in Cape Town. The things that had ignited and nurtured our early passion were all present: diversity, culture, nature, beauty, challenge, and wonderful people. South Africa is one of the most beautiful places in the world—the country spans a variety of stunning landscapes, unique flora and fauna, and a rich tapestry of cultures. It is a land of complexity and diversity that we couldn't hope to understand. Although Mandela was democratically elected in 1994, the pain of apartheid was deeply evident when we arrived in 1997. Living in such a divided society was confusing and at times scary. There was little trust between many sectors of the population and violence occasionally erupted. For the first couple of years there were bombings at ATMs and restaurants, and it was not safe to drive on the roads at night. The inequality and the attitudes that bred these events were staggering. During our time there we witnessed healing, though the extreme disparities in wealth and privilege continue to divide the country. As a family, we thrived in our lives there, which is why we stayed for 16 dynamic years.

Our early years of parenting showed how deep and aligned our values and our collaboration were. From our birthing plan to sleeping arrangements to education, we intuitively agreed on approaches that neither of us had experienced previously. Randall was an engaged and present partner, actively involved in all aspects of child rearing. We had both often worked 50-60 hours a week in our jobs in the U.S., but once our daughter was born he limited his work hours to weekdays only—no nights or weekends unless he was traveling. His commitment to the family never wavered, and I rarely lost sight of my gratitude for him and for our partnership. I did, however, begin to lose sight of myself, and the slow creep of self-alienation had long-term effects on our partnership.

As with many new parents, we became engrossed in the demands of daily life and many times lost sight of what had brought us together. As we became consumed with our parenting challenges, and struggled with our limitations as parents, the brightness of our vibrant connection dimmed. Fortunately, the container of our marriage that we had cultivated so beautifully at the start was there to help us. The dear soul of our marriage carried on, silently guiding us in creating a meaningful life for our family that reflected our shared values and aspirations. Its support was there even when we were unaware of its presence and value.

On a personal level, the first few years abroad were a confusing period for me. Within the space of the previous five years, we had moved from San Francisco to New Zealand, gotten married, backpacked around the world, settled in Boston for two years, navigated the sadness and confusion of an ectopic pregnancy, moved to South Africa, and had our first child. Randall had a busy professional life waiting for him in Cape Town, while I struggled to find my place. I taught in the architecture department at the University, but once I had a child I was in constant inner turmoil about where my loyalty lay. When I was preparing for my courses, I felt I should have been with my daughter. When I was with her, I agonized over my work and trying to address it with the same intensity and integrity I had before I had kids. I know this is common for new mothers, and I was not alone in my concerns. Yet by the time our daughter turned one, my perception of myself was in complete disarray. I was a congregate of disparate parts with no connection to a guiding center or "self."

Despite our clear intention to start a family, we were unprepared for the reality of doing this thousands of miles away from family, friends and a familiar medical community. Having children catapulted me into a new role, which was both exciting and yet felt alien. I longed for the company of old friends who knew me well, and who could help me bridge the gap between how life was and this new reality. Many of the ways that I defined myself fell away—the strong, resilient, independent, creative professional was gone, and I hadn't made a conscious choice to let go of her. Because my life had been one long identification with one achievement or another, I now had no way to define myself, no hook to hang my hat on after we moved. Being an architect was a very strong identification, both because I valued the work and also because I had a credible label through which the world could know me. When I chose to step back from teaching part-time at the University—temporarily, I thought at the time—I lost a big crutch that supported how I claimed my value in the world. Randall was delving deeper and deeper into a secure and fulfilling career, whilst I was lost in my own wilderness. Though I often had concerns about my ability to be a good parent, I did not foresee the utter loss of identity I experienced when I became a mother.

Now I am not so sure that this crisis was just that I stepped back from architecture and all the ways it supported me. Perhaps an even larger issue was a deep-seated apprehension about motherhood. I was thirty-six when our first daughter was born. I was conscious of how hard women had fought for the right to work and to be respected professionally. At times I felt obligated to uphold the gains won by the brave and fierce female professionals who preceded me. I also had worked hard, sacrificed, and devoted myself to succeeding in a male-dominated field and I was conflicted about leaving my career path once more. Unconsciously I delayed the decision to have children as long as I could. And yet because I had waited so long, having children brought such precious delight to my life. I feared letting these tiny little beings down. I knew that, as a profession, architecture is a demanding master. I did not think I could practice the kind of architecture that inspired me and also become the parent I hoped to be, one who could raise happy, secure, and resilient children. I sensed that trying to do both would be a compromise where every side got less than they needed, including me.

I was fortunate to be able to spend gentle, unhurried days with our children. I had time and space to grow into a role that did not come naturally to me. But I did not consciously and intentionally make the choice to leave my profession. A part of me did not understand the value of full-time parenting, and this part became a constant nagging voice of doubt in my mind. There was a subtle war going on within between the established educated professional "achiever" and the fledgling healthy internal "mother" that I was creating. Although a part of me mourns the road not taken to a life-long architectural career, I have been deeply blessed by the road I did take to be with and grow with my family. Over time, I have been able to do several building projects that have given me the creative challenge and satisfaction that I love from design and construction. Overall, I believe this journey subtly nudged me towards discovering and healing generations of trauma around parenting.

Finding our Way Back

Parenting was a new invitation to healing for both of us. Although I floundered often in the early years, I also experienced so many sublime moments with my children that I reclaimed some of the joy and curiosity I had lost in my own childhood. I allowed myself to appreciate the simple acts of taking a walk, cooking, observing dung beetles, and play. I slowly began to disidentify from the part of me that believed my worth was based on significant external achievements. I was reparenting the child within as I learned how to parent my girls. Over time I came to see that I was reclaiming a sacred part of myself as I dedicated myself to growing into motherhood.

As my priorities and identity shifted, so did my relationship with Randall. We were asked to get to know each other as new parents, and as lovers with different commitments than just one another. While we were focused on developing our abilities to be the parents we hoped to be for our children, we sometimes fell short in being the partner we had committed to being for each other. I was often overwhelmed and disoriented by my changing role and struggled to find a place of ease within. Once I had children, a loud voice of self-doubt about being a "good enough mother" was joined by the internalized voices of generations of mothers, sisters, and aunts, forming a cacophony clouding my intuition and clarity. I needed to find my way back to myself and a connection to my inner wisdom.

Had we been able to see the patterns in our relationship, we would have realized that our prickly interactions were inviting us to turn towards very old wounds and to help one another heal. Instead, as these old wounds were activated, we retreated from one another in subtle but persistent ways. Our reactive behavior reinforced core beliefs in each other about the unacceptable nature of our needs and our inherent unworthiness to have these needs met. When repeatedly identified with these beliefs, we were unable to stay present with each other and were no longer available to be a compassionate partner. Over time, the repetition of this pattern shifted the wounds that originated in childhood, to ones perpetuated by the relationship.

Wisely, we sought help. We found a kind, empathic counselor to guide us in finding our way back to one another. It was through this counselor that we first experienced the profound healing power of sustained Presence. Our sessions were like lanterns lighting the way back to the familiar, nurturing vessel of our marriage. I cherished them not just for the psychological help, but for the fact that, for one hour, we had someone's undivided attention supporting us. We no longer felt so alone, so confused, and so alienated from each other. We began to emerge from our closed-off places and our life began to settle down as we approached the birth of our second child in Cape Town.

Even in dark times, both Randall and I clearly had the will to orient towards personal growth to the best of our ability. We read, talked, went to therapy, and meditated. We loved getting out in nature as a family, offering us a way to tap into what united us. We especially enjoyed trips to game reserves. Sitting in the grandeur of nature and watching the animal world carry on around us brought ease and wonder. With the girls silently climbing around the vehicle and watching in awe as an elephant, giraffe or warthog meandered across our path, we settled into witnessing the natural flow of life and were enveloped in a sense of timelessness. These moments gave us the chance to see things, as Assagioli wrote, "from the aspect of eternity."

The Soul as Healer

> It is our highest intention that in one another's presence
> we will nurture the unfolding of our true selves.

As we moved beyond the challenges of establishing our family in a new country and parenting very young children, we gradually relaxed into a calming rhythm of family life. If we consider the relationship as having its own "egg diagram,"[7] then we had so far done a decent job of harmonizing many parts of our connected psyche, at least those parts of which we were conscious. In addition, our simple life was not particularly stressful—our kids went to a nurturing local Waldorf School, Randall worked from home, and I was involved in school affairs and other activities that nourished me and allowed me to be available to the girls. We chose not to have a TV, so our home life was filled with reading, stories, games and art projects. We spent a lot of time outdoors, the kids were excellent at entertaining themselves through creative play, and we did not worry too much about "getting ahead" in life.

Our biggest blessing during this time came unexpectedly. Since moving to South Africa we had been uncomfortable with the standard practice of hiring domestic workers for housework and childcare. Our house was so small we could clean it in an hour and having someone else in our house felt foreign to us. The politics of the system were problematic for us, yet the reality of hiring someone who needed a job to support her extended family made it personal. Little did I know that in hiring someone I would find a beloved soul sister and a second mother for my children. Euphemia was a calm, resourceful, humorous presence who helped keep our ship afloat. Sharing twelve years together with all the ups and downs of raising children and navigating our lives forged a lifelong bond. She was a spiritual ally to our journey as a couple and a family.

Euphemia's support was fundamental when I developed fibromyalgia a few years after she started working for us. Having a chronic illness meant rearranging our schedules, our activities, and our expectations. I can't overemphasize what a gift it was to know that the details of daily living would carry on reliably and with care. The girls knew that Euphemia was available to them during the day even when I was not. Randall knew that he did not have to take over the tasks of keeping a house running. Although this experience was debilitating for me, between Randall's commitment and Euphemia's help, the disruption in our family was minimized. I was reminded of the saying that it takes a village to raise a family. We were blessed to have such a village.

My multi-year efforts to regain my health and vitality led me to a course called "Bridging Polarities Through Art,"[8] a remarkable precursor to my study of Psychosynthesis. These two approaches to personal and spiritual growth, both of which address the transformation of polarities within the psyche leading to greater self-knowledge and inner harmony, invited me to awaken to my soul and my transpersonal potential. Bridging Polarities is an approach to art-making that allows unconscious insight and wisdom to emerge through intuitive artistic expression, encouraging deep listening to the process. It is also a wonderful opportunity to get past the judging mind that often stops people from exploring art as a healing modality.

Through creative exercises with clay, soft pastels and wet-on-wet painting, I experienced myself not through what I had achieved or accomplished, but through the soul qualities expressed in these explorations. In other words, as I identified less as a "doing" person, my "being" qualities, such as awareness, sensitivity, joy, insight, curiosity, and compassion had the opportunity to arise. It was like coming home to myself, back to a place that I was seeing for the first time. Bridging Polarities was not just an exercise in art-making, it cultivated a paradigm shift in how I viewed myself as a human being and an embodied soul.

In his book *Holy Fire: The Process of Soul Awakening*, Tom Yeomans describes how, in the journey of soul incarnation, "we gradually shift identity to soul as the center and guiding principle of our life and make choices accordingly."[9] Bridging Polarities woke me up to qualities of my soul buried beneath my conditioning. I caught glimpses of my true Self and became curious about what got in the way of expressing myself in our relationship and in the world. As Yeomans writes, "we don't have to go anywhere special to be in touch with our souls; we need only to clear away and heal the obstacles to that experience and learn how to express it in our unique ways."[10] During my training an image came to me of a fledgling plant in a garden choked by weeds. In the image, a small clearing surrounded the little plant, enough for it to breathe, receive sunlight, and be seen. I knew I was the one who had made the clearing, and my core essence was the plant. I needed only to keep the weeds away and let the rest unfold. Through this I began to live up to my vow to "nurture the unfolding of our true selves." My last few years in Cape Town were a dynamic exploration of art, healing, and reconnection to subtle soul qualities, all of which fed back into our relationship.

Vulnerability as a Path to Soul Connection

As our children grew and needed more freedom, we realized that it was time to leave South Africa and settle in the United States. Our return was a steep learning curve for all of us. The U.S. had changed significantly in our absence, and although Randall and I were born there, we returned as strangers in our own land. It once again took a couple of years to find our way together and as a family with two teenagers. We were heartened by the resilience and adaptability of our children, who had never lived in the U.S. We were reassured that they felt safe enough in the world and could find the resources they needed to adjust. We were the committed couple we had always been, and we were still eager for growth and insight. When our children reached late teenage years, with college and an empty nest on the horizon, we found ourselves up against "the last frontier" of the well-worn but subtle defense mechanisms that we had learned to live with over the years. The consequences began playing out in unhealthy family dynamics.

We were aware that the patterns in our family life had their roots in our own relationship as a couple and, beneath that, in multigenerational patterns we had inherited. Not able to fully articulate and transform the patterns, we again sought help. In the course of expertly facilitated therapy, which started with cultivating safety within the relationship, we gingerly turned to face persistent barriers preventing us from being fully honest and present to one another. We slowly opened towards the soul container of our marriage as a source of support and guidance. Working with a therapist provided the security we needed to bring our painful feelings to each other. It was challenging and scary work which required a lot of energy and will.

During this work, we were invited to give voice to our deepest vulnerabilities and fears about what made us feel unseen, unvalued, or existentially alone. It was a process of bringing our most wounded and shamed parts to light. I had learned early in life that having, or—worse—expressing, an emotional need was seen as a character flaw, resulting in rejection, scorn and humiliation. I had tried numerous ways to deny an unbearable longing for secure connection to Randall because that need seemed so unacceptable to my inner child. When he was not able to respond or stay present to that poorly expressed need, a confusing cascade of complicated emotions shut me down. I withdrew emotionally and often slipped into depression. These conflicted parts shielded and isolated me, by convincing me that I could live without relying on a healing connection (which was there in all but the darkest times), because there were so many other wonderful things about our marriage.

Step by step, we explored our triggers and behaviors around deep-seated wounds and were gently encouraged to share our experience with one another. We stuck with it even when it took weeks to be willing to share our fears and desires out loud. Just as we had learned as children to protect ourselves, we had unconsciously created the same protective patterns in our relationship—and they definitely were no longer serving us. Our patterns separated us not just from each other but from the wonderful healing space at the heart of our marriage. A significant turning point in our therapy came as we opened to the possibility that we could stay present to one another even when in these scary places. It took a lot of coaxing for me to even consider it. I began to understand what John Welwood meant when he wrote: "Living with someone we love, with all the joys and challenges, is one of the best ways to grow spiritually. But real awakening only happens in the charnel ground where we acknowledge and work with our wounds, fears and illusions."[11]

As we dismantled our invisible fortresses, a palpable sense of ease and energy began to flow back into our relationship. I am so grateful that we had the will and courage to turn towards our difficulties and transform our dance. Painful as the difficulties were, they were an invitation from the soul to heal, and we were doing the healing not just for us but for past and future generations. During these times the spiritual grinding stone was doing its heaviest work, identifying and polishing the bits of our psyche that were blocking our path to profound soul connection. This work requires courage, honesty and commitment. It is not necessarily comfortable. It is wise to work with a skilled couples therapist who can provide a safe container and be a loving witness to what wants to emerge.

I realize now that the very vessel for our transformation was what had united us at the start. We needed a reminder to trust the vessel, even if we were not always able to fully trust each other. When times were challenging, our marriage was solid enough to hold what was happening between us until we individually felt our feet on firm ground. Once we were able to face what kept us in our protected silos, we could turn back towards each other with warmth, openness, and curiosity. Our relationship took us to the door of our own personal process, and then it was our choice to do the work that would allow us to show up fully for each other.

Releasing the Energies of the Soul

Embarking on and continuing my work as a student, coach, and trainer of Psychosynthesis has helped me develop new insights into my own path and the path of marriage. My husband has also studied Psychosynthesis for his personal benefit, so we have a shared language and framework for understanding and growth. Our training and commitment to the Psychosynthesis process helps us to know our parts (and each other's) and reminds us that there is more to us than these disparate parts. In turn, we are able to have more understanding for our partner and the needs underlying their behavior. Our path asks us to practice radical self-compassion and self-care so that we can stay present even when we want to protest or run and hide. The spiritual grinding stone continues to wear away what no longer serves us, and we are freer to open to what is seeking expression through us: joy and gratitude, appreciation for one another, and the inspiration at the heart of our relationship.

As my trust in the soul of the relationship strengthens, I welcome the words of Assagioli: "The soul knows all about it, and is just waiting for you to find out."[12] When I am able to get out of my own way, and allow the energies of my soul more expression through actions and intentions, I am more aligned to the commitment I made to Randall on our wedding day:

> I will strive to make our marriage a safe place for you to bring your hopes and dreams, a sanctuary from which we can both go forth into the world. I will hold out my hand for you in times of sadness, and celebrate with you in your joys. I hope always to be a source of inspiration, consolation and admiration.

The relational work we have undertaken has encouraged us to embrace rather than resist our marriage as the "spiritual crucible of transformation." We celebrate knowing that what we intended on our wedding day has guided us every step of the way, even in times when confusion obscured our vision:

> May we always have a special sense of our mission in life together, and may we never tire of the endless possibilities of exploring our shared existence. May we find constant reward and challenge as we pursue the ongoing adventure of partnership in our life together.

Our life together is indeed an ongoing adventure, one infused with the potential that comes from trusting ourselves, one another and the guidance of what unites us. Our challenges are no longer seen only as problems to be fixed, but as invitations to release what is limiting us. We trust that the qualities of our sacred connection emanate into the world around us and impact our family and our community. To recognize and to embrace the transformative potential of our partnership has been the journey of a lifetime. I am eternally grateful to walk alongside my life partner, aligned with and guided by the soul of our relationship.

Tom and Anne

Anne tells the rich story of her over-50-year marriage
to Tom, which spans many decades of deep cultural
shifts. Their relationship survived her transformation
from traditional wife to feminist partner as they used
Psychosynthesis to navigate challenging emotional and
spiritual waters. Now in their 80s, they continue to be
creative through teaching, mentoring, and writing. The
peaceful contentment of their current life is inspiring, and
Anne's commentary about the spiritual journey of relationship is especially beautiful.

CHAPTER ELEVEN

Learning To Love: From 1964 to Yesterday Afternoon

Anne Eastman Yeomans

Part I: A Story of Two, Told by One

In 1964 when I was 24, at a very inopportune time in my life, as I was already engaged to be married to someone else, I fell in love with a handsome, charming, and deeply intelligent man. I have spent the last 57 years learning to know Tom, myself, and us as a married couple.

This is a story of two, and I can only tell it from my viewpoint. I'm sure there is much I still can't see, and don't understand, even though I have put a lot of my attention on our relationship for years. As the old expression goes, *love is blind*. There is definitely truth to that.

Our First Real Meeting

Sitting in the dark on the grass behind a house where a party was going on, we shyly spoke about many things that were important to both of us, books we had loved, scenes from D.H. Lawrence novels that we both remembered, experiences in college, adventures, traveling in Europe, our families, our lives, our hopes and dreams for the future. We were young.

That night I found myself sharing things I had never told anyone before. They were things I cared so much about, but which had found little resonance over the course of my life. By the quality of his listening and his responses, I could tell that what I said didn't puzzle him, nor was he judging me to be strange or weird. What's more, he seemed to be interested and perhaps even to understand. *There is something beautiful and rare here*, I thought silently to myself.

I was speaking to him about my inner world, a deep and private internal experience that I had been aware of since I was young. My name for it was "the secret world." Later that evening as I listened to him speak, I noticed that he was looking at the ground as he talked. I realized that he also felt shy and cautious about sharing the deep places inside himself. I wondered if he knew about "the secret world" too.

As we sat together on the grass in the dark behind the house, which was still alive with the sounds and lights of the party, time seemed to disappear. When it began to rain gently, we didn't run for shelter. We could hear thunder and see lightning in the distance, and we stayed. Something about this moment, this sense of connection, and of being understood, held us both. Two deep and lonely souls were finding each other. It was the beginning of a long journey, with many adventures, many trials, and so much learning.

Before this moment, our lives had circled each other. We had crossed paths a number of times. We had even been in the same room once in college, but had never spoken to each other. Mysteriously, we both remember that moment. We had a number of friends in common, but we were in different social circles and were coping with college life in very different ways. This night, sitting in the rain, with the thunder and lightning in the distance, was our first real meeting, and it changed each of us forever.

These lines from Mary Oliver come to me now:

> Not anyone who says, "I'm going to be
>   careful and smart in matters of love,"
> who says, "I'm going to choose slowly,"
> but only those lovers who didn't choose at all
> but were, as it were, chosen
> by something invisible
> and powerful and uncontrollable
> and beautiful and possibly even
> unsuitable—
> only those know what I'm talking about
> in this talking about love.[1]

"The Times They Are a-Changin'" —*Bob Dylan*

For the story of our relationship to make any sense at all, I need to place it within the huge cultural shifts of the mid to late 1960s when we first met. We were in college during the time of the Civil Rights movement. John Kennedy had just been elected president. Though Tom and I did not yet know each other, we both remember Robert Frost trying to read his poem at the Inauguration while the wind blew his papers. We were ignited by the hope this new young president brought to the nation. It was the time of the birth of the Peace Corps. We heard his call when he said, "Ask not what your country can do for you—ask what you can do for your country."

We believed him when he said, "the torch has been passed to a new generation." We, like so many others, were inspired by his words and by his outlook, so full of possibilities.

Then, suddenly, he was gone. The shock of his assassination and, in the next five years, the assassinations of Robert Kennedy and Martin Luther King, shook us all profoundly. Hopes were dashed. The country mourned in a way that had never happened before in the years I could remember.

The Civil Rights movement continued, followed by a new awareness of the atrocities of the Vietnam War and the protests against the war, the women's movement, the sexual revolution, and the environmental movement. Over the same period, there was also an expansion of consciousness through psychedelics and meditation, as well as through a host of new psychotherapies, sometimes referred to as "the human potential movement," of which Psychosynthesis was a part. It was an extraordinary time of change, like nothing we had ever seen before in our lives. The epicenter of so much of this was San Francisco and that is exactly where we headed the very night after our afternoon wedding in the suburbs of Chicago in July of 1965.

As one of my college friends said to me many years later, "When we graduated we were all trying to do it right, find a good husband, get married, live by the social norms, but within two years, all the rules had changed." She was right. That huge cultural upheaval had many implications for the relationships between men and women, and for us as a young couple just starting out.

Changing Relationships Between Men and Women

When I married Tom in the summer of 1965, I was thinking, "Here's a good man. I want to learn to love him well, create a beautiful and welcoming home, have a family, and maybe do some part-time teaching while I raise our children." I was *not* thinking, "Who am I? What do I care about? What do I want to do with my life? Is there work outside the home that I want to prepare myself to do? How will I do that and be married and have children?" If the year had been 1970, I would have been asking those questions, but in 1965, when we married, they were nowhere in my mind. Nowhere!

In one sense, you could say I really wasn't an "I" yet. I had little "agency." I was looking for a man, and planning on being his intelligent and devoted wife. Without really being aware of it, I was also thinking I would find my worth and identity through him, even though I had been a leader in both high school and college. The real journey to find myself was still ahead, and with it would come challenges to our relationship and to the unconscious contract we had entered into with our marriage.

As Dylan sang, "The times they are a-changin'"—and it was true. By the early 1970s, I was asking new questions, and so were a lot of other women around me. By this time we were living in Santa Barbara, California, where Tom was going to graduate school. We had two little boys and I was home taking care of them. I was still in my young woman's dream of married life, but it was beginning to unravel. It took several years, and a lot of pain and fear, but slowly I began to realize that part of why I was feeling so unhappy and alienated was that I was listening and giving to everyone except myself, and that my sense of myself before being married had pretty much disappeared.

Climbing Out of Patriarchy

I remember being at a graduate school party where wives were invited, and a beautiful young graduate student sat down beside me. She was very engaged in working on her doctorate in education. Unlike me, she was not married and not a mother. She asked me about my life, and at one point she leaned very close to me and whispered, as if she were bringing a message in code from the outside world, "Anne, a lot is happening out there for women." She was, of course, referring to the women's movement. I remember that moment to this day. At the time I'm not sure I fully understood what she was talking about, for I was still immersed in babies, diapers, and dishes, but somewhere inside me, I knew not to forget what she had said.

Not long after that conversation, my lovely dream of married life began to crash. I had fantasies of hurling things against the garage wall. I put away all the big knives on the top shelves in the kitchen (I didn't understand why, but I knew I felt better when I couldn't see them!). Tom was going to the university each day to work on his doctorate and, though it is hard for me to believe now, I was making sandwiches for him to take with him before he left. I'm not sure where that impulse came from. He had never asked me to, nor do I ever remember my mother doing anything of the kind. It probably came from imagining what a "good wife" would do and trying so hard to be one. But all that giving was rapidly wearing thin, and we both still remember the day I resigned. I said, "I'm not making those sandwiches anymore, and anyway, if you knew what was in them, you wouldn't want to eat them: They are filled with nails and screws."

Feminism was in the air, and though I wasn't ready to embrace it all, it was affecting me. It brought with it a clearer articulation of the presence of patriarchy in our society. It included a profound reexamination of the power dynamics between men and women, as well as awareness of the constrictions of gender roles as they had been defined up until then. Patriarchy as a social structure is a system which gives more power and value to men than to women. Ultimately it limits all of us, and, when we are unaware of it, it stands in the way of the equal, mutual and respectful relationships between the sexes.[2]

I sometimes refer to these years in my own life as the years of "climbing out of patriarchy," both the patriarchy of the outer world that gives more value and power to men than to women, but also out of "the internalized patriarchy" that I and many, many women had taken inside themselves, without even being aware of it. [3]

I had a real encounter with my own internalized patriarchy at one point early in my marriage. It is not an easy story to tell, for it brings with it both shame and embarrassment, but I tell it with the hope that it will help other women see something within themselves that is limiting them, as this was severely limiting me without my knowing it.

Here is what happened: One day I heard a voice in my head clearly say, "You are nothing. Find a man who is something and then you will be something too." I was shocked. It had apparently been there all along, and I had been struggling with its impact without realizing it. Being able to recognize this voice and its devastating message meant I was no longer controlled, or unconsciously identified with it in the same way. I would have thoughts like this again, but now, I also would have the possibility of recognizing them and choosing not to believe them.

An unconscious thought like this feels generational. I imagine my mother and my foremothers back through time had similar thoughts, which were probably unconscious to them as well. There is great freedom in finding an internalized thought of self-negation and making it conscious. This was a very significant step in my own "inner liberation."

The Middle Years

I call this next period the middle years, or the "householder years" as the Hindus say. They took place first in California and later in Concord, Massachusetts.

It was during the California years that we discovered Psychosynthesis, an approach to psychological and spiritual growth, which had been developed in the early 1900s by the Italian psychiatrist Roberto Assagioli. We were completely inspired by his vision and the power of his conception of the human being. We worked tirelessly with a group of about twenty others to teach and practice Psychosynthesis, both in San Francisco and in other parts of the country.

These middle years were incredibly full and busy. As we look back now, we wonder how we did it all. We were raising two lively boys whom we adored and wanted the best for. We were attending soccer games and school meetings and getting dinner on the table. All four of our parents, who lived some distance from us, were aging and needed our help. Both Tom and I were working by now as psychotherapists and teaching training programs and workshops, which often involved travel.

With so much activity, there was inevitably plenty of stress in our relationship, and little time for romance or downtime. We had to steal time for both, and we did. From time to time, when we were living in California, we would leave San Francisco for the East Bay and spend 24 hours at the Claremont, which was a grand old and, at that time, affordable hotel, where we made love, ate well, and slept late. In the morning we walked the streets of Berkeley and talked and talked. It was always renewing and brought us back to the depth and passion of our original bond. How reassuring to find that our deep connection was still vibrant, and that, even in 24 hours, we could find it again. It was as if we were the ones who had been gone, and the love between us was there waiting for our return.

Tom and I were held together by our many responsibilities to our family and to work we loved and shared. At the same time I was continuing to forge ahead to find my voice, to listen for my own path, to claim my value as an equal partner in this relationship, and to dispel the voices of the internalized patriarchy, which I had swallowed without knowing it. I was relentless in my pursuit of my larger life, making up for lost time.

These became challenging and stormy years for us. There was a sea change afoot in our couple. I desperately needed witnessing, needed the experience of being seen and affirmed as a person and as a deep, passionate, intelligent and creative woman. Tom, who was intent about his own career trajectory, wasn't able to offer that in the way I needed during this period.

In 1982, New England called us home, and we moved back to the East Coast to live in Concord, Massachusetts. We both had roots in the East, and Tom, who always had a sense of a full circle, knew that at some point we would return.

It was at that time that I began to immerse myself in female-affirming environments. I began to read and study Women's Spirituality, returned once to California to study for three months, and considered entering a doctoral program there. I facilitated women's circles for many, many years and was a co-founder of a nine-month program in Women's Spirituality, which later became an organization called The Women's Well.[4] I was letting my interests and my newly found passions lead me at last. Having birthed and nurtured two children, I was now intent on giving birth to my Self, and supporting the women in my classes and my groups to do the same.

All the while, profound change was taking place between Tom and myself. That level of change is never smooth and even; it can't be. The whole system between us was shifting. We had outgrown the container that held our relationship. An unconscious contract was being disrupted, and a new balance of equality and mutual respect was emerging. I was the catalyst for this momentum. Tom was trying hard to understand and respond, yet the parts of him that counted on the old ways were frightened and resistant. He was also very preoccupied with the demands of an expanding career as a therapist and in training professionals in Psychosynthesis in both North America and Europe. Couples therapy helped both of us navigate through some of this turbulence. This story of our middle years is, of course, a condensed version of a very complex period in our lives.

Part II: Psychosynthesis: Stories and Practices

Psychosynthesis has never been easy to talk about because it is such a large framework and offers a remarkable number of tools, techniques and practices. Sometimes people mistake a part for the whole. It is a little like the story of the five blind men and the elephant, with one person thinking Psychosynthesis is guided imagery, another that it is meditation, and someone else thinking it is subpersonalities.

Basically, psychosynthesis (with a small "p") is a way of describing the process of unfolding and growth that is inherent in all life. It is the urge in all living things to move toward a greater wholeness and to express more fully the essence of who or what they are. It is the same process that animates the seed to become the sunflower, the acorn to become the oak tree, the caterpillar to become the butterfly, and the child to become the mature human being.

I think it is time for those of us who have practiced Psychosynthesis to realize that this unfolding process also moves two people in a committed partnership toward a more honest, mature, respectful and loving relationship. Just as an individual will inevitably meet his or her blocks and challenges to that deep process of growth, so too will a couple meet theirs and have the opportunity to work them through in order to move forward. As we bring awareness to this unfolding process within us and between us, we can learn to cooperate with it and to trust it. Psychosynthesis, as a field of psychological theory and practice, offers many different tools, techniques and practices to enhance and support a couple's evolution.

How did this orientation help us? First and foremost, it confirmed and strengthened what we both had already sensed was true: There exists a deep process of unfolding within all human beings and thus within ourselves, and we could learn to pay attention to it, to make time for it and to trust it, including trusting that this attention would bear fruit.

Psychosynthesis provided us with a shared orientation. It gave us a context in common, a set of principles and a language for talking about them. It also meant that, as individuals in a committed relationship, we were not only interested in our own awakening, but in learning how to encourage and support the growth and awakening of our partner.

Our Particular Story

We found Psychosynthesis in the early 1970s. As two young seekers in our early life, we had always been asking what I call the "big questions": Who am I? Why are we here? How do we go deeper? What is life all about? We each had those questions even before we met.

After we married and relocated to the Bay Area in California, we soon found ourselves in the epicenter of "the human potential movement." Tom was trying to figure out his career, and his goals were determining where we would go next. He first taught at a school outside of San Francisco, and then decided to go to graduate school. I was in the support role of wife and mother. By 1970, and several graduate programs later, we moved to Santa Barbara, where he studied for a doctorate in Education and Psychology at U.C. Santa Barbara. There he was introduced to Roberto Assagioli's book *Psychosynthesis*. When he saw what is known as the "egg diagram," Assagioli's picture of the psyche and its different levels of consciousness, he knew immediately that this was what he had been looking for all along.

At the time, I was a person who knew things more immediately through my lived experience, rather than through my mind. So my "aha" about Psychosynthesis came not through a diagram, but through a long guided daydream in a Psychosynthesis workshop, led by Jim and Susan Vargiu. I had an experience of meeting an Earth mother and a deeply loving father inside myself. I wept as I experienced the healing power of the symbolic processes within. After that first workshop, I knew with complete certainty that this work was profound and that we needed to pursue it. Tom agreed wholeheartedly.

Tom was still in graduate school in Santa Barbara when we learned that the Vargius, who had studied in Florence with Roberto Assagioli and then were part of the group that introduced Psychosynthesis to the Esalen Institute in Big Sur, were offering a training program in Psychosynthesis in the Bay Area.

Though it seems impossible now, we drove the 300 miles to those training weekends from Santa Barbara with our three-year-old, Peter, chattering away in the backseat. Nothing was going to keep us from what we both sensed would change our lives in deeply meaningful ways. And indeed it did.

After the training we continued to study with the Vargius whenever we could get up to Redwood City where they lived. Then, in the fall of 1972, with their encouragement, we traveled to Italy with our boys—Peter, now four, and Benjamin, just nine months old and still nursing—to study with Assagioli.

Roberto Assagioli was an Italian psychiatrist living in Florence, who had been a contemporary of Freud and Jung and who had developed the basic tenets of Psychosynthesis in 1911, as a medical student at the age of 23. When we met him he was 84. Roberto, as he was lovingly called by many of those who went to see him, was fond of saying "one thing for one person, and for another, quite the opposite." And that is the way he worked with us.

To Tom, the scholar and graduate student, he said, "I don't want you to read any more books while you are here. I want you to spend more time in silence and contemplation. Just walk in the countryside, open yourself to the beauty of the Italian landscape and visit the art museums of Florence. I want you to enjoy the many gifts of this city, and its art treasures." There was a day when Tom spent the whole afternoon sitting in a yellow canvas chair behind our pensione in Fiesole looking out across the hills dotted with olive trees, toward the red tile roofs of Florence beyond, silently opening himself to life's mysteries.

To me, he said, "Take this article on women I have written. Some women have liked it a lot, but others have had a very strong negative reaction to it. I want you to read it and critique it. I'm an old man now and I need your help with it." How pleased I was with my new assignment! I, who had spent many days in my life reflecting on life's mysteries, was now closeted in my hotel room working with focused consciousness and great intensity on the article Roberto Assagioli had given me. I was working with words, with my mind, trying to articulate my experience, trying to put form to what had been intuitive knowing for so long. Our children were exploring Florence with a young American, whom we had hired to take them out each day.

The meetings with Roberto Assagioli in the fall of 1972 were a privilege and a gift beyond measure. His keen intuition and his uncanny ability to see deeply, allowed him to clarify where we were in our life's journey and what the tasks ahead would be for each of us.

"This is your work," he said to Tom; and "This is your work," he said to me. For one person, one thing, for another quite the opposite. He was right then, and almost 50 years later we would both agree he is still right. He had named our respective life tasks.

Masculine and Feminine Principles Within our Relationship

When I apply the principles of masculine and feminine[5] to our relationship, I would say that in the beginning of our marriage, I was very identified with the feminine, and Tom was very identified with the masculine, and in love with the feminine in me. I, in turn, admired him so much and counted on him for planning, direction, and solving outer world tasks and challenges. As a very shy person, I also counted on him to take the lead socially, and at times, to even be the life of the party.

We had each projected aspects of ourselves onto the other partner and had fallen in love with them. In the course of our long marriage, we would need to take back those projections, find the disowned parts of ourselves, learn to embrace them, and eventually to integrate them. This of course was no small task. It is, in fact, a major task of our lifetime together.

There was a therapist along the way who said to us at a point of crisis in our marriage, "You will become each other." In many ways, that has been true.

How did Psychosynthesis Help?

I consider the following five principles and practices from Psychosynthesis essential to the strength and well-being of our relationship. They do not belong only to Psychosynthesis, but to many psychological and spiritual traditions that emphasize self-knowledge and self-awareness.

> 1. *There is an unfolding process within everyone, and the direction of its movement is from fragmentation and separation toward greater wholeness and integration.*

Because we came to Psychosynthesis together, we shared this orientation. How did it help us as a couple? I know it helped me have faith that when Tom was going through difficult times, his struggles were part of a deeper process within himself, a process that I trusted profoundly. Sometimes I trusted it more than he did. On my best days (which of course were not all days), that trust helped me let go when I might have worried or thought I should give him advice. Sometimes it helped me to remind him of that inner process, or say something like, "Have you meditated today or talked to the wise person inside yourself?" (a Psychosynthesis practice for accessing inner wisdom). Sometimes the expression of my trust was silent. As we know there are non-verbal ways of being with someone, a touch or a loving smile, that convey, *I know you will find your way.* Learning to offer this silent presence to another is a great gift.

This first principle also gave me a way to explore the processes of change within myself. In my essay "Self-Care During Dark Times"[6] I describe a period of profound transformation in my own life and the lens I used to come to understand it. This principle places trust in the inner process of awakening within each of us, and it assumes that, just as the acorn holds the pattern of the oak tree and will guide it, the essence of me, or my Self, holds the pattern of my unfolding as well. The same holds true for my partner. So as committed partners, the work of the relationship is learning how to support the unfolding process within the other, as well as to ask for and to receive one's partner's support for our own inner development. In other words, can we find the place in ourselves that wants our partner to be all that they can be? I once heard Stephen Levine, the late Buddhist teacher, refer to this experience as "going to God together." This generosity of spirit comes not from guilt or obligation, but from a full, generous and awakened heart.

> 2. *There is an inner life in all of us that is rich with symbols, wisdom and guidance. We can cultivate the practice of turning inward to access this deep wisdom and intuitive knowing and learn to let it guide us.*

Do you remember "the secret world" that I referred to earlier, the place inside myself, which I knew as a child? That secret world was my name for the experience of my inner world. I have found deep strength in this world of dreams and visions, in the power of symbols and the imagination, and in the practice of learning to listen for inner guidance and trusting what is invisible. How did this help us as a couple? For one thing, in an extroverted, action-oriented, materialistic culture like our own, if you have those tendencies, it can feel lonely, and at times even a bit crazy or weird. To have company in trusting what cannot be seen is a precious gift.

Tom and I have both been keeping journals and writing down our dreams for many years. We tell each other significant dreams, as well as hold with respect the symbols that have come to have meaning and guidance for each of us. I can say, "Remember that dream that I had about the girl standing by the inlet, and how at the end of the dream she suddenly looked up and saw the sun so bright and powerful and burst into tears." Tom will know what I am talking about, even though that dream is probably close to 50 years old and is still teaching me. On my side, sometimes when I am listening to Tom talk about what is going on in him, an old dream of his will come into my mind unbidden and I will tell him. Or another time, when he was troubled about something, I saw an image of his father, and he realized he was dealing with a way of being he had inherited from his dad that was no longer useful. This kind of insight comes when you decide to trust intuitive knowing and to be open to the inner world.

A word of warning: Do not forget the place for discrimination in this kind of work. One can get overly identified or attached to this way of knowing, and misuse it. The work with inner wisdom is a practice, and like all things, we get better at it with time and attention.

3. *Self-awareness matters, and it matters a lot.*

This principle involves the practice of learning to self-observe. It is learning to look at one's own experience in the moment with clarity and with compassion, rather than with criticism and self-judgment. It is an essential skill for relationships. It involves a commitment to knowing what's going on inside you, and learning about your own reactivity in relationship to your partner. This is both a moment-to-moment practice and the practice of a lifetime, for it is never over. We can always practice self-awareness. Rumi writes in one of his most beautiful poems, "Don't go back to sleep."[7]

How did the practice of self-awareness help us? The examples are myriad. One of the most important places in the awareness work of a couple is learning to look at what we project on the other. By projection, I mean seeing outside oneself what is really within oneself. I came to our relationship with a big father wound. I knew this, but in many ways I didn't know it, nor did I understand how it might impact my relationship with my husband. (But how could it not!) I had inside me a girl who never had had a loving, steadfast, and truly trustworthy relationship with her father, the first man in my life. My father was a man with his own deep wounds and he was not able to love in a generous, or reliable way.

I came to the marriage with an unfulfilled longing for a connection with a father I could count on. Over time I grew to understand this more. I learned that when Tom disappointed me, there was the first level of whatever caused the disappointment between us, and then there was the deep well of disappointment under it, which seemed at times bottomless. That wound came from the first 25 years of my life. It had the power to pull me under and sink me for a long time. I also had times of touching a fury that was so much more than what I knew the present situation merited. Yet it was there. The source of that fury is still unknown to me, but I continue to be very interested in it.

The late Mary Butler, a therapist in Chicago, said to me that the more she worked with couples in the present, the more she came to believe that 90% of the trouble was from the unresolved issues in the past. It was a very useful concept, and we began to learn to say to each other, "I think I was in my 90%." As you can imagine, it was often quite hard to admit. Sometimes it took a few days or so before we could actually say it. The first impulse is to insist that what is wrong is all about right now, and it is all the fault of the other person. In truth, both the 10% and the 90% need our skillful attention.

Another pattern I brought from my relationship with my father was that I learned that the only way to know him was to vanish my own needs and become a harmless presence. Only then would my father feel safe enough to talk. As a result, I became a very good listener and a skillful questioner. I knew how to give my full attention to a man, without registering my own needs.

Like all unconscious patterns, the more I was able to recognize and understand it, the more freedom I had from it. As I did, I was able to begin to disidentify from it, and to work to seek a relationship of more balance and mutuality.

What were Tom's projections? This is a place where the problem of a "story of two told by one" comes in. If I were to guess, his projection was about the feminine, about sensitivity, intuition, and vulnerability. It was safer for him to see his vulnerability in me than in himself. Then he could take care of me, but not have to feel vulnerable. I sense that I was also, at times, his muse, and inspiration for some of his creative work.

As we recognized these projections and their power over us, we were more able to meet the present together, and to speak directly about what we felt and thought and what we truly needed. It's a work of a lifetime, but as we grew in awareness, the relationship got better, more alive, more honest, and a lot more fun.

4. *The practice of presence toward oneself and another.*

The practice of presence is completely related to self-awareness. In fact, it can be thought of as another way to say the same thing. Learning to be present to myself requires turning inward and beginning to observe my experience moment to moment with compassion and non-judgment. A daily practice of mindful meditation helps to develop this capacity.

In a relationship the question becomes, "can I be present to my partner or spouse, and what keeps me from that?" Ultimately the question is, "can I be present to myself and also to my partner at the same time?" That is "the advanced course," and the one that is never really over.

Certainly, Tom's and my ability to be present to each other has grown tremendously over the years, as our self-knowledge has grown. We have even learned to say to each other, *I need your full presence now. Can you listen to me and not give me advice, or try to fix me, but just be here with me as I speak about what is on my mind?*

In the beginning of our marriage, Tom felt that when I was unhappy, he needed to do something to help. He would often offer solutions like "maybe you should do this" or "maybe try this". It took a while for us to figure it out, but over time, I became aware that, for the most part, what I really needed was his being there with me, not his solutions. I needed his presence. In turn he began to look at how oriented he was, as a man, to problem-solving and finding solutions when someone was having trouble, especially his wife. He learned to say to me, "I have some thoughts about this; do you want to hear them?" This approach gave me a choice and made a tremendous difference. Sometimes I did want them, but not always.

I have my own version of this. I was a good listener—in a way, too good. As I have said, I learned early on to listen to my father by actually disappearing myself and being there for him. I became skilled at turning away from the information in my body, my feelings and needs, and giving my full attention to another. It was a completely unconscious pattern, and I think I did it often early in our marriage without realizing it. Over the years, I began to be able to observe this pattern, understand where it came from, step back from it, and give birth to a more balanced way of being present. This included listening to myself and my own needs, as well as to what was going on for Tom.

It was a long process, and, as I have said earlier, the shift created a deep change in our relationship. Tom lost me as "the selfless other" as I began to listen to myself and give credence to my own needs, feelings, and thoughts. It was a turbulent time for us. The system between us was being profoundly changed. Of course, we were not the only couple in America making that shift. It was going on in the collective as well.

Now we can both look back on that time and realize that it was an absolutely essential step that allowed each of us to differentiate and individuate in new ways; it was completely needed in order for our relationship to grow and deepen. Our capacity to be present to each other has grown exponentially as a result.

5. The practice of learning how to speak to each other with respect, clarity and care, even when it is difficult.

In common parlance, this practice is known as learning communication skills. Our friends and colleagues Rich and Antra Borofsky sometimes call it the practice of Giving and Receiving. Like the previous practices I've mentioned, it is enhanced by our own self-knowledge and by learning to speak directly about our own experience without blame or shame. This would include learning to know what we are feeling, knowing what we need, and learning how to ask for it. It would also include learning about our own reactivity and becoming more aware of our partner's needs, vulnerabilities and strengths.

It also involves listening, not just with our ears and with our head, but with the whole body, including our heart. I remember a couples therapist saying to Tom, "can you stop and really receive what Anne is saying?" He stopped, and took a breath. I spoke again, and this time he took in what I was saying with his in-breath. I could see it happen. I could see the energy of my words enter his body. Something in him softened. How relieved I felt. I needed so much more than his hearing the words. I needed him to receive my words in a way that would impact him, perhaps even change him.

Here is another example from our life together where we needed all the communication skills we had ever learned and more. At one point along the way, when our children had either finished college or were about to finish, I began to focus more fully on my own work with women and women's groups. I learned about a graduate program in California, which I was very interested in pursuing. At the time, Tom was running training programs in Psychosynthesis and Spiritual Psychology on the East Coast and in several countries in Europe.

I proposed that we move back to the West Coast so I could go to graduate school there. This was a break from earlier patterns in our marriage where I had always followed the trajectory of Tom's interests and career, as both of our mothers had followed their husbands. My proposal created a major crisis in our marriage and led us straight into couple's therapy. Our goal in the therapy was to find a way for me to try out the program for a semester, and to identify some agreed-upon ways of staying in touch. (This was before the Internet, Skype, or FaceTime).

It was a stormy time for each of us and for our couple. It was a time that brought up some of our deepest fears, and as well as plenty of reactivity in our conversations. I was listening to my own self in new ways and giving validity to the call of my own path and my deeper Self. I was asking Tom to come into relationship with me now as a person no longer only identified as his wife, but as a woman who had a path of her own and a responsibility to listen to it.

Now, looking back, we both know that, though that time was very difficult, it was essential to our maturing, both individually and as a couple. My core learning was to claim my life as valuable and important, which included facing my deepest fear—that if I let go of Tom, I would lose him. His challenge was to experience new levels of vulnerability and to face his unconscious dependence on me, of which he had been quite unaware.

The result was that we grew in consciousness, and we survived. In fact, we more than survived. We became more whole in ourselves, and also more deeply connected to each other. Learning to communicate with respect was fundamental to our process.

It is in these times of crisis (*dangerous opportunity* as the Chinese say) when couples sometimes lose each other, separate or divorce. We worked on staying connected to each other while I claimed more of myself and my own path. Slowly, we learned to find that balance. I am so glad.

In my therapy practice, I often say to people who are struggling in a relationship, "Is this the person you want to do the work with?" I think it is such an important question, because sustaining a long-term relationship does indeed take work.

Part III: Where We Are Now

Is it all work and no play? Of course not! I have written about some of our most challenging times to show how Psychosynthesis helped us navigate them. Yet there is of course an essential place for fun, pleasure, the daily rituals of connection, for hugs and kisses, both tender and passionate, and for the laughter that heals.

These days we laugh more than we used to. Way more. We both work hard, but we take time out for walks, dinners out, movies, cooking together, kisses. Sometimes we dance in the kitchen. We always sit down to eat dinner together when we are both home. We set the table and often light candles. It might seem like nothing, but I've been amazed to learn how many people don't eat together in the evening. For us, preparing and sharing the evening meal is a time of pleasure and connection.

We also have tea together when we are both home in the late afternoon. Sometimes we say to each other, "I will be home for tea." If we can't be there, we will often call each other and just check in at teatime. Nothing like a little caffeine and a cookie at four, say I! It wouldn't be everyone's pleasure I am sure, but it is one of ours. Having tea is a pause toward the end of the afternoon, where we catch up with each other, and tell the stories of the day. Often we make tea in a teapot and use cups that have been warmed. It is a ritual, which draws on our English and Scottish roots. Our ancestors did this too.

I call this one of the "small rituals." There is a pattern to it that we both count on, and it is one of the forms of daily connection between us. Think about your small rituals, your rituals of connection. I imagine you have them if you look. If not, create some. They can be simple, but they can become something you and your partner count on, a time that brings renewal and pleasure, and through which you reconnect and feel closer.

It has been 55 years since we first met. Our life is much calmer now. In 2005 we moved to an old farmhouse in the country in western Massachusetts. We have a big garden, rows of berries, and we can see cows in the field across the street and occasionally a fox or a flock of wild turkeys. We know more about the ways of the natural world than ever before. We both love it here, and we don't want to leave. The balance between us has shifted to be more one of mutual respect and support. Though we are still working, Tom now has a much lighter schedule and is painting, and I was surprised to find that there were poems in me that wanted expression. He went through his own deepening crisis, which allowed him to be more present to me and to the relationship than in the early years. We enjoy each other's company more than ever. Our boys are married men now, with their own families, living in other parts of the country. Psychosynthesis has been integrated into our lives and our work in both explicit and implicit ways.

We have had the great privilege of many years together. In hindsight, I think we needed every minute. There are no adequate words to express what a precious gift it has been to have a partner in the long journey of awakening, including through very challenging times of change and growth. If you are so fortunate to find someone to travel with you, to live life beside you, with whom you share a core of values, and a commitment to growing in awareness, to waking up even through the hard times, don't lose them. This kind of company is precious. This is something I knew intuitively that first night, sitting outside in the dark.

It doesn't mean the road isn't rough and bumpy, and that it doesn't have some very challenging and unexpected turns. It means that you and your partner, if you are fortunate to have one, can learn to be a match for it. If you stay connected to each other, and are willing to keep learning and growing, you will become wiser from living through those times, and you will be closer to each other because of meeting those challenges together. Your capacity to love and understand will grow and deepen.

Death Makes the Heart Grow Fonder

Now we are both over 80 and we live with a profound new aware-ness: the awareness of the presence of death. We have lost and are losing dear friends, family members and colleagues. This is a poem I wrote about this time, in 2009:

The Last Trimester

We are in the time now when people die—

not mothers and fathers,

who have been gone for a while, but good friends and colleagues,

people we have worked beside for years,

siblings, who have been here always,

classmates and cousins,

those we have loved

and those we have struggled with.

Not that people aren't being born— ah yes, adorable, tiny ones

with faces full of hope

are arriving every day,

but foreground for us now

are those who are going away.

Yes, I know death has happened before,

but then we thought it was the exception,

not the rule.

We know that, unless we die together, like the two characters in the poignant movie *The Notebook*, one of us will die before the other. The other will be alone in ways he or she has not been for over fifty years.

In new and vivid ways, we know that this life is not forever. As my poem expresses, that has always been true, but now that truth accompanies us. We wish each other and our close friends good health as well as happiness on birthday cards. I never said that in my 30s. The awareness of death changes everything and teaches us to let go of things about each other that used to bother us. We count our blessings. We complain when our bodies hurt and then we quickly remind ourselves it could be much worse. We "knock on wood" more than ever.

I haven't let go of everything, but I am more skillful and less reactive now. I'm glad about that, and I'm sure Tom is too. He is more in touch with his sensitivity and is aware of how challenging it was to keep that alive, as a man born in the 1940s. As we all know, it was a time when the gender roles were narrow and prescribed for both men and women. As Tom has claimed his sensitivity and vulnerability, he is able to be more present, to listen more deeply and to express his love for me more directly. Like so many men, the patriarchy gave him a certain kind of power, but no room for him to own and share feelings, vulnerability and the more sensitive parts of his nature. As I have said, patriarchy limits us all.

The Learning, the Wonder and the Mystery

When I look back now it is so clear to me that these 55 years have been a journey of learning. What a wonderful frame that is for a committed relationship. Maybe that is, in fact, what commitment means—the willingness to learn together.

Our relationship has been a journey of finding and losing, a journey of getting up again and finding again, a journey of adventure and discovery. It has been a courageous journey for which I am very proud and forever grateful.

You can read all the books written on couples, and there are now more than ever. You can take training in Psychosynthesis, non-violent communication, internal family systems, somatic experiencing, sexual enhancement, and yet none of them can explain why two people come together, and what they are here to learn and to figure out. It is a wonder that Tom and I even found each other in the first place, that we had the courage to break social expectations and to marry—a wonder that we stayed connected through a time of enormous cultural change, and a wonder that we have had this much time to learn to know both ourselves and each other.

When we left Roberto Assagioli for the last time in the fall of 1972, he said to us, with a smile and a twinkle in his eyes, "Remember to leave a little room for the mystery." Here is my offering on behalf of the mystery inherent in relationship:

A deep bow–

To the mystery of two who choose to take this journey together.

To the mystery of what they will learn from each other, and what they will teach each other, and learn together.

To the mystery of my being here with you and of your being here with me.

May all couples open to this mystery and grow in awareness and love.

POSTSCRIPT

Put Your Marriage Among the Stars

Piero Ferrucci

During my training with Assagioli I was called to the military service (at that time compulsory for every Italian male citizen). Luckily, for most of the time I was stationed in Florence, and managed to see Assagioli in the late afternoons and weekends. Perhaps because he knew I was alone in the city, he often invited me for lunch on Sunday.

Lunchtime included three people: Assagioli, his wife Nella, and me. Meals were served by Assagioli's faithful maid, Carmela. The trouble with this setting was that Assagioli was deaf and his wife was in the final stages of dementia. What Nella said usually did not make much sense. Assagioli would at times make notable or surprising statements, but without any specific context. I, for my part, easily felt awkward in almost any social situation. So the conversation resembled more the Theatre of the Absurd than an actual discourse. And yet I would come out of those lunches in great spirits, and always looking forward to the next. That largely happened because I could see how Assagioli treated his wife, always including her with a smile or a gentle remark. I was touched by how kind and caring with her he was. That was what life offered him at that time; that was what he would make the best of.

Let's face it: sooner or later every relationship, one way or another, comes to an end. How do you walk that final stretch, often the hardest and trickiest? Assagioli did it in an admirable way, with patience, humor, and heartfelt caring. About Nella I cannot say much. I met her towards the end of her existence. Once a vital and intelligent woman, I am sure she must have suffered immensely from the persecution her husband had been subjected to, not to mention the death of their son.

Later, in recalling these (for me) precious moments, I understood what a great experiential lesson that had been, much stronger than anything I would learn from theory. This is the School of Marriage, a significant part of the greater School of Life. Every situation, so the teaching goes, inherently contains the possibility of learning deep lessons, or of tapping hidden resources. In the School of Marriage we are challenged, given riddles to solve, and obstacles to face. Here we find an enormous variety of learnings: about ourselves, about coexisting with a mate and children who may be hugely different from us; about supporting one another, and walking together the easy or rough paths of existence. This is the School of Marriage, the only school where, as poet Charity Nduhiu says in her poem of that name,[1] you get your certificate before starting the course.

If there is one learning I got from Assagioli above all else, it would be caring for the quality of a relationship. In the couple, in education, in psychotherapy, everywhere. That is the one value from which all else derives. Do you want to be a good psychotherapist, do you want your marriage to work, do you want your students or your children to flourish, do you hope to get along with your friends and associates, and with yourself? Then what you want to care about most is the quality of your attention, your kindness and warmth, your capacity to understand and to be patient. That is what counts, in marriage as everywhere else. Not the details of what you do or don't do. Who does the cooking and how money is dealt with, what you do with the in-laws, and who takes the children to school, all the usual matters, important and unimportant, become so much less heavy if we view them in the light of the great transpersonal qualities: love, peace, awe, honesty, and so on. Not that it is easy; in fact, it requires a lifetime of work.

Now here is a piece of good news. There is a shortcut to this high goal, a way of making life easier for us, as Psychosynthesis vows to do. And that is to perceive the other as a Self. The Self, as we all know, is that part of us which is not immersed in time but lives in timelessness. It has no age, it has no gender. It has no preconceived ideas or agendas. This thought in itself is tremendously liberating. Apply it to yourself to begin with: you are a Self. Then apply it to any relationship, and the context is shifted. If you see the person before you as a concrete entity in space and time, who may have strong differences with you, who did not come to this earth with the purpose of pleasing you, who may have ideas and projects that clash with yours, you can find yourself in trouble, because both of you will be limited by mental structures. If you rise above this, and see the other as a timeless Self, you perceive them as inherently free; you see infinity, you see sacredness; issues of gender, privileges, structures, expectations, disappear. What seemed to be a gigantic issue becomes a much easier task, which we can tackle. With a bit of good will.

Assagioli took this idea very seriously. He called it *namaskar*, the Sanskrit word meaning "I salute the divine in you." At some point he suggested I apply it to my clients in therapy. But he did not just suggest it, he reminded me of it. The next day he asked me: "Did you use *namaskar*?" No, I had forgotten. After a while he asked me again: "Did you do it?" No, I had forgotten again. From that day on I was more diligent.

But what happens if we don't do that? It is easy to forget, and to follow the habitual way. What happens if we see one another not for what we essentially are, but for what we are not; if we take a fragment for the whole, the mask for the underlying face, the transient for the eternal? As we relate with one another in this faulty way, we have multiple cases of mistaken identity. Now, imagine living for twenty years with a fictional version of your husband or wife or children; or a heavily fallacious one, as with distorting mirrors. Or imagine a society in which everybody sees other people for what they are not, exchanging them for their surface traits, subpersonalities or roles. This is indeed a big risk, and it is always present.

The remedy, however, is simple (at least in principle). We can learn to see the Self in each of us. Most importantly, in our mate and in our children. We can manage to perceive their inner beauty, maybe a beauty that is forgotten or concealed—but it is there. We can learn to see again their creativity, their capacity to love and to be generous. Their honesty. Or whatever other quality may be the note expressed by their Self. Sometimes all of this is buried, deep and forgotten; at other times it is out in the open and active. In all cases we can train ourselves to see it—and to see it is to affirm it. That is the best way of being honest with each other: to go beyond the façade, the roles, the games, and to perceive each other for what we truly are.

There is one other inner device Assagioli was fond of suggesting for elevating the quality of a relationship: enlarge your context. He used to give as a wedding gift to his students a star globe with all the constellations, which could be lit from the inside. The idea was to light it up and then to remind yourself of the immensity of space and time, of all the stars and the lives that populate our galaxy and beyond, so as to put in perspective our concerns and projects. Even if you do not have a star globe, what works is the thought behind it. Assagioli used it at times in meditations with students. The "right proportions" idea is just one way of doing what Psychosynthesis continually prompts us to do: change our perspective, see ourselves from another person's point of view, that of the wise person, our Self, or the stars. If we can't shift perspective, we risk getting stuck. The moment we can, transformation is possible. It's all about flexibility of mind.

There was of course a touch of humor in this idea of putting your marriage among the stars. Your all-important ideas and concerns and demands, your kids, your everyday worries, your quarrels too—put them in the context of the universe, and then think again. Assagioli was amused by the term "Local group," used by astronomers to denominate our galaxy (100 billion stars) together with the Andromeda (one trillion stars), and Triangulum (40 billion stars) galaxies, and a few others; and who knows how many of those stars have planets sustaining life and intelligence. Remember, this is just our immediate neighborhood! What about the rest, the immensity of the known and unknown universe, let alone the multiverse?

So: place your marriage among the stars, and that will help you regain serenity and consider the greater whole that embraces you. It will allow you to take a breath and see, with a greater sense of proportion, our human doings as one brief episode on a small planet traveling through immense space-time. I can guarantee that, seen among a multitude of stars and galaxies, in the midst of immensity, your relationship with your mate and children will take on a radically different feeling.

NOTES

Chapter One: Assagioli's Seven Core Concepts and the Life of the Couple

[1] Rilke, R.M. 1929. *Letters to a Young Poet*, Random House.

[2] Assagioli, R. 1991. *Transpersonal Development: The Dimension Beyond Psychosynthesis*. Crucible.

[3] Assagioli, R. *Archivio Assagioli,* Istituto Di Psicosintesi, Firenze, Italy.

[4] Rabbi Hillel the Elder. First Century C.E. in *Pirkei Avot*, from a section of the Jewish Mishna.

[5] Buber, M. 1923. *I and Thou*. Various English translations available.

[6] Rumi, J. *A Great Wagon*. Version by Barks, C. and Moyne, J. 1999. in Open Secret: Versions of Rumi. Shambhala

[7] Alcott, L. M. 1868. *Little Women*. Various editions available.

[8] Assagioli's "egg diagram" portrays an expansive, dynamic and holistic vision of the human psyche, including both its conscious and unconscious elements as well as the influence of the collective unconscious. This map of the psyche encapsulates the organic process and movement towards greater levels of psychological integration and spiritual maturity, with the self as a central organizing principle and unifying center that is distinct from the contents of consciousness. The dotted lines in the diagram suggest that the process of psychosynthesis supports healthy circulation in the psyche, a sort of "psychological osmosis", and that over time a person may experience profound healing and personal transformation at all levels.

[9] Muir, J. 1911. *My First Summer in the Sierra*. Houghton Mifflin.

[10] See the seminal work by Thomas Yeomans: Yeomans, T. 2020. *Holy Fire: The Process of Soul Awakening*. Concord Institute.

[11] Assagioli, R. 2000. *Psychosynthesis: A Collection of Basic Writings*. Synthesis Center.

Chapter Two: A Marriage of Strong-Willed Partners

[1] Assagioli, R. 1965. *Psychosynthesis: A Manual of Principles and Techniques*. Psychosynthesis Research Foundation. The Viking Press. p.141

[2] See https://www.arica.org.

[3] See https://lynchcancers.com.

[4] *Psychosynthesis: A Manual of Principles and Techniques*, p.24.

[5] See, for example, www.arizonataichichuan.com/links.htm.

Chapter Three: Three Candles: Strategies for a Marriage

[1] Assagioli, R. 1964. Synthesis in Psychotherapy. Address given at the Sixth International Congress of Psychotherapy, London, England, August 1964: 3. Available online at http://synthesiscenter.org/articles/0115.pdf.

[2] Cited in Polt, W. 2011. Polarization, no! Polarities, yes! A call for sharing our keys to interpersonal synthesis. *AAP Newsletter*, Spring 2011: 6-8.

[3] See https://quoteinvestigator.com/2018/02/18/response/.

[4] See Lashley, C.O. 2012. Listening to student concerns: An instructional strategy to expand student perspectives. *Journal of Early Childhood Teacher Educators*, 33: 190-201.

[5] Assagioli, R. 1974. *The Act of Will*. New York: Penguin.

Chapter Four: Growing Together: Reflections on Our Marriage as a Psycho-Spiritual Path

[1] A Zen Buddhist saying.

[2] From Roche, L. 2014. *The Radiance Sutras*. Sounds True. (Translation of the Vijnana Bhairava Tantra)

[3] Huxley, L.A. 1987. *The Child of Your Dreams*. Compcare.

[4] From Rumi, "Spring Giddiness". Available online at at: https://a-poem-a-day-project.blogspot.com/2014/02/day-561-let-beauty-we-love-be-what-we-do.html.

[5] In the poem "Birdwings". Available online at https://lotusheartmindfulness.com/lotus-heart-blog/2019/5/8/birdwings.

Chapter Five: Saying Yes! Two Women, A Love Story

[1] Heteronormativity is the term that is used to describe a set of social norms about sexuality, gender and relationships. (With thanks to my good friend Dr. Angie Fee for the information below.)

Common heteronormative assumptions include:

- There are two, opposite sexes – male and female, with different gender roles, masculine and feminine.

- Women and men are "made for each other," with vaginal penetration of the penis seen as "the" sex act.

- Normal relationships are monogamous and must be sexual.

- Male and female sexuality are seen as naturally different. This is continually produced and reproduced in social practice.

In Western society, heterosexual discourse is based on dualism, e.g.:

- Biological bodies are either male or female.

- Gender identity is either feminine or masculine.

- Sexual orientation is either heterosexual or homosexual.

Chapter Six: Love and Loss

[1] Feurman, M. Your Attachment Style Influences the Success of Your Relationship. Available online at https://www.gottman.com/blog/attachment-style-influences-success-relationship/.

[2] https://kennethsorensen.dk/en/subpersonalities-and-psychotherapy/.

[3] Battista, J. 1996. Abraham Maslow and Roberto Assagioli: Pioneers of Transpersonal Psychology. In B. Scotton , A. Chinen & J. Battista (Eds.). *Textbook of Transpersonal Psychiatry and Psychology*: 9-18. Basic Books:

[4] See https://psychosynthesisresources.com/NieuweBestanden/whatissynthesis.pdf, and Assagioli, R 1974. *The Act of Will*. New Viking/ Penguin.

[5] https://psychosynthesisresources.com/NieuweBestanden/coupletocommunity.pdf

[6] Ibid.

[7] Ibid.

[8] Assagioli, R. Life as a Game and Stage Performance – (Role-playing). Available online at https://psychosynthesisresources.com/NieuweBestanden/life%20as%20a%20game.pdf.

[9] Assagioli, R. 1965. Psychosynthesis—Individual and Social. Online at https://psychosynthesisresources.com/NieuweBestanden/individual_and_social.pdf.

Chapter Seven: Navigating Relationships

[1] His Holiness the Dalai Lama. 1999. From Ethics for the New Millennium. Riverhead Books and Gillon Aitken Associates.

[2] The CDC-Kaiser Permanente adverse childhood experiences (ACE) study is one of the largest investigations of childhood abuse and neglect and household challenges and later-life health and well-being. See https://www.cdc.gov/violenceprevention/aces/about.html.

[3] Bowlby, J. 1900. *Attachment and Loss*. Available online at https://archive.org/details/attachmentlossvo00john.

[4] See Hoffman, K., Cooper, G. and Powell, B. 2017. *Raising a secure child*. Guilford Press.

[5] In addition to those cited above, the following texts have been specifically useful to us in preparing this chapter: Gilligan, C. 1982. *In a different voice*. Harvard University Press; Gottman, J.M. 2011. *The Science of Trust*. Norton.

Chapter Eight: Our Marriage: Enriched by Awareness and Will

[1] Bergler, E. 1994. *Divorce Won't Help*. International Universities Press. The book was first published in 1948.

[2] 2016. Parenting with Wisdom and Compassion: Bring Out the Best in Your Family. Quality Parenting, Culver City, CA.

[3] 2010. *Bring Out the Best in Your Child and Your Self: Creating a Family Based on Mutual Respect*. Quality Parenting, Culver City, CA.

[4] Rinpoche, S. 1992. *The Tibetan Book of Living and Dying*. Revised and updated version edited by P. Gaffney and A. Harvey available online at https://www.freespiritualebooks.com.

Chapter Nine: Synthesis and Service: Living Our Gifts in a Same-Sex Partnership

[1] In Sweasey, P. 1997. *From Queer to Eternity: Spirituality in the Lives of Lesbian, Gay and Bisexual People*. Continuum:28

[2] Wilber, K. 2000. *A Theory of Everything: An Integral Vision for Business, Politics, Science, and Spirituality*. Shambhala.

[3] Dönges, S. and Brunner-Dubey, C. 2005. *Psychosynthese für die Praxis*. Kosel Verlag. There is no English translation available of this book.

[4] Mattman, U. 2006. *Coming In – Gays and Lesbians Reclaiming the Spiritual Journey*. Wild Goose.

[5] Brown, M.Y. 2004. *The Unfolding Self*. Allworth.

[6] Ferrucci, P. 1982. *What We May Be: Techniques for Psychological and Spiritual Growth Through Psychosynthesis*. Putnam.

[7] Websites of the communities where Emmanuel and Urs were and are engaged, and mentioned in this chapter are: Solidarity Fund: https://solidarityfund.jimdofree.com/; Holy Rood House: www.holyroodhouse.org.uk.

[8] The guided imagination is based on an exercise devised by Roberto Assagioli and further developed by Piero Ferrucci in *What We May Be* (see note 6), on which my version is based but with my comments.

Chapter Ten: Marriage as a Crucible of Transformation

[1] Kingma, D.R. 1991. *Weddings from the Heart*. Mango Media: 60.

[2] The Ideal Model is a technique through which one identifies a core, authentic self-image, unhindered by images we carry of ourselves as being less than or greater than, or determined by what others may expect of us. Kenneth Sørensen writes (p. 20), "An Ideal Model is an authentic self-image guiding one's imagination and patterns of behaviour. It is a technique that combines self-awareness, will, imagination and passion with the aim to become the best version of you." Sørensen, K. 2016. *The Soul of Psychosynthesis*, Kentaur Forlag.

[3] Quoted in Firman, J. and Gila, A. 2007. *Assagioli's Seven Core Concepts for Psychosynthesis Training*. Available at: https://synthesiscenter.org/PDF/Seven%20Concepts.pdf.

[4] Kingma, *op cit*: 47.

[5] Assagioli, R. 2012. *Psychosynthesis*. The Synthesis Center: 19.

[6] *Ibid.:* 19.

[7] See Chapter One for Assagioli's egg diagram, and note 8 to that chapter.

[8] See https://www.bridgingpolarities.co.za/.

[9] Yeomans, T. 2020. *Holy Fire: The Process of Soul Awakening.* Concord Institute: 96

[10] *Ibid.:* 99.

[11] Welwood, J. 2017. "Intimate Relationship as a Spiritual Crucible", in *Lion's Roar*, Nov. 9, 2017. Available at https://www.lionsroar.com/intimate-relationship-as-a-spiritual-crucible/.

[12] Assagioli's advice to Tom Yeomans, *op cit.:* 47.

Chapter Eleven: Learning to Love: From 1964 to Yesterday Afternoon

[1] Oliver, M. 2015. "Not anyone who says", in *Felicity,* p. 65. Penguin Press. Reprinted by permission of The Charlotte Sheedy Literary Agency as agent for the author. Copyright © NW Orchard LLC 2015 with permission of Bill Reichblum.

[2] For a rich exploration of the effects of patriarchy on both men and women see Gilligan, C. and Snider, M., 2018, *Why Does Patriarchy Persist?* Polity.

[3] By internalized patriarchy, I am referring to the fact that we have taken the preferred values of patriarchy inside ourselves and, because of that, we often value the masculine side of our nature more than the feminine. This could be said of both women and men.

[4] See www.womenswell.org.

[5] I want to make it clear that when I speak of masculine and feminine principles, I am speaking of different energies that belong to all of us, to both women and men alike. In defining

them I am using the concept of the masculine principle to indicate reason, logic, linear thinking, words, forward motion, getting things done, manifesting. And when I speak about the feminine principle I mean the receptive, the non-linear, the non-verbal, the space between things, attention to relationship, the ability to see patterns, the dreamtime. As well as valuing men more than women, a patriarchal society like our own has also valued the qualities of the masculine principle more than those of the feminine principle. You can see the potential for confusion here. Sometimes I even question the usefulness of these words, but I hope my effort to define them will help the reader.

[6] "Self-Care During Dark Times". In Kuniholm, J. (ed.). 2018. *Sharing Wellness: Psychosynthesis for Helping People*. Cheshire Cat Books.

[7] The poem is available online at, e.g., https://www.poetryverse.com/rumi-poems/dont-go-to-sleep.

Post-script: Put Your Marriage Among the Stars

[1] The poem, "School of Marriage" is available online at https://www.poemhunter.com/poem/school-of-marriage/.

BIOGRAPHICAL NOTES
ON THE CONTRIBUTORS

Preface: Molly Brown

Molly Brown, MA, MDiv, lives in Mt Shasta, CA with her husband Jim. They are parents of two sons, Greg and Cassidy, and grandparents of Ben and Summer. Molly and Jim studied with Roberto Assagioli in 1973. As an educator, writer, and mentor/life coach, Molly draws on psychosynthesis, ecopsychology, and the Work That Reconnects. She co-directs Spiral Journey, a Work That Reconnects facilitator development program, edits *Deep Times: A Journal of the Work That Reconnects*, and runs a small publishing company, Psychosynthesis Press. Website: MollyYoungBrown.com.

Foreword: Thomas Yeomans

Thomas Yeomans, PhD, is the founder and director of the Concord Institute and co-founder, with Russian colleagues, of the International School, a post-graduate training institute in St. Petersburg, Russia. He completed training in Psychosynthesis in 1974, which included work with Roberto Assagioli in Florence, Italy, and since then he has worked as a psychotherapist, teacher, and trainer of professionals in Psychosynthesis and Spiritual Psychology throughout North America and in Europe and Russia and, more recently, as a spiritual guide/mentor. He has published writing on Psychosynthesis and Spiritual Psychology, as well as three volumes of poetry and a children's book. He is also a painter and musician. Currently he consults with practitioners in the fields of Psychosynthesis and Spiritual Psychology and teaches occasional training seminars in Soul Process Work.

Chapter One: Jon Schottland (and Lyn Sperry)

Jon Schottland, MA, has worked for twenty years as a psycho-synthesis trainer, therapist, educator and mentor. He studied at the Concord Institute and later served as president and senior trainer at The Synthesis Center for many years. He has also been an adjunct faculty member and guest lecturer in transpersonal psychology at Sofia University and American International College. He is the founder of Synthesis Northeast and currently teaches in the psychosynthesis and leadership development program at the Psychospiritual Institute in Delray Beach, FL. Jon has dedicated his life and work to personal and group development, including the human potential to experience healing, love, beauty, fulfillment, harmony and belonging. He currently works, writes, hikes and plays tennis in Brattleboro, VT, where he lives with his wife Lyn and their two sweet dogs.

Lyn Sperry, MFA is a professional coach certified through the International Coach Federation who loves to provide support for neurodiverse adults and college students. She supports them in tapping into their creative and organizational potential to achieve meaningful goals. She has 28 years of experience coaching and teaching writing to students with ADHD as an associate professor at Landmark College, a college for neurodiverse students. Lyn has presented to college faculty and academic advisors nationally and internationally about using coaching techniques to improve student outcomes in the classroom. Currently she coaches adults and college students in her private business. Lyn loves the woods of Vermont and spends time playing tennis, hiking, and enjoying poetry and travel. She lives with her husband Jon and their two dogs.

Chapter Two: Janet Messer (and Stephen Messer)

Janet R. Messer, PhD, is a licensed psychologist who has maintained a private practice doing transpersonal/humanistic psychotherapy with clients for more than 40 years. She taught Psychosynthesis to laypeople and professionals in Eugene, OR for many years. She also served on the faculty of the Southwest College of Naturopathic Medicine in Tempe, AZ, where she taught student doctors about mind-body medicine and supervised psychology interns. Janet provided leadership on the Steering Committee of the Association for the Advancement of Psychosynthesis for six years, two of them as co-chair of the organization. She presents at conferences locally and nationally, about topics related to psychotherapy and spirituality, particularly about Psychosynthesis. Janet loves to dance, act in plays, cook and eat, hold babies, and be outdoors. She lives with her husband, Stephen, in Chandler, AZ, close to her adult sons.

Stephen Messer, ND, holds a master's degree in science education from the University of Pennsylvania, and a Doctor of Naturopathic Medicine from the National College of Naturopathic Medicine. He is a founder and past president of the Homeopathic Academy of Naturopathic Physicians. He served on the board of directors of the National Center for Homeopathy, and as the Dean of the Center's prestigious Summer School. In 2000, after 21 years of practice in Oregon, he relocated with Janet to Arizona and the Southwest College of Naturopathic Medicine, as Professor and Chair of Homeopathic Medicine. He has received numerous awards, but he considers his greatest accomplishment the large number of ND graduates whom he has had the privilege to train, both in the classroom and in the clinic, who are now among the vanguard of physicians bringing about a resurgence of excellent homeopathic practice in North America.

Chapter Three: Cynthia Lashley and Walter Polt

Walter Polt, MA (Columbia University), co-created Intermountain Associates for Psychosynthesis and its training programs. His long experience in individual and group counseling and coaching has taken place in a variety of settings, including hospital, community mental health, and private practice. His numerous professional articles and newly revised book, *The Anger Makeover,* clear up confusion about conflicts, especially in relationships. While the book teaches skills, his coaching and online course called "The Plus Side of Anger" grow those skills into habits. They boost the new knowledge into mastery, replacing ground-in, primeval neural grooves with purposeful brain pathways. This work has increased his boundless joy and gratitude in life and especially his marriage.

Cynthia Lashley has a PhD from Loyola University and Erikson Institute in Chicago, an MS from Wheelock College, Boston, and a BS in Special Education from Southern Connecticut State University. She has used mindfulness and key constructs from Psychosynthesis personally and professionally with children and an array of practitioners. They include student teachers, administrators, caregivers, teachers, and community groups that work with young children and families. Recently retired, she has presented around the United States and at international conferences. She has authored and co-authored several articles in peer-reviewed journals.

Chapter Four: Diane and Jeff Rossman

Jeffrey Rossman, PhD, is a psychologist in private practice, providing psychotherapy to individuals, couples and families and consultation to business-owning families. For many years he was the Director of Behavioral Health and Life Management at Canyon Ranch, a world-leading health resort, and a consultant to executives and business-owning families at the Harvard Business School. Jeff earned a PhD at Adelphi University and completed a clinical internship in the Department of Psychiatry, Harvard Medical School. He also completed a five-year training program in Spiritual Psychology at the Concord Institute, where he became grounded in the psychospiritual principles and practices that inform his work. Jeff is the author of *The Mind-Body Mood Solution* (Rodale Press, 2010) and numerous articles in professional journals and the popular press. He enjoys practicing Qi Gong and meditation, playing basketball with friends, and hiking with his wife and their adult children.

Diane B. Rossman, MA, MFA, has maintained a private practice of Spiritual Psychology for over 35 years. She has co-facilitated training experiences in soul-work, led grief groups, and worked with children, teens and adults in exploring the beauty and power of words through reading and writing poetry. She is a published poet and an enthusiastic student of the harp. Diane and Jeff live in the Berkshires in western Massachusetts, not far from their adult children.

Chapter Five: Chris Dennler and Judith Firman

Chris Dennler was born 1957 in Switzerland. Her first profession was as a psychiatric nurse. After some years working in the emergency department and in a women's prison, she became a teacher of psychiatric nursing. She trained in Psychosynthesis in Switzerland between 1987 and 1991. In 1992 she worked as a Psychosynthesis therapist, trainer and supervisor in Switzerland, Germany and Austria. She had further education in intuitive massage, polarity and psychodrama. In 1997, she founded the Center of Psychosynthesis in Bern with her wife, Judith Firman. After their marriage in 2006, she moved to England. In 2011, they closed the

Center in Bern and she built up her private practice in England, where she worked one-to-one online with an international clientele. She retired in February 2022.

Judith Firman is British, born in 1947. She trained in Psychosynthesis in San Francisco between 1976 and 1979. After leaving the USA she became co-director of The Psychosynthesis and Education Trust in London (1981–1996.) She also taught in various Psychosynthesis centers in Europe (Austria, Holland, Germany, and Switzerland). Alongside this, she had a private practice as a Psychosynthesis psychotherapist and supervisor. In 1997 along with her wife, Chris Dennler, she founded the Center for Psychosynthesis, Bern (Switzerland). She became a business coach in 2000 and, over the last 22 years, she has worked in both private and public companies at director and board level. She also trained and supervised business coaches. Most recently, she has worked with numerous clinicians implementing the use of a coaching style with patients the UK National Health Service. All her work is informed by Psychosynthesis. She now works reduced hours.

Chapter Six: Shamai Currim (and Ahmed Nooruddin Currim)

Shamai Currim, PhD, is a retired psychotherapist, educator, and educational consultant and has done volunteer work in hospice/palliative and home-care services, prisons, and seniors' residences. She is a graduate of Psychosynthesis Pathways of Montreal and has served for many years, in many varied positions, on the Steering Committee of the Association for the Advancement of Psychosynthesis, the BOD of the International Organization of the Helen Prize for Women, the BOD of the Association of Early Childhood Educators, and as the Executive Director of Eduporta International Education Agency. She was a chosen attendee at the Leadership Training Course at the Canadian Jewish Congress and the first recipient of the Ross-Seaman Memorial Leadership Award at Concordia University. Now in her senior years, Shamai has immersed herself in the arts and is a director and professional member of her local art association. She has presented at numerous conferences, has been published in many peer review journals, and is the author of "Meaghan's Story". Shamai currently divides her time between Canada and Israel with her new husband.

Ahmed Nooruddin Currim, MD, PhD, (1940-2017) was born in Bombay, India and traveled to Switzerland for his secondary education. He studied engineering mathematics and chemical engineering at the University of Michigan, received an M.A. in physics from Harvard University, and a doctorate in mathematics from the University of Colorado. He completed his medical degree at the University of Brussels and received his license to practice family and internal medicine as well as passing the exam for the Connecticut State Homeopathic Medical Board, where he later served as the chairman for many years. He taught seminars in Materia Medica, homeopathic philosophy, and repertory to many groups of medical practitioners, including physicians, nurses, and naturopaths, and presented at international conferences. As a soulful person, Ahmed made himself always available for his patients and friends. His published books include *The Collected Works of Arthur Hill Grimmer* and *Guide to Kent's Repertory*.

Chapter Seven: Judith Broadus and Vincent Dummer

Judith Broadus, PhD, is the mother of three grown children, and recently and joyfully welcomed her first grandchild. Judith has a doctorate in psychology, with a major focus on counseling and women's issues. She completed five years of training with the Kentucky Center of Psychosynthesis in the 1980s, later serving as a co-trainer in mindfulness-based professional Psychosynthesis training. She developed a strong interest in meditation after an introduction to meditation in Psychosynthesis and continued training in meditation with Transcendental Meditation and Shambhala Buddhism. She wrote an article on Psychosynthesis and Buddhism (2008), exploring similarities, differences and inseparabilities between the two systems. She has chosen to focus on self-care as her "growing edge." Judith is currently semi-retired and continues to study the interface of meditation, developmental psychology, health behaviors and psychotherapy. Her intention is to ground the knowledge in her body through practice, centered in her heart.

Vincent Dummer, PsyD, is a native of the Netherlands and has been a licensed psychologist in private practice in Lexington, KY, since 1983. Currently, a large part of his practice consists of assisting highly creative and gifted individuals with emotional and interpersonal difficulties, utilizing insights from attachment literature. He has served as a part-time staff psychologist at a state psychiatric hospital and was a co-director and supervisor of an A.P.A.-approved doctoral internship program. He completed his Psychosynthesis training from the London Institute of Psychosynthesis in 1983, and served as a trainer and director of the Kentucky Center of Psychosynthesis from 1983-1988. With Judith Broadus, he conducted a three-year professional training in mindfulness-based Psychosynthesis and produced a video interview series, "Psychosynthesis Portraits." His research interests have been in psychological growth in adulthood. He has been a practitioner of meditation and Buddhism since 1992.

Chapter Eight: Ilene Val-Essen (and Ed Schuman)

Ilene Val-Essen, PhD, MFT, has been in private practice since 1975. An innovator in the field of parent education, she blends Western psychology with Eastern philosophy, bringing a unique voice to the global community. Her first book, *Bring Out the Best in Your Child and Your Self,* helps parents create a family environment based on mutual respect. *Parenting with Wisdom and Compassion* supports parents to reach toward their higher self during the roughest of times, when understanding and an open heart are key. She contributed a chapter on "Transforming Family Life Through Psychosynthesis Coaching" to *The Call of Self: Psychosynthesis Life Coaching* (Ed. D. Firman, Synthesis Center Press, Amherst, 2018). Through her Quality Parenting program, which has been translated into Spanish, Dutch, and Swedish, parents discover that family life can be so much easier and deeply rewarding. Ilene lives in Culver City, California, near her children and grandsons.

Ed Schuman worked as a documentary film producer, writer, and director, creating award-winning PBS documentaries, including one that aired on Frontline. He also earned numerous international awards, receiving the prestigious Columbia DuPont Award for Broadcast Journalism and an Emmy nomination. He co-founded Dimension Films, where he developed award-winning educational films. Decades later, he co-founded Success Stories, L.L.C., focusing on programs that prepared prisoners for release. When retired, he used his creative energy to dive into writing and performing comedy songs, developing his improv skills at Second City, and advancing his photography hobby.

Chapter Nine: Urs Mattmann (and Emmanuel Grassi)

Urs Mattmann, Acc MBACP, reg. Social worker SWE, is a counselor/psychotherapist, clinical supervisor and spiritual director. After studying business and theology, he graduated as a social worker in 1988. From 1997 to 2002, he trained as a Psychosynthesis therapist in Switzerland, before moving with his partner to London in 2005. He has since had a small private practice (www.ursmat-tmann.com), while working in the drug and alcohol sector until 2020. In Switzerland, he had worked in the mental health sector. In recent years he has specialized in trauma work using Emotional Freedom Technique, Somatic Experiencing and EMDR. Urs is currently employed by a Centre for Health and Pastoral Care in North Yorkshire: (www.holyroodhouse.org.uk). He has contributed to several books and published one on spirituality for gays and lesbians. In the 1980s and 1990s he was very active in the Christian L.G.B. movement. Strongly interested in faith and spirituality, he has facilitated retreats for years.

Emmanuel Grassi has been the partner of Urs since 1986. He originally trained for the Swiss Railways as a teenager and worked there for 20 years before becoming a support worker for people in need (mental health, learning disabilities) in Switzerland. In 2005, he left with Urs for England, where he worked until his retirement in the learning disabilities sector in London. He is currently a volunteer at Holy Rood House in North Yorkshire. Since the 1990s, he has engaged in Ikebana (Ikenobo school/meditative Japanese flower arranging) and gained diplomas, having trained at the Ikenobo Center in Kyoto, Japan. He loves cooking.

Chapter Ten: Amy Spalding-Fecher (and Randall Spalding-Fecher)

Amy Spalding-Fecher, MA, BCC, is the Director of Synthesis Northeast, a Psychosynthesis coach-training program in New England, a lead trainer at the Psychospiritual Institute, and a board-certified coach. Amy trained and practiced as an architect before she studied Psychosynthesis. She has worked with individuals and groups both locally and in South Africa, where she lived for 16 years. She weaves decades of meditation practice, dharma study, mindful self-compassion, and transformative art practices into her work. Amy trained in Psychosynthesis with Didi Firman and studied women's spirituality and circle work with Anne Yeomans. She has been mentored by Thomas Yeomans in Psychosynthesis, spiritual psychology and the embodiment of the soul process in everyday life. When not teaching or coaching, Amy loves hiking, yoga, kayaking and being in nature. She has traveled extensively with her husband of 28 years and their two daughters, including seven months driving overland in an outfitted Land Cruiser from Cape Town to London.

Randall Spalding-Fecher, PhD, has worked in almost 30 countries over the last 25 years on using carbon markets and climate finance to support development in low-income countries. After leading a research group at the University of Cape Town, he moved to development consulting for a Norwegian company focused on climate policy, market mechanisms and development. More recently, he has been supporting multiple initiatives to bring greater integrity and quality to the voluntary carbon markets. He completed the Psychosynthesis coach training with Synthesis Northeast in 2020 and is a long-time meditation practitioner. Randall lives in Amherst, MA, with his wonderful wife, Amy, and enjoys playing classical piano, hiking, biking, spending time with his family and drinking oat milk lattes.

Chapter Eleven: Anne Yeomans (and Tom Yeomans)

Anne Yeomans, MA, LMHC, has been a psychotherapist and a group facilitator for more than fifty years. She trained in Psychosynthesis in Palo Alto and San Francisco (1971-1975), and in 1972, she and her husband Tom studied with its founder Roberto Assagioli in Florence, Italy. They were teachers and trainers in Psychosynthesis for many years. Anne has also taught workshops and courses on non-violence, the process of reconciliation, healing dialogue, and women's spirituality. The principles of Psychosynthesis underlie all her work. In the 1990s, she began to facilitate women's groups and women's circles, and co-founded The Women's Well in Concord, MA (womenswell.org). She has facilitated women's circles in the U.S., Canada, Europe, and most recently in Russia. Currently, she lives in Colrain, Massachusetts, with her husband Tom. They have two grown sons and five grandchildren. She is also a poet and a social activist.

See the note on Tom Yeomans above, under Foreword.

Postscript: Piero Ferrucci

Piero Ferrucci was born in Turin, Italy, in 1946. He graduated in philosophy at the Università di Torino, then did didactic training with Roberto Assagioli, the founder of Psychosynthesis. He is a registered psychotherapist, and a trainer at the Società di Psicosintesi Terapeutica in Florence. He has written several books, translated into various languages, among which are *Inevitable Grace, Beauty and the Soul*, and *Your Inner Will*, and has edited *The Human Situation* (lectures by Aldous Huxley). He lives and works in Florence, Italy.

SELECTED BIBLIOGRAPHY

Assagioli, R. 1965. *Psychosynthesis: A Manual of Principles and Techniques*. New York: The Viking Press.

Assagioli, R. 1974. *The Act of Will*. New York: Penguin.

Broadus, J & Stewart, G. 2011. (Eds.) *Conversations in Psychosynthesis: Trauma and Recovery*. Vol. 9, Oct. 2011. Bethany, OK: Cowan Printing Co. Association for the Advancement of Psychosynthesis.

Brown, M.Y. & Macy, J. 2014. *Coming Back to Life: The Updated Guide to the Work that Reconnects*. Gabriola Island: New Society Publishers.

Brown, M.Y. 2010. *Lighting a Candle: Collected Reflections on a Spiritual Life*. Mt Shasta CA: Psychosynthesis Press.

Brown, M.Y. 2009. *Growing Whole: Self-Realization for the Great Turning*. Mt Shasta CA: Psychosynthesis Press.

Brown, M.Y. and Treadway, C.W. 2009. *Held in Love: Life Stories to Inspire Us Through Times of Change*. Mt Shasta CA: Psychosynthesis Press.

Brown, M.Y. 2004. *Unfolding Self: The Practice of Psychosynthesis*. New York: Skyhorse Press.

Brown, M. Y. and Sartor, L. 2004. *Consensus in the Classroom: Creating a Lively Learning Community*. Mt Shasta CA: Psychosynthesis Press.

Ferrucci, P. 1982. *What We May Be*. Los Angeles: Tarcher.

Ferrucci, P. 2010. *Beauty and the Soul*. New York: TarcherPerigee.

Ferrucci, P. 2015. *Your Inner Will*. New York: TarcherPerigee.

Ferrucci, P. 2016. *The Power of Kindness*. New York: TarcherPerigee.

Lashley, C.O. 2012. Listening to Student Concerns: An Instructional Strategy to Expand Student Perspectives. *Journal of Association of Early Childhood Teacher Educators, 33*(2): 190-199.

Mattmann, U. 2006. *Coming In: Gays and Lesbians Reclaiming the Spiritual Journey*. Glasgow UK: Wild Goose.

Messer, J.R. 2006. The Therapist's Body in Therapy: A Personal Reflection. In B. Roth, J. Messer and P. Clay (Eds.) *Psychosynthesis and the Body: Conversations in Psychosynthesis,* Vol. 6: 67–69. Albany, CA.: Association for the Advancement of Psychosynthesis.

Polt, W. 2021. *The Anger Makeover: Discover your Power to Reform Your Relationships*. Cheshire, MA: Cheshire Cat Books.

Rossman, J. 2011. *The Mind-Body Mood Solution*. New York: Rodale Press.

Spalding-Fecher, A. 2018. Reverence for Psychosynthesis. In D. Firman, (Ed.), *The Call of Self*. Amherst: Synthesis Center Press.

Val-Essen, I. 2010. *Bring Out the Best in Your Child and Your Self: Creating a Family Based on Mutual Respect*. Culver City: Quality Parenting.

Val-Essen, I. 2016. *Parenting with Wisdom and Compassion: Bring Out the Best in Your Family*. Culver City: Quality Parenting.

Yeomans, A. 1977. Self-Care During Dark Times. In J. Kuniholm (Ed.) *Sharing Wellness: Psychosynthesis for Helping People.* Cheshire Cat Books 2018.

Yeomans, A. 1977. *Psychosynthesis: A personal experience with a holistic system.* New *Realities* magazine, 1, (2).

Yeomans, A. Womenswell.org

Yeomans, T. 1999. *Soul on Earth: Readings in Spiritual Psychology.* Colrain, MA: Concord Institute Publications.

Yeomans, T. 2020. *Holy Fire: The Process of Soul Awakening.* Colrain, MA: Concord Institute Publications.

ACKNOWLEDGMENTS

*If the only prayer you ever say in your entire life
is thank you, it will be enough.*
— *Meister Eckhart*

We, the four editors of this book, would like to acknowledge our fifteen fellow writers who have collaborated on this long-term, multi-faceted project. We are so grateful to each other for the unwavering good will, the generosity of time, and the range of skills which enabled us to persevere through the uncertain terrain of birthing a book "by committee" without a map. We know who we are!

We wish to acknowledge Jan Kuniholm, who initiated the idea of gathering stories about couples seen through the lens of Psychosynthesis. We would also like to express our appreciation to one of our authors, Ilene Val-Essen, who kept this vision alive. Her tenacity and conviction drew us back together when we had lost our faith in the original project. Our book would not exist without her.

We would like to acknowledge Phyllis Clay, who wanted to be part of this effort and drafted a short chapter before her untimely death. We are grateful to Molly Brown for her wise, courageous voice. Her articulation of the through-line from person to planet sets our stories in the context we intended. Our deep appreciation goes to Tom Yeomans for his willingness to reflect on and write about the couple relationship within the context of Roberto Assagioli's vision; and to Piero Ferrucci—who knew Assagioli better than any of us--for his generosity in sharing his "Roberto memories" and the reminder to place our relationships "among the stars."

A deep bow to all those who helped to transform our manuscript into a book. First and foremost, to Jennifer Browdy, our professional editor and literary midwife, whose expertise shaped our words into a cohesive whole. Her belief in our book buoyed our spirits.

To Tim James, who painstakingly assisted with the copy editing.

To Asya Blue, who artistically assisted with the interior and cover design.

To Genevieve Mackenzie, for her assistance with proofreading the final manuscript.

To Molly Brown and her Psychosynthesis Press company, for publishing the book.

To an anonymous donor, who generously offered a significant financial contribution to the publication expenses.

Our greatest debt of gratitude goes to Roberto Assagioli, the founder of Psychosynthesis, whose vision and faith in the spirit within each of us and among us, has profoundly inspired and influenced our lives. We dedicate this book to him and to the spirit of Synthesis he perceived and offered to the world.